# STORM COUNTRY

**Random House**

**New York**

# STORM COUNTRY

## A Journey Through the Heart of America

## PETE DAVIES

Title page photograph: Superstock

Library of Congress Cataloging-in-Publication Data
Davies, Pete
    Storm country: a journey through the heart of America/Pete
Davies.
        p.      cm.
    ISBN 0-679-40885-1
    1. United States—Description and travel—1981–   2. Davies, Pete,
—Journeys—United States. I. Title.
E169.04.D37 1992
917.3—dc20    92-53636

Manufactured in the United States of America
98765432
First North American Edition

*for Susan and Carl*
*who let me go in the first place*

*and for all the people*
*who were good to me when I got there*

The introduction first appeared in British *ELLE,* November 1990, and is reprinted by permission of Hachette Magazines Ltd.

For my account in Chapter 8 of the Wounded Knee massacre I am indebted to Jack Utter's memorial pamphlet, "Wounded Knee & The Ghost Dance Tragedy," published by the National Woodlands Publishing Company, Lake Ann, Michigan.

The tornado survivors in Chapter 11 are quoted in the *Wisconsin Magazine of History,* Volume 73, Number 4.

# Contents

# Introduction:
# The Trunk of the Tree

*March 1990*

I stopped outside the Little House on the Prairie, the log cabin where Laura Ingalls Wilder's family lived in the year 1869–70. It sat squat and plain on an empty county road, a small fleck of history stranded in the void of the Kansas landscape. It was closed.

There was no mud on the road, no hayspill, no water, no traffic. Yet as I sat with the engine idling, for no clear reason a solitary pickup two hundred yards down the road ahead suddenly spun off the asphalt, cannoning down into the wet dirt ditch. The trailer fishtailed. Sprays and divots of black earth and bright grass flew up against the ocean of fire and blood in the sunset sky.

So I drove on over. A big woman was getting down, and two kids; they were acting like they threw the truck in the ditch every week. The woman said she had no idea what had happened, was glad the kids weren't hurt—and could I get them home to Havana, across the railroad and 75? Her little girl said, "Hi, I'm Crystal. And he's Jesse."

Havana was a church or two, a broken-up brick school with cattle in the yard, shotgun shacks lining dirt roads with the paint long peeled off the boards; random junk and rusting cars lay strewn around the satellite dishes. It was another little place like Valeda or Liberty, places that looked like God just scattered them down there, and told the people to go to it—which they did, and no one ever thanked them. Outside the church in Angola the sign read WHEN BROKEN, WE NEED MENDING. GOD'S GRACE IS THE GLUE.

So I set them down at their house in Havana. Of course now they had heat and power, and phones and pickups and TV—but under that fierce red sky, in all that land, it still felt like a Little House on the Prairie.

Because all the junk in the world, out there, can't make you more permanent. A tornado pays no mind to who you are—it just explodes your house anyway . . .

I was staying in Coffeyville, Montgomery County, Kansas—a town of maybe thirteen thousand people spread out by the Verdigris River. To get there you go north on 169 from Tulsa, bang into the heart of America.

Least that's what I thought. I got there by a bootstrap calculation: I took the farthest points north, east, south, and west in the continental USA—the Lake of the Woods, Minnesota; Eastport, Maine; Key West, Florida; and Cape Flattery in Washington—and the lines I drew on the map said dead center between those four, I'd find Coffeyville.

It turned out that the official geographic center of the forty-eight states is a concrete stump five hours' drive northwest of the place, by the settlement of Lebanon. But by then it was too late, I was hooked—Coffeyville would do me just fine.

Colonel Coffey set up his trading post for the Osage Indians in the 1860s. A surveyor named Blanton laid out the town; they tossed a coin to decide which one it should be named for. There was natural gas, and William Brown made his fortune from it; his mansion is a wondrous Kansas oddity of mahogany, marble, and Tiffany glass, marooned on a roadside hill.

Gas and the railroads brought in industry, brickyards, glass plants; a 1907 magazine listed among the town's splendiferous facilities "2 Ice Plants, 1 Neckyoke Factory, the Largest Zinc Oxide Plant In The World, 2 Opera Houses"—one cultural, you gather, and the other one bawdy.

William Brown's cold room was cooled by one-hundred-pound blocks of ice, brought to the house on wagons. Guests were taken to the third-floor ballroom in an elevator that, weights and all, was operated manually by a massive black butler, who'd previously been a prize-fighter.

There was a fainting room. At 100, 110 degrees in high summer, there was a likelihood of fainting at a dance.

Today, dancing in Coffeyville's a riot. You might go first for a drink at Butterfield's, known generally just as The Lounge, or The Back Room. Then you dance at Shenanigan's, to country and rock—from fiddles to Billy Idol—and weave through a whooping throng of rough and happy leviathans. I played pool there with a drunk kid with slab-of-meat hands, fingers so thick you could tether a horse to them. The men wore cowboy hats. The kid said if I beat him, he'd *bust* my ass.

Where you probably don't go is the 14th Street Bar, out by the stockyard on Fishworm Flats, known also as The Hole. The way the police chief put it, "You'd stick out like a sore thumb in there. People'd *know* you're not from here." The way other people put it, they had knives and guns in there, and a tendency to pull them.

And let me tell you: I had one of the best weeks of my life in this town.

Damon "Sam" Willbern was the proprietor of Red Nose Sam's Jewelry, Gun & Pawn: "We loan money on anything that doesn't eat and can get through the door." He was described to me as "the most respected black sheep of the community"—and he said you'd have to be deaf, dumb, and blind not to have a good time in Coffeyville. Sure, there were people who complained—but there were people in this world who'd complain "if you hung 'em with clean rope."

When I asked him about the 14th Street Bar, he roared with laughter. "Hell, I used to *own* that place. The one and only man who brought go-go dancers to Coffeyville."

And was that good for business?

"You ever see sardines in a can?"

John Vest worked for Sam. He'd bought a burn-out in a street of wrecked row houses for five hundred dollars, and was doing it up. We drove past another wreck a block away and he said, "That's where that stabbing happened. Well," he laughed, "more of a hacking really. Man, she took a machete to the guy."

John's people came to Coffeyville in '57, because the school system there's good. He and Fritz Green took me out to Indian Bluff, a crumbly sandstone stack with views, when you'd climbed it, halfway to eternity. Then we went to the Saturday auction at the stockyard.

On the electronic board they clocked one bull at 2,620 pounds. Up close he was a monster, pawing up the shit and the mud on the pen's concrete floor. Three men got it in one gate and out the other, the auctioneer rattling through the invisible bids all the while like a tenor robot on speed. Big men with arms crossed on big bellies wore jeans, boots, Stetsons, or seed caps; the bulls backed and grunted, as the gates clanged and banged.

Back outside John remarked, as a new car passed, "Now there's a fifteen-thousand-dollar car. If there's one thing people are split on round here, it's cars. Basically there's Chevrolet, Ford—Found Off Road Dead—or foreign." Himself he had, he said, an Italian car. "A Ren-*olt*."

Me, I had a rental Toyota. With the radio on to preachers, to country, or to K-Double-Q-F 92.1 Coffeyville, the Edge, I trashed it down those dirt county roads; I sprayed it through the mud and dust of a landscape so magnificent, so blindingly enormous that when I stopped and stepped out, I felt merely particle-sized—an atom in the eye of the Lord.

I heard a railroad man talking about what it takes to pull mile-and-a-quarter-long freight trains over the low rolling hills, the hogbacks. It was March. Massive plowed fields glistened black with rain, or sunk flooded under sheets of grey and brown water. Other fields were rich green with new shoots; pasture blew with pale yellow and rust-orange grasses. Swollen creeks and rivers filled high, dense with silt; oak trees ran in stark leafless stands round the horizon, among dogwood and bodark and golden rain.

Brilliant red cardinals flashed on wires and branches; big red-tailed hawks swung lazy on the wind. Clouds marched by in a gleaming immensity of blue—then the sun dropped low and the yellow veils of last light gathered, until clouds and sky all ignited together into a red and orange firescape of shadow and vapor. Across the tracks from downtown, the grain elevator reared up gold against the indigo east.

So no one should be surprised that God gets good ratings in these parts. Kansas is one of His more imperious performances.

There are sixty-eight churches in Coffeyville, from the Fire Baptized Holiness Church and the River Of Life Tabernacle, to Methodist and Baptist places of a quiet but substantial brick solidity. I went to the Baptists'.

It was moderate stuff—no speaking in tongues. The text was from Revelation, on the theme that if your faith was lukewarm, "God will spew you out from his mouth." The pastor told his full house that people laughed at a man hot in his faith, called him Holy Joe, called him *nuts*. "Well, I may be a nut—but at least I'm screwed on the right bolt."

And he told them emphatically, with all that declamation, that oratorical fluency, "Jesus says, I—KNOW—YOUR—DEEDS." They sang, "Wherever He Leads I'll Go"; the preacher came down before them. A woman stepped up to reaffirm her faith, and he took her hand. With bowed head held close by bowed head they whispered together, hymn-cloaked.

After the service the first woman I'd spoken to in Coffeyville, a kindly middle-aged bank teller from whom I'd sought directions, came to ask how I was. She had, she told me, been thinking of me all week, and hoped sincerely that all was well.

All did go well; it went better all the time. A girl took me to where her grandparents had a small lake, and a cabin beside it made neatly from an old trolley car. Trams ran between the towns here until after World War II, before the rule of the automobile, and this one still had its original ads: WHAT ARE YOU DOING TO OPPOSE COMMUNISM? ONE SURE WAY IS TO HELP RADIO FREE EUROPE.

From the end of the little pier we fed bread to the catfish, which they took from our hands. One was known by name, for an obvious reason— Old One Whisker. Round the water there were persimmon trees, which seemed deliciously exotic.

And in the heart of America, the things you do like this seem daily to become more enchantedly unreal until—wind rustling through bare branches by the side of the grey lake, the catfish lapping at your fingers—you realize you're more wonderfully, empty-headedly relaxed than you've ever been in your life.

You realize, basically, that the rest of the world is just *so very far away*.

Coffeyville bar talk: "Hey Carey, how ya doin'?"
"Oh, fine—keepin' outta trouble."
"What ya doin' in here then?"
"Aw hell . . . I *like* to fight."

Allen Twitchell had big gouged grazes down his forehead and his nose. What the hell happened? "It's a short sad story. I got drunk. I fell out of my car. I landed on my face."

The car was a battered Firebird that he drives, occasionally, into the sides of buildings. You needed a screwdriver to get it in gear, don't ask me how or why. It reeked of gas, and rumbled like an angry bear. He had the Nicholson role in *One Flew Over The Cuckoo's Nest*, he was directing it for the Coffeyville Community Theatre. He was sports editor on the *Coffeyville Journal* and he was, said Carey Borum—whose card showed an eagle marching along, pieces of Borum Steel pipeline tucked beneath its wing—"a scholar and a talented man."

Carey tried to give me his new $350 camera—there were pictures of buffalo on the film in it, a herd out by Havana, pictures he felt I should have for my work. So hell, just take the camera . . . When I wouldn't have it, he pulled out a grapefruit-sized wad of hundreds, and tried to give me the value of the thing in money instead.

Certainly, it would have been unwise to try and stop him buying drinks. He'd already decided that the monocled Danish journalist passing through (researching Wild West stuff—the Dalton gang was shot here) was a Russian spy. So he told him, with feeling, "You don't know *shit.*" Allen cooled him down. Carey said he was a trained killer, CIA; the scar on his forehead was from 'Nam.

Holiday tips in Kansas: Watch out for snakes and tornadoes—and don't talk about gun control.

Frank was an ex-pilot, also ex-'Nam, now a chewing tobacco sales manager. He was headed three hundred miles northwest to Odin, to the family farm—four generations of German Catholic homesteaders since the 1860s. He said, "Let them shoot each other in New York, what the hell do I care? That's not America." And once we'd crossed the sticky moment where he'd thought I might be radical—gun control, indeed—he invited me to come slaughter some cattle with him. He was going six hundred miles round trip, just to stock up his freezer with some home-grown T-bone . . .

Allen said when they built Coffeyville, they put a great big magnet under the sidewalk downtown—and then you got born there with a metal plate in your head. So maybe you went away—but you always came back.

Red Nose Sam Willbern said, "We're not exactly *mañana,* but we sure as hell ain't right now either—not like the damn Yankees. Those people think everything sucks west of Jersey."

Police chief Allen Flowers said he'd been in Philadelphia once for six months, thirty-some years ago, and he had a fine old time—but then he realized, and he laughed, "Man, you got to *work* out there." So he came back and started in the police. Back then there were bars he could go in to bust up a fight, but where—being black—they'd not serve him afterwards. He had to go round the back for his coffee. He said the world was a better place now, and the fishing in the Verdigris was great. "Sure, we got the same problems everyone got—just less of 'em, less often."

John Vest said people said hi to you on the street here. "My cousin, he's from California, he's a bit [he tapped his head], says people don't talk to other people. But here, they do."

And the boosters (Glen Welden the city manager, or Maurice Weinberg at Weinberg's Western Wear), they said the people here were honest and hardworking, and stood up for themselves, and for America. "We're the backbone of the country. We're the trunk of the tree."

And they are good people; I think they fixed me with one of Allen's metal plates. There are girls there with slow-drawling voices that flow like honey on shining glass—and then they laugh and they tell you, amazingly, that accents like theirs are *trash.*

They stay fit playing racquetball at the Olympic Rec, with the sound in the background of the pins crashing down along twenty-four bowling alleys. They looked so well and young, the children they'd had at nineteen seemed now, ten or fourteen years later, more like brothers and sisters than children. And some had traveled maybe a few of these central states—but none had been to the coasts, or farther. One had been to Chicago, and hadn't liked it; she'd felt, she said, like she had to look over her shoulder all the time. But they tried to save money; they imagined other places far away with a pragmatic wistfulness, and made plans to get to them someday.

So what did they want from life? The boys, I'd been unblinkingly informed, wanted "beer and pussy, not necessarily in that order." As for the girls, my informant told me, "They like to dance, and they like to laugh." Then he thought about it hard before concluding, "And they like *sincerity in bed.*"

And me—what did I want? What was I doing, bang in that heart of America?

Well—I'd been needing a haircut too long. So I got me one from Mike Wilson at the 9th Street Barber's Shop, and he did a good job. Then I drove back down to Tulsa, not wanting to leave.

# STORM COUNTRY

# 1.

# Under the Weather

*May 1991*

I didn't want to leave, but that didn't mean I couldn't go back. There was, I felt, far more of a story out there than could ever be told in the three thousand words of a magazine piece—a story of landscape and weather, history and people . . .

The bus left New York at 8:45 on a Saturday evening. It was 1,447 miles to Tulsa; 34 hours—2 nights and a day. I could have flown, but I wanted to feel the weight of the land, the space and the mass of it, the long crawl through time. And I wasn't alone in that.

Among the Greyhound motley, the fat and the mad, the poor and the ever-hopeful, Melissa joined the bus in Harrisburg, Pennsylvania. She was eighteen, a tad on the plump side, but pretty—and she was going to Minot, North Dakota. When I asked her why, she answered simply, "A man."

She'd known him for three days, then for three weeks after that they'd talked on the telephone. She said, "A girlfriend was trying to mend my broken heart, she fixed us up to meet . . . and we talked on the phone, and it's like he's falling in love with me. I don't know if I'm falling in love with him, but I'm on the bus . . . I guess I'm just an impulsive kind of person. And I want to see America, before I go any place else; I want to go to Europe, but I want to see America first. Though I don't believe I'm really doing this right now, to be honest with you."

Then she said, "All my friends, they say there's nothing out there. But there is, there's history—that's our history out there. I always wanted to see it out there, since I was a kid I wanted to see it. And what have I got to lose?"

She went to sleep as we rolled through the wet Appalachian dark, this cheerful girl skittering like a hockey puck over ice across the vastness of America. It occurred to me that if a British girl went as far for a man as Melissa was going, that man would be Russian.

She changed buses in Pittsburgh. From there my route was through Weirton, Steubenville, Wheeling, past bluffs rising along the Ohio over the broken-up steel towns. Rusty bridges lanced into tunnels in the tree-dense rockface; huge barges slipped under the grey skies of Sunday morning past convolutions of red pipe, past tank farms and slag piles, past railyards and crack-windowed factories.

Motel signs said WELCOME HOME BOYS. The town of Brilliant announced BRILLIANT WELCOMES OUR HEROES. Mr. William's House of Hair Fashions in Wheeling had a hand-written sign proclaiming VICTORY: THANK GOD & THE USA. The Big Boy restaurant across the street said WE SUPPORT OUR MILITARY EVERYWHERE.

Cambridge, Zanesville—dots of buildings in a long, rolling world of pale and leafy green. Still the sky was grey, indistinct. But *USA Today* promised high 80s beyond St. Louis, with widespread thunderstorms— and by Columbus the sky came good, clearing high and blue. It was 11:45 in the morning. In the terminal I slumped before one of the postcard-sized TVs on the armrests of the seats; I listened over a Sunday babel of news and preaching to one black man ask another where he was headed to.

And the other guy replied, "I don't know. I just don't know."

Behind the shuttered bar a paper flag announced WE ARE PROUD TO BE AMERICANS.

From Columbus I sat with Mike from Miami, Oklahoma. He'd been in the military from 1973 to '77 in Japan, the Philippines, and Vietnam during the evacuation—on an aircraft carrier he'd watched the choppers bring out the last refugees. Then he went back to Oklahoma and sold fruit door to door, oranges and lemons, apples and grapefruit, roaming with two other guys in a truck from Texas through Oklahoma, and on north into Kansas. "We had to tell folks it was Texas fruit—California had the Mediterranean fruit fly then—but it wasn't Texas, not all of it." One guy would drive, while the other two worked down each side of the street.

He worked in construction after that; but you'd put up your piece of a building in a month, then there'd be nothing for the next six. So he got a job in a wood factory, making bases for sports trophies. It lasted a year and a half, until the supervisor came and said, "If you find another job you better take it. 'Cause we're shutting the doors next week." He went ranching for a year in New Mexico then; but he got cabin fever, he needed to see a tree. So he hitched to Ohio.

He'd been doing this and that in Ohio ever since. It was, he said, a decent state; up here there was work, not like in Oklahoma. Right now he was working in a residential care home in Dayton, "Looking after eight old paralyzed guys. It's good money, but it ain't work. Making up eight beds, how long's that take you? And helping them eat, cleaning up after them—it ain't work. But I like it, I take time to talk with them. Some of the old boys get gripy—seems the older you get, the gripier you get."

Himself, he had no gripes. He'd been around; he'd liked California for the beaches and the girls, and the fact that you could drink at eighteen— and he'd liked Tijuana, because down there you could drink forever. He looked well enough, for a man of thirty-six, given what sounded like a diet consisting solely of beer. He was the proud owner of a TV he'd bought for $48 from his landlord, so he figured when he got into Dayton he'd drop by the store, buy twelve, go home to the TV—then be up to work at six, to look after his old boys. He was saving $150, to contribute to a car for the girl he'd stayed with in Columbus; she'd contribute the same.

I said, "You can get a car for three hundred dollars?"

"Put it this way," said Mike. "You can get a better car than the one she's got now. Anyhow," he asked, "how d'you like the USA?"      .

I said I liked it—and that this was my seventh time in the country. Then I told him where I come from in Wales.

He asked, "D'you have TV there?" And he asked, "Is that England a democracy there too?"

But when I laughed he said I should listen, there was a lot of people in the world didn't know too much about it. He did his basic training in San Diego in '73. "And one day," he said, "we're on smoking formation, they give you five minutes to smoke a cigarette. And we're all standing in line there passing the tin—'cause you ain't allowed no ash on the floor, no butts on the floor—and there's a recruit right by me from California. And he says to me, D'you have cars in Oklahoma?"

Mike's dad had been a Chevy man, and so was Mike too. He was a scrawny guy with a moustache and a seed cap, and a really bad smell on him—he'd been fishing the night before, and the bait and the muck was still pasted on his jeans. He was married twice, walked out twice. He still had a mother and a grandmother in Miami, but he'd not seen them since '82, '83. They talked on the phone now and then.

He described seeing a balloon rally in Albuquerque one time. He said, "Them balloons was humongous. A whole field of them, just rising up together—I sure'd have liked to get a ride in one of them things. But I couldn't afford the sucker."

Then he paused—and a most American persistence of hope stood vivid in his next three words.

He said, "Not that time."

In Dayton he got off, and shambled away through the bright gap of daylight at the terminal gate. Like so many people I was to meet, his life, it seemed to me, was fresh out of a country song.

We rolled through Richmond, Indianapolis, Terre Haute in Indiana, through Effingham and Vandalia in Illinois. In St. Louis I changed onto the bus for L.A.; near midnight of the second night we started out across Missouri.

I woke briefly in Joplin at 5:15, then again at 6:40, twenty minutes out of Tulsa on the Will Rogers Turnpike. It looked a misty dawn, chill and dank under a low grey sky—but when we stopped at the depot it was close and warm, the air of early Monday thick and sticky already.

A Jamaican cabbie took me out to the airport—I had a car booked there. He said that on Friday a tornado had touched down on the south side of Tulsa; no one was hurt, but a few houses got blown out. In April in the counties round the city, he said, twisters had killed five or six people. He said especially in the evenings, if the weather was close, humid and still, temperature in the 80s, and you saw cloud coming in and felt the wind get up—then you turned on the radio, you kept your ears pinned and eyes wide.

"If you on the road," he said, "and you see one coming, quit the car. That thing just take a car right away. It *so* destructive."

I said I was fascinated, and he chuckled.

"That one *dangerous* fascination."

I felt wasted, sleepless and unshaven, groin grimy, torso clammy, mouth furry, my head leaden with a dull slow throb—but I felt electric too. New York wasn't just thirty-four hours away, it was on some whole other planet—because I was back in the heart of America now, with its savage weather and its sentimental music. It's the nearest thing I know to going to the moon—*and I love it.*

At the airport I lucked out with Alamo, the same way I was going to luck out all the way down the road. They had no economy models on the lot that morning, so they gave me a "fun" model instead, a low-slung and punchy white Chevrolet. Touch the pedal and *whoomph* . . . east on II, east again on 244, then north onto 169, eyes sticky and pulsing in the muggy morning murk, too buzzed out to be ready for country music yet, tuned instead to 94.1 the Hawk, "Nonstop Classic Rock," the Who, the Byrds, T. Rex, and the wipers took water off the windshield out of the hot grey air—and I was whooping, just whooping like a maniac to the music as I got out of Tulsa and away over the thin and rickety bridges, over Bird Creek and Horsepen Creek and Caney River, through Oologah, tornado-struck just a couple of weeks back, through Talala and Watova and Nowata, cackling and singing my way into the great, flat, watery, tree-spattered blank of northeastern Oklahoma.

Lilac flowers stood pale on the verges. The road was a ribbon, straight ahead and behind in the windshield and the mirror. A sign said COFFEY-VILLE 12 MILES. Eleven miles later, I crossed into Kansas.

At the *Journal* Allen Twitchell looked taut and uneasy. It was Monday, he was getting married on Friday, and the girl's parents weren't letting her stuff out of the house—her clothes, her stereo, her records. She'd gone round there with the police to try and get this all dealt with; Twitch was waiting for news. He was thirty-four, the girl was eighteen, and her parents were mad.

But he was, he said, trying to get himself respectable these days. He'd even sold the Firebird, and got a little Geo Prism instead. "I sold the Firebird to a seventeen-year-old who never had a car before, because only a seventeen-year-old who never had a car before could think it'd be good to go around in a car like that."

I said I needed a vehicle myself. I needed, for this journey, a seriously *American* vehicle: I needed a pickup truck.

I scanned the small ads in the *Journal,* and in the *Independence Reporter.* There was a V6 turbo for six hundred dollars, "drives good, looks rough." There was a truck over three thousand dollars, "lots of chrome"—but that was too much money.

In short, there was nothing—but it didn't matter. I knew that there was, in Coffeyville, the ideal man to fix me up—so I drove a half-block down 8th Street from the *Journal* to Red Nose Sam's.

John Vest behind the counter, Red Nose on his stool, slow Irving in the shadows at the back; rifles on the racks, electronics dangling wire on the shelves, dusty lights and boxes and a jumble of pawned goods, the TV tuned to CNN—it looked like nothing had even minutely moved or changed in the fourteen months since I'd been there before. John and Red Nose looked up, and both grinned; they slapped thighs and said in unison, "Aw shit. Look what the cat dragged in."

It was good to be back.

But they didn't figure I'd find the reliable truck I needed inside of three or four thousand. I'd need power steering, two-way radio, air. "If you can't afford it," said Red Nose, "you got 2/60 air. Two windows down at sixty miles an hour." And that, he said, just wasn't the same at all.

Six weeks later I went through McCook, Nebraska, the temperature reading 100 on the signs outside the banks. I shut off the air, wound down the window—and it was ugly, like sticking your head close into the hot, dry blast of a powerful hair dryer. So let me tell you—in the heart of America, you need air.

"You need air," said Red Nose. "I'm serious as a heart attack. What you're doing, you need air."

He took me to lunch at the Pig Stand to discuss the matter further. We went in his truck, of course—he disdained to ride in my rental car, on the grounds it was no better than "a motorized shoe skate"—then we went to do business at Perl Chevrolet.

Now Red Nose—surprise, surprise—once had a one-third interest in a used car lot himself. In the old days, he said, before government paperwork ruined every damn thing, there were two kinds of guarantee. There was a 30/30 guarantee—thirty feet, or thirty seconds. And there was a 50/50 guarantee—if it breaks in half, you get to keep both halves. But at Paddlefoot Perl Schmidt's, he said, I'd get a deal that'd stand up.

Paddlefoot himself, said Red Nose, was retired, at least in theory; being a city commissioner, "He has to go round saying he's retired, 'cause Perl Chevrolet sells cars to the city." So the business was run by his sons instead, and they were both out—but I explained what I wanted to DJ Morse, and he showed us an '81 Ford F100 half-ton sitting shiny on the lot. It was a white truck with a pale blue stripe along the side, and a daft kind of quilted silver camper on the back—a topper, an Okie box, with little shutters and diamond windows.

"You could sleep like a baby in that thing," said DJ. "I'll throw you in a foam mattress."

I drove it out with Red Nose to Dearing and back. Red Nose said it ran like a sewing machine, which apparently meant good. And to me—

sticking the automatic into drive then rolling smooth down the road, left elbow hanging out the wound-down window, right hand touched lightly to the power steering, the V8 slowly rumbling under the hood of this wallowing whale of a vehicle—well, it was perfect, utterly perfect. It was, said DJ, "a land yacht." But it cost three thousand dollars . . .

Red Nose said he'd fix me up—so the next day we went back to talk it through with John Schmidt. Red Nose said, "We think we've worked out a deal that'll help you boys out."

John said, "Hell, that's scary."

He sold me the truck for two thousand dollars, on the understanding he'd buy it back for a thousand dollars when I was done. Then I asked him, looking at the paperwork, what the "implied warranty" meant.

"It means soon as the taillights get out of our vision, it's your problem."

An hour after that the large and amiable Nancy Nipper had got me insured, and at Billie Lewark's county office I'd bought a license tag. Canceling those things at the end of the trip, I got refunds—so you're looking at fully legal and covered ownership of this vehicle, for the duration of the journey, at less than $1,350.

As John Schmidt said, signing my check when I brought the truck back, "What a deal. Isn't America a wonderful country?"

Right there and then, it did feel that way.

The truck had 117,843 miles on it. In ten years in Kansas, that's the equivalent of one careful lady owner. Red Nose said he hoped it wouldn't lay down and have pups on me, but he didn't think it would, and it didn't; nothing went wrong with it at all. Given what I did to it, that's the very definition of reliable.

DJ showed me round the engine. Power steering fluid here, automatic transmission fluid here, oil here, change the oil and the filter every two thousand miles. "I know you're not a gearhead," he said, "but I know you know it's got to have oil."

What's a gearhead?

"You grow up in this town, you're one of four things. You're a gearhead, a redneck, a jock, or a longhair. Or if your skin's a different color . . . well, we know those names too."

In less than forty-eight hours I was the proud and rightful owner of a pickup truck. Red Nose followed me down to Tulsa so I could hand in the rental car, then drove me back up. In the meantime I set to figuring how things went for the town of Coffeyville.

Not good, is the straight and simple answer. It's not, I should say first, a typical Kansas town; the gas- and oil-based industries built since the beginning of the century make it less dependent on agriculture than a lot of other places—but that hasn't helped.

At the turn of the eighties, nearly half of Coffeyville's 4,000 jobs in manufacturing went up in the economic smoke of the Reagan recession. A town that once topped 20,000 people, and had 15,575 in 1980, was down in the new census to 12,917—with recession ending the decade the way it began, and no serious chance of a turnaround in sight. In that regard at least, Coffeyville's vengefully typical.

Because all across Kansas—all across the heart of America—the small towns are shriveling. And with them there withers too the whole mythic notion of what America is, of family values and small-town virtues, of hard work and trust, of fellowship and community. From Coffeyville and all the other little places, hunting for a living, the people go to Wichita and Tulsa, to Oklahoma City and Kansas City or farther, to Dallas and Denver, to San Francisco and L.A. They vanish in the random and faceless mayhem of the murderous cities, and the endless identikit of their sprawling suburbs.

And America vanishes with them, feeling helpless and bewildered and angry, and not knowing who to blame . . .

Of the three girls I'd danced with in Shenanigan's a year back, only one was still in town.

And Shenanigan's was closed.


At the Pig Stand, Red Nose called "hi" to a tall man in dungarees who told Red Nose not to speak to him in public—he had, he grinned, his image to consider. Now this guy, said Red Nose, was a self-made man. He used to be in banking—but now he was in garbage, and had his own route.

The man was named Blake Allen; we met him again the next morning in the alley behind Red Nose's store, his truck grinding past the dumpster bins. Red Nose told him I was interested in tornadoes, so Blake said down at Tyro ten years ago a twister hit a creek there, took a right along the course of it, went a quarter mile south of his house, took out his neighbor's barn, jumped the road, then hit a trailer home. "There was nothing left but the axles. Just exploded that thing." So now Blake goes out riding the bush on his mule, and he'll be looking up the trees for coons—and now and then, even today, he'll still come on big sheets of tin wrapped like foil high around the trunks and the branches . . .

"You're so big," said Red Nose, "that mule ought to be riding you."

"You ain't seen my mule."

Red Nose shook his head. "Can you believe he used to be a loan officer? In a suit and tie? Hell," he said, as Blake clambered back into the rattling cab of his truck, "there's more money these days in trash than there is in banking." He gave a sorry little laugh, at the bad way the world was turning.

"There's more money," said Blake, "in anything than there is in banking."

"Too true. Banking just ain't no fun anymore."

Well—there's a degree of personal resonance in this. Red Nose was raised in Alice, Texas, by a grandmother and two aunts until he was nine, after his mother died young in São Paolo, Brazil. He came to join his father in Coffeyville in 1933—and in 1937 his father, after an early career in the milling business running exports to South America, founded the First Federal Savings & Loan Company, and the Coffeyville Loan & Investment Company. One of the town's big bankers, he became president of the Chamber of Commerce in 1942.

And now his son runs the pawn shop. . . . Mind you, since they put up the Wal-Mart out on 169, it's the busiest shop left downtown. It was, said John Vest, "the poor man's bank."

The radio said there'd been fifty twisters in the state that spring already; the weathermen were looking for a record, and the count was up nationwide. The worst day was Friday, April 26; Oklahoma that day had eighteen tornadoes, while fully thirty tore through Kansas. In Oklahoma three people died, and in Kansas twenty-five, including fourteen at the Golden Spur Mobile Home Park in the Wichita suburb of Andover. Over two hundred more were injured, and about fifteen hundred left homeless.

The week before I got to Coffeyville, another tornado traveled seventy miles along pretty much exactly the same track as the one that tore up Andover. That, said the experts, was a million-to-one event.

Red Nose took me and John Vest to his house on the Grand Lake o' the Cherokees. He was doing way over fifty-five, but when I asked about that he said, "Hell, in this country everybody's got speeding tickets. There ain't a swinging dick in America that hasn't sped—if you ain't speeding, you ain't going nowhere."

But he slowed down as we went through Oologah, and started pointing things out. Stands of trees looked like they'd been bombed, shredded, and stripped. "That was a house," said Red Nose, "and this. This was a church. This was a store." There was nothing left but the foundations. In all, thirty homes had been flattened.

We passed a big new school, the roof all battered and torn. Brick walls had been pulped, the building was unusable—and behind it, the buckled wrecks of the school's buses were parked out in ragged lines. The twister had hit the bus barn, and of the twenty-four buses, every one had been damaged or destroyed; on the morning after, six of them couldn't even be found. Word had it, said John, one of them got dumped in a creek *four miles away.*

That same Friday evening, LaRita White and her four children were heading back to Coffeyville from Dewey, Oklahoma. On 75 north of Copan they ran into a hailstorm, so she decided to turn back. But the weather seemed to clear, so she turned around again—and ran, this time, into hail the size of softballs. Once more she turned back for Dewey—but now the rain and the hail got so dense, she was forced to pull over. And then . . .

White told the *Journal,* "I never figured we were going through a tornado. We never even saw the thing coming or heard it coming, the next thing we knew we were up in the air. The tornado picked us up—we were turning around, and it just dropped us on the side of a hill. The whole time this is going on we were just praying. I don't know how long or how far up in the air we were—I have never heard anything like it. All the damages to the car are what was in the tornado with us. I mean, it was loud. It was just so violent. The tornado was just coming in and ripping that car all apart. My daughter kept saying, 'We're going to die, we're going to die.' I said, 'No, Nicole, we're not going to die, just keep praying.' We just kept calling Jesus."

There was so much grass inside the car afterwards that White said, "It looks like a garden."

I tried to find LaRita White—but unfortunately, like 2,658 other people since 1980, the lady had left town.

People couldn't figure out why Twitch was marrying this girl.

Twitch said he loved her, which seemed good enough to me.

Fritz Green said her parents weren't mad meaning angry, they were mad meaning *crazy*—they'd got God in a big way. Fritz figured they'd detain her, she wouldn't show. Or she would show, and the parents would too—with guns. As best man, he was wondering if he should pack a weapon in his tux.

The girl was named Sharon. She said her mom told her Twitch was an alcoholic, he'd been married before, he had a daughter, he probably had AIDS, and he was definitely a demon.

"Apart from that," said Twitch, "I'm a really great guy."

We had dinner at his parents' place on a county road out of town. A pale crimson sun died into a lilac sky over thirty acres of wheat before the peeling white porch; barn swallows nested in the eaves. Twitch's dad, Virgil, sat on the swing and told how, when he was fifteen, he'd ridden fence in North Dakota one summer with a Creek named Dutch Wells. It was only ninety miles, he said, from the place he'd been working to the Canada line, and he wished he'd gone and crossed it. That way, he said, he'd have seen another country.

Night came down, and the lights of the oil refinery on the edge of town glittered bright over the trees on the horizon. "That's our skyline," said Twitch. He paused and added, "We had two refineries in this town once."

He roamed the end of the garden in the gathering dark. Among the flares of the fireflies he had a tad more to worry about, I suppose, than most men in their last bachelor days.

Fritz asked, "You ever been to a wedding in a flak jacket before?"

John Vest had bought himself a second wrecked house for two thousand two hundred dollars, three doors down from the burn-out he had already. He got the money from a win on the Indian bingo down in Tulsa—so I went with him and Bruce, a supervisor for a chain of convenience stores, Mary, who worked in one of them, and Missie, who worked in a cemetery, to see if he could win big again.

"What's that on the road up there, Bruce?"

"Motorcycle. Looks like a Honda Goldwing. Either that, or the fastest bag lady you ever saw."

John's a little guy, shambolic and cheerful with a big dirty grin. His friends call him Tripod (though not to his face), which you can work out for yourself. Bruce, on the other hand, was very, very large—and these were old buddies here. It was Bruce who got John drunk the first time in his life; John danced with chairs. Back then you got five burgers for a dollar, so they bought ten—Bruce had two, reached in the bag, and it was empty. "Hell," says John, "I thought I only had seven."

"I don't know if he ate them or threw them at people."

Bruce figured he was seven hundred dollars ahead on the bingo, from twelve trips in the last month—eighty-five miles each way. He had a key

ring that said, depending which corner you pressed, FUCKING JERK, FUCK YOU, YOU'RE AN ASSHOLE, EAT SHIT. We streaked down 169 to a soundtrack of tinny electronic cursing mixed with the sporadic shrieking warble of the radar detector, the dash chirper. Going through Oologah again, I noticed a few pieces of furniture this time—a wardrobe, a table, a chair—dumped alone in the flattened fields and pasture. Then Tulsa came up on the horizon, a stubby scatter of futurescape similarly dumped on the banks of the Arkansas.

Built on Indian land there—so the gambling was legal—the Creek Nation Tulsa Bingo Hall could take thirteen hundred people. It was a rectangular box, slow tonight with only five hundred players (the great majority white) sitting hushed and intent over their cards at rank upon rank of long narrow tables. The balls whispered and clattered in the bowl, the numbers coming up fast so you really had to concentrate. You played to fill in lines across your card, or shapes—an arrow, a kite, two stamps, a block of eight, a crazy T—with a speedball blackout thrown in now and then. It was mind-numbing; it was desolate. A withered woman at my table with a pile of black hair like frozen rotted cotton candy must have spent hundreds of dollars on the cards laid out around her and on a vast pile of pull-tabs—little one-armed bandits. She ripped at the tabs with an expressionless, remorseless, robotic intensity.

Then there was Megabingo—fifty-five halls in fifteen states from California to Vermont all linked up by satellite, playing together for a possible $1,000,000. The hall grew more hushed than ever, the caller reverent with the numbers on the monitor screens. And then—"All halls stand by please, we have a bingo"—someone in Santa Fe picked up $5,000.

I talked with Frances Mesnard, a slight and pretty half-Indian woman who was managing the place that night, and with Bob Kulp, a fat, sweaty type from Gamma International Ltd., the gaming outfit that runs the Megabingo network. Last week's total payout had been $245,000, when typical sales would be twice that. The Creek Nation got half the profits, which, Frances said, obviously benefitted the tribe. The hall opened seven years back; before that, they played mainly in churches.

You could have an armed guard to escort you to your car when you won. When John won the money for his second house, the guard even came to the rest room with him.

Kulp worked out back in a computer-jammed trailer by the satellite dish. He talked a grandiose vision of global bingo, of Alaska, Canada,

Venezuela all wanting in, of doing a demo for the Japanese . . . The average customer, he said, was a forty-year-old lady.

Back inside I went to stand on the stage. The view from there was weird, like looking down on an exam room. As he gathered each ball the caller flourished it with an airy little wave, then set it down with the number lined up into a lens for transmission to the screens around the hall. He had the strangest way of saying, kind of calm and bored and sinister all at once, "This game is *clooowhhsed*."

But then, so are large swathes of the American economy—Coffeyville, after all, isn't bucking any trends. And in the fairyland that economy's now become, with the federal government, many cities, and the majority of the fifty states running deficits so big no one dares even look at them anymore—well, gambling's a thing government reaches for with the same frantic hope of the crazy woman with her pull-tabs.

So down the Mississippi you can gamble on the riverboats again—revenue masquerading as heritage. In the bars of Nebraska you can play keno, a kind of simpleton's bingo. Or you can give your money to the Indians, and to Gamma International, in the burgeoning network of their bingo halls.

Back in Coffeyville I went wearily for a whiskey at Butterfield's, and was enormously pleased to find that one thing at least hadn't changed. Loretta, hands-down winner of my award for Best Barmaid in the Heart of America, was still working there.

That was the good news. The bad news was that Loretta had cancer.

Turns out—according to a local history written by Tillie Karns Newman in 1961—that the first settler to join the Osage Indians on the banks of the Verdigris was, in fact, a black man. He came from Texas in the early 1860s, and his name was Lewis Scott, or Scaggs. He settled on the east bank, across the river from the Black Dog band of the Osage; in 1866 his brother Abe brought his wife, eight children, and a span of mules to join him.

James A. Coffey came two years later from Humboldt, sixty miles to the north, hauling wagon trains of merchandise, and a grand piano from Kansas City. Seems Humboldt, when its population hit 250, was getting too big for him—and he moved on from Coffeyville too, in the end. The influx began the next year, 1869, leading to much confusion and claim-jumping, and the establishment as a consequence of Claim Protection Clubs. These were judge, jury, and executioner too. "It was not uncom-

mon to find after a protection hearing a defendant hanging from the limb
of a strong tree near the roadside," Ms. Newman wrote.

As for the Indians, in theory they had eight million acres—but the
government wanted them shifted onto a "Diminished Reservation" in
Indian Territory (now Oklahoma), so an offer was made of 20¢ an acre
for their Kansas land. A treaty was signed on Drum Creek on May 27,
1868, after Chief Black Dog's initial objections (a representative named
Sidney Clarke subsequently caused sufficient fuss in Congress about this
steal to push the price up to $1.25 an acre) and a Quaker agent named
Isaac Gibson then "gently led his wards from Coffeyville . . . it was a slow
process. The Osage were reluctant to go. All their possessions were
packed on ponies and dogs. Long poles, or travois, hung from the backs
of these animals loaded with skins, robes, cooking equipment, and food
supplies. Some Indians walked, some rode ponies, but there was much
mourning and wailing in protest."

In 1872, a Cherokee named Chouteau started giving out handbills
round the town laying claim to the land on which that town was now
so rapidly rising. He was murdered.

Coffeyville was incorporated in 1869; the Leavenworth, Lawrence, &
Galveston Railroad arrived in 1871, and cattle began pouring up from
Texas to the railhead stockyards. A nearby settlement called Parker had
hoped the railroad would go there instead . . .

In 1871, the influx of restless cowboys driving cattle caused the opening of
numerous saloons and dance houses; this brought in the usual gang of
gamblers, thugs, and all-around toughs who constituted the patrons and
hangers-on of such places. These gentry took sides with Coffeyville against
Parker. Almost daily threats were made that they were about to raid and
wipe Parker out of existence, and the experiment was made on several
occasions. Among the frequenters of 'Red Hot Street' . . . was a notorious
gang known as the Adams gang. They had frequently boasted that they were
going to Parker to shoot up the town. One morning word came that they
were actually advancing on the city, and preparation was made to give them
a warm reception. They were heard riding across the river bridge and soon
appeared on Oak Street . . . they were met by a committee who told them
that they were not wanted, and their attention was called to the gleaming
guns protruding from every corner and doorway along the street. This ended
the interview, and the Adams gang withdrew.

Without the railroad, of course, Parker died anyway.

But consider, meanwhile, the extraordinary, the fantastical, the exponential growth of American life and raw vigor at that time: from one black settler, to a railroad and cow town in less than a decade. Bridges went up over the river; Captain Napoleon Bonaparte Blanton opened a ferry service across it, and a hotel in town. People poured in in the hundreds; churches went up, and schools. At first, one of Coffey's daughters taught school in their kitchen—but there was a tax-supported school by December 1871, only three short years after James Coffey first arrived.

One hundred and twenty years later, the state governor vetoed a tax raise designed to put more money into Kansas schools. Red Nose remarked, "We don't teach our people to read and write and make change anymore."

I went out to Ruth and OB Johnson's to feed the catfish again. OB'd put thirty or forty weed-eaters in the lake to keep it clean, some sort of Chinese fish. The catfish came slopping up for their bread; squirrels shot about on the lawn, and cardinals almost luminously red settled briefly on the birdseed, darting about. Ruth showed me the pecan and the oak and the persimmon trees again, and the walnut trees she'd grown by setting walnuts in the lawn a dozen years back.

The house was on a knoll above a dirt country road, just across the line into Oklahoma; they'd built it there twenty-two years ago. OB said he'd seen two tornadoes—not close, no thanks—and he showed me the storm cellar. The ceiling was thick concrete laid over substantial steel girders—you could, he said, drive a bulldozer through the living room overhead, and the place would stay sound. So when they got what he called "hairy broadcast" out there, they went downstairs and slept it out.

He said if you do see a tornado, just pray you keep seeing it. Because once it got too close it'd fade, the world'd go dark—but by then, I said, you'd be lying in a ditch praying. He laughed. "That'd be right."

I'd figured them to be in their sixties, these two—so I was gobsmacked when Ruth told me OB was seventy-eight, and herself not far behind him. They seemed two of the kindest, the most decent people I ever met. OB'd worked forty years straight at the Acme Foundry & Machine Co.—and he'd just now got new corneas, he said, so he was back to 20/20, near as good as his working days; he was quietly happy over that. Ruth said the only thing she regretted was that she hadn't traveled—but she had a friend who did her traveling for her, so she heard about the world that way.

Their granddaughter later told me, "They would carry a Popsicle stick ten miles rather than throw it on the ground. If OB paid even a nickel less than he should have on something, if he got home and realized that, he'd turn right around to go back and settle."

Down in the tramcar cabin, Ruth showed me two 7-pound bass her son had caught, stuffed and mounted. The lake glimmered outside. "There's an old boy up on the next hill," she said, "came here as a babe in 1901, he'd remember better than I would—but there was a teapot dome here, they found oil here in the twenties, and they had five lease houses put up for the pumpers. And they used spans of mules to dig out the lake for a sludge pit—so that's how come we got it here now."

She watched OB turn and turn around the lawn on his mini-tractor mower, and changed the subject fondly to say, "You know, for a man of seventy-eight that man is remarkable to me. He does more work than most men of fifty or sixty—and he never does it grudgingly. Though he likes machines," she smiled, "so I guess that does help."

"Every day's Saturday with her," said OB.

It was broiling hot, high in the eighties, the sun burning in a dazzling blue sky over the oak and elm around their land. Far in the West, a great slow anvil of thunderhead formed up through the late afternoon, marching northeast along the horizon. Severe thunderstorms were predicted—but they didn't come to us. Bullfrogs roared down by the lake, as the evening came down.

OB said now, that lake was clean as a whistle. There was still oil to be had here, he said, and the companies had contracts that promised they'd make no mess getting it out. But there was no way you went for oil, there wasn't some of it got to leaking some place—and he wasn't taking no chances with that lake.

I felt the way I did a year before; Ruth and OB's place seemed again a little pocket of paradise in the heart of America. I tried hard not to let it feel punctured, when Ruth told me that lately the house had twice been burgled.

The night of the Big Scare, Friday, April 26, the tornado that spun LaRita White and her kids up through the air in their car tore past Copan, twenty miles southwest of Coffeyville. On the edge of that town the Handi Mart, Ruth's Country Kitchen, and the Copan Bait Shop were flattened. Cars were flung five hundred yards; sixty-year-old Nada Packard died when the car she was in got blown across a field.

I went by there with Gretchen Pippenger from the *Journal,* and gawped at the foundations left clean after the debris had been swept away. The Handi Mart sign—on a hollow metal post seven or eight inches square, thick metal too—was flung down on the scoured forecourt. It had sheared clean off at the base, the metal torn through like a strip of paper twisted in half in your hands.

Twitch's bachelor party was at Fritz and Angie's place, a few miles west of town up a hill off of 166. That April night, said Fritz, Angie was in the closet screaming—but Fritz is a weather buff, and he stood outside in that storm saying exultantly to himself, "Yeah! I can see *everything!*"

He and John Vest the year before had taken me up a bluff over the east side of town, and told how when the warnings were issued, they'd get up there hoping to see a twister pass. Gretchen said she used to do that too; but now she'd seen and photographed up close the kind of damage they do, she wasn't so sure she'd go looking anymore. "Maybe I'd still like to see one—but from a *long* way away. Because they can change direction," she said. "Those things can come *after* you."

I stood with Fritz and Twitch in Fritz's front garden; I tried to imagine the sky and the wind howling black and ferocious, on fire with lightning, dumping rocks of ice at 100 miles an hour. In the Dalton Museum there's a cast of a hailstone 17½ inches in circumference, dated September 3, 1970; it lays claim to the world record. We're talking melon-sized hail here: imagine what it'd do to your greenhouse. Or your head.

And all through the trip I heard ads on the radio for hail-damaged car sales—in eastern Colorado one time, an announcer raving enthused at the prices of "these dimpled darlings" . . .

But right then it was a calm cool night, the crickets whirring in the cornfield on the other side of the dirt road. Under the starry sky in the mass of the land, loud the way it was with bugs and birds, I felt suddenly like I was back in Africa—some place wild, anyhow, and impossibly remote. Then the other guys rolled up, and we got drunk and played poker.

I told a teacher I'd be out in western Kansas soon, when the wedding was done. He said he used to work in Dodge City out there, and every weekend he'd split, just get out on the plains. "You find a little rise, stand up there, and everything for thirty miles around is lower than your ankle—and it's like . . . I'd spend whole afternoons out there just watching beetles cross the road. You never hear a car, a truck, nothing—not fifteen, not fifty miles away. Man," he said, "it's *scary* out there."

Then all of a sudden, I don't know how, parked on Fritz's lawn in the cool and cricket-busy night, we were talking Vietnam. The teacher said everyone his age, everyone—if they didn't go themselves, they all had friends, people they knew, lifted up and shipped off into madness. And he said, or murmured, "They'll never be happy again. Never be happy again. Not crazy or anything—just never be happy again."

Lightning bugs flared through the corn. The teacher said how Coffeyville once was a queen of a city, how in the twenties there was way over twenty thousand in this place. "Before they got the oil down in Tulsa this was the biggest thing south of Kansas City; hell, Tulsa used to come *here* to play. One Fourth of July early this century, six thousand people got off the trams into Coffeyville just for that one day."

And now? Now they were planning a civic pride campaign called, with a kind of blithely unthinking aptness, Operation Prairie Storm. Central to this exercise was the tearing down of 150 abandoned and derelict houses . . . but there's a lot of ways to flatten a house. Between tornadoes, wars, and the relentless march of free-market economics, it's no wonder Americans are an impermanent lot—ricocheting like Melissa on her way to North Dakota round the huge and scary land.

I slept in the back of the truck. When I woke up, head like a brick, the grey sky was hammering down hard rain. I drove slowly back to town, with a weird and nervy memory sinking in that I'd made an agreement. I'd agreed to give the bride away . . .

Anyone got a flak jacket?

But what the hell, I was honored. If the rest of her friends were so gutless they were scared of getting shot in the church . . . like I say, what the hell—I was honored.

I was also hung over, late for a little ceremony I'd planned to attend, and so late for a meeting with the police chief that I'd missed it altogether. The ceremony was the dedication of Coffeyville's 911 number—and it seemed to me amazing that a town of this size, even this shrinking size, should have gone so long without a unified emergency number.

The police chief's secretary grinned, and said things wouldn't change much. "I'll still get the same bullshit calls, people asking about the weather. And I'll still tell them the same thing."

Which was?

"Look out the window."

Glen Welden the city manager was there, among other local worthies jammed into the foyer of the police department. I remembered interviewing him the year before, and how it was definitely one of the more boring hours I've spent with a tape recorder. He'd got out the map and told me all the places you could get to if you got out of Coffeyville. Bald and sly and trimly bearded, he looked like the storekeeper in the Westerns—the guy in the black frock coat who plays both sides, and measures the main characters with his eyes as they pass by for the size of their coffins.

I wondered how the worthies would feel if their town was called Scottsville, or Scaggsville. After a cheerful encounter with a black guy in the street one time, Red Nose had said, "I get on better with the brothers than I do with the white boys. I'm too outspoken. And," he said, with an arch significance, "I know where the bodies are buried."

Well—he loved to play his role of town scoundrel, but at least he spoke straight—and he said, in essence, that the town was fucked sideways, and going nowhere real fast. It was, in short, a town seriously under the weather—with more jobs under threat even now, as work at the local branch of a national company got relocated elsewhere. . . .

"If people can't make a living," said Red Nose, "you can't have a community. A community needs air, water, and money. Well, air and water we got—but money we don't. 'Cause once you've lost your locally owned newspaper, your radio station, your banks, once the chains have moved in—then you got a problem. 'Cause then nobody gives a shit."

He had only one hope. Looking out over the moonlit water on Grand Lake's thirteen hundred miles of shoreline he said, "When California runs out of water, the people'll come back." And the money'd come back with them. . . . In the meantime, metaphorically at least, he'd been doing a bit of coffin measuring himself. "What Coffeyville needs," he said, "is a few expensive funerals."

I only hoped, with this wedding, mine wouldn't be one of them.

At the 911 ceremony, I talked to the ambulance man who'd found LaRita White. He was coming back from Bartlesville, unaware that there'd been a tornado—though he figured now, most likely, he'd not been a lot more than five minutes in the wake of it—and suddenly he came to all this debris on the highway, leaves, and bits of trees. "It looked like fall in a country lane. And they were standing on the verge with the car in the ditch so I asked, Did you have a wreck? And they said No, something picked us up in the air. And I'm going, Awww . . . but then I look around and I start to see. I mean, there was a piece of a tree sat right on the front seat in there."

And they only just now got a 911 number?

There was a thing that worried me about this wedding, or about marriage in general, something more in the long term than the possibility of aggrieved God freaks spraying lead down the aisle—and that was ... well, that was marriage itself, in this impermanent country out here.

The boys, I'd been told, wanted beer and pussy; the girls wanted to dance, and to laugh. But this crude idyll, it seemed, took on a very different aspect once rings were on fingers ... The way the boys told it, the girls underwent overnight transformations just as soon as they'd said, I do. A boy would go to bed on his wedding night with the girl of his dreams—then wake up in the morning to find he was sharing the sheets with a nagging harpy.

An oafish country song kept playing on the radio, in which the singer whined that he was just a simple man, all he wanted was a job and a piece of land—so he was working and he was tired, and *why don't you give it a rest?*

One guy I knew freaked himself out once, when he grabbed hold of his woman so hard he left big bruise marks down her arm. He told himself, Whoa boy ... ain't nothing worth getting that crazy.

The woman in question talked fast and high. "He says he loves me, but I need more than just him saying that. I need respect. I don't call him bad names. He says he loves me—so why does he call me bitch?"

At Fritz and Angie's, when the women got back to join us drunk men in the small hours, I ended slumped on the kitchen floor between one couple, watching the perspectives of their dispute bat back and forth across me, and it was like sitting in an echoing chasm.

He talked about how she was always on his back, and she didn't pick up the house, and she didn't have to work.

She talked about their debts, the need to keep a budget, the money he spent on beer, and how she wanted them to get ahead, and how of course she had to work.

So I looked vaguely for a bridge of reason, or compromise—but forget it, I didn't make a dent, not a scratch. And Twitch stood watching—a great way to end up your bachelor night. Except of course he knew all about it, having been married once before. And if someone shot him tomorrow, I guess he'd not be worrying too much anyhow.

Five days later, an editorial in the *Daily Oklahoman* fretted how three out of four marriages in that state now ended in divorce. More locally, in northeastern Oklahoma—beginning a mile south of Coffeyville—the record was worse.

The figure for Tulsa was nine out of ten.

We gathered at the First United Methodist Church, across from the library on West 10th Street. The wedding was to be at eight in the evening.

Gretchen, who was twenty-two years old, turned up with her boy-friend Bart, and they were a good-looking couple. She said people kept asking her when they were going to do what everyone else did, and get married—but she said she was too smart for that. Bart, looking through the big glass windows of the entrance hall, calmly opined that it was raining "harder than a cow pissing on a flat rock."

Twitch's brother arrived, and asked an amiable fireman named Wayne if he could tie his tie for him. He didn't, he said, get to wear a tie all that often.

Wayne said Sharon's parents were "crazier than a pet coon. If they turn up, it's gonna be fist city round here." He had, he said, thought seriously of packing his Colt.

Fritz said they'd been ringing the preacher, threatening to "rebuke the demon."

A short, round woman with a gorgeous smile turned up and said cheerfully, "Hey, you should talk to me. I'm the only happily married woman in Coffeyville. Mind you," she then added, by way of explanation, "I'm Italian. From Chicago."

Twitch wandered around acting superhumanly calm, keeping an eye with his mother on Shannon, his exquisitely pretty little eight-year-old girl. The service was to be in a small chapel to one side of the entrance hall; the reception afterwards would be in a spartan white room in the basement.

Outside, the sky was leaden and grim, the air heavy with black water. Wayne said his Mom saw a tornado once—said she called it, "Wicked-ness in its purest form."

The guests milled loosely round the hallway. Sharon downstairs looked radiant, but nervous as hell. "Is Allen nervous? Is he excited? Do I look okay?"

You look great.

"I had my hair done. Several times. Look," she said, "the flowers smell. Look, see—they're plastic, but they smell." She swished her train back and forth behind her, petrified of tripping on it.

At eight a boy sang a song solo to the guests filling the little chapel. I took Sharon upstairs with the bridesmaids, and walked her down the aisle, and gave her away. She shook like a leaf from beginning to end—but no wind came strong enough to blow anyone away, and there were no interruptions, and it all went off smooth as silk.

Diving outside for a cigarette afterwards, I found the clouds in the sunset sky had turned during the wedding into an awesome heavy lid of orange and mauve; the sun fell in the west through a torrent beneath the cloud's edge of turquoise and fire. In the east, against a soupy background of indigo, a massive rainbow arched up bright into heaven.

The weather, after all, isn't always malevolent.


*Road Addiction*

Five weeks later, I got in my truck and followed Robert Carver out of Ellsworth Air Force Base in South Dakota, past the B-52 and the two armed men at the gate—then I hurried the few miles south to rejoin I90 heading west.

In the next two weeks, I drove 4,367 miles.

I90 goes round the north of the Black Hills, past Sturgis and Spearfish to Wyoming; the hills were pretty, a jaggedy ruck of green slope and pine. The storm that had threatened earlier in the afternoon had passed by; the sky was a cathedral of clear evening blue, fading to whitish violet where the dome of air met the land.

Across the line I left the interstate and gassed up at Beulah, a little motley of houses tucked into a dip in the road. In the dust in front of the weathered wooden porch the gas station had one ancient pump; it was also a bar and store. I microwaved some kind of Texican sandwich, a mess of fiery chili and processed meats, stuck a can of Classic Coke in the cup holder, and headed on west.

Eastern Wyoming's an empty expanse of buckled, arid, short-grass prairie; it rolled away on all sides, shattered and worn, a bleak and lovely ocean of land. I pulled into a rest area somewhere between Sundance and Moorcroft, and stared across thin grass and red earth past a knot of trees round a distant ranch; Devil's Tower rose solitary and eerie on the northern horizon, a mysterious thumb of rock in grey silhouette against the lilac edge of the sky.

Wind plucked and tugged at the truck, rocking the half-ton like it was no more than a fragile bit of dust. It was 8:15. In the west, two thunderheads climbed the reddening sky side by side, the anvils spreading wide and sweeping my way.

By 8:30 the anvils had merged. The two squat cloud towers beneath were tinted a sinister, marbled yellow in the falling sun. A Burlington Northern coal train rumbled by, the metal of the black-loaded cars flashing orange. The merged anvils were like a huge burning horseshoe. I got the National Weather Service out of Gillette on my Weatheradio; they were issuing a Severe Thunderstorm Watch.

I drove maybe forty miles farther into the blackening night, then followed signs to the Crazy Woman Campground in Gillette. Murky clouds spilt hurriedly by in the last light; where I parked for the night the wind came roaring and groaning over a scrubby rise, stirring the trees to a ceaseless noisy hissing, a great stage whisper of sibilant alarm. The truck bucked and rocked in the wind. On DJ's foam mattress I had trouble falling asleep, and when I did, I dreamt uneasy dreams.

I woke at five, threw water on my face, gunned the engine to howls of outrage from various unhappy campers, and set off across sixty-eight empty miles to Buffalo for breakfast.

I had reached a point of madness; I had road addiction, and would drive now till I dropped.

# 2.

# Storm Chaser

Seventeen miles west of Coffeyville, Wayne the fireman and maybe seventy other people pitched two camps for the weekend on open land by the Caney High School, one Confederate, one Yankee. An Indian guy sat by Wayne's tent, making black powder cartridges in little tubes of stiff white paper. He had a replica 1858 Remington; Wayne had a replica 1851 Colt Navy, and a Mississippi Zouave rifle. Hot dogs sizzled in a huge old pan on a grill over the campfire. The temperature was high 80s; in their heavy wool uniforms they must have been burning up. Horses grazed around the white tents and tepees. Everything, said Wayne, drinking from a tin cup, was as authentic as they could manage. They'd have a battle at noon. A small boy asked who the star would be; Wayne told him, "We're all stars." All he needed to get his set of gear complete, he said, was a canteen and a bayonet.

Over in the Yankee camp, a man with gleaming buttons and epaulettes said, "You won't find a beautiful old uniform like this in that mangy old reb camp."

People wore the blue or the grey according to which side their forebears fought on. Wayne said, "Most people here are, I wouldn't say educated necessarily, but people who think, and read—people interested in our history. And for Americans, this is the pivot point of our history. Everything that went before led up to this, everything that's happened since is a consequence of it. It fractured everything in one way, and brought everything together in another. So it's a patriotic feeling to be here—you watch the battle and you'll see guys riding out there with tears welling up in their eyes, because this means so much to us. If you don't understand this, you're not an American."

Of Lincoln he said, "We've had presidents come and go, but he was the one. We'd not have what we have today without Lincoln."

Red Nose was a Nixon man—"All he did was get caught."

His buddy Phil Bernhart said he went to Eisenhower's funeral up at Abilene. "Only time I saw three presidents—two alive, and one in a box. Lyndon was there, and Tricky Dicky. And obviously Ike was there."

Phil was a Democrat; Red Nose castigated the Democrats' Works Progress Administration of the thirties as "two a-coming, two a-going, two a-shitting, two a-mowing," and cursed all their subsequent works too.

"You got to remember," said Phil, "this is just a lot of Republican propaganda."

"He's got Roosevelt tattooed on both cheeks of his ass."

"The only mistake Roosevelt ever made was putting Ronald Reagan's daddy to work and keep him from starving."

The battle was to be fought on the hill by the cemetery.

Some guys, Wayne said, did this twice a month all through the summer.

The rebel infantry formed up, then marched across the road and up the hill. Once there, they fanned out off the open ground into the edge of a long stand of woodland. People from the country all around lined the cemetery road, watching as other men at the camps mounted horses, then rode towards us under the blazing blue sky. The Caney water tower gleamed silver in the sun, high above the radiant green of the springtime land. Union infantry crept low through the grass towards the rebs in the trees and bushes; cracks of blank rifleshot burst against the wide silence, and puffs of airy smoke drifted over the field. Then, with scattered whoops and yelling, the two groups of cavalry charged against each other in a thunder of hooves on the earth, swords drawn, pistols sharply popping like whiplash. Out in the field now and then an infantryman flung an arm to the sky, spun around, and fell. Sweat-lathered, the horses pounded past, leather slapping, spurs and tack jingling.

A Confederate officer came by on his huffing, wide-nostrilled horse when they were done, and called to the crowd and the excited pointing kids, "Like to thank y'all for coming. Y'all come on back to camp now if you'd like to, and we'll show you the equipment. Everything's the original, or the closest reproduction you can get to if it ain't—from the underwear up."

Someone in the crowd called back, "Is that Kentucky or Tennessee bourbon you got in your flask there, sir?"

The rider smiled back, "Good Missouri flat-belly corn."

In the hospital tent women in hooped skirts bustled around men acting wounded with bloodied bandages and slings, letting out the odd moan, or a gasp for water. Children stared in rapt silence, clutching their mothers' hands and clothes. One man had a mocked-up stump, lying on a board table by a box of gruesome blades. A surgeon wandered by saying, "Do we have any laudanum?"

"Help me turn this man over—and be *easy* with him now."

"He's a Yankee."

"He's a wounded man. Son, what's your name?"

"Reece."

"And where you from?"

"Nevada Territory."

"Well, we'll see and make sure you get back there."

Other women prepared vegetables in the kitchen tent next door, hacking them with battered old knives into steaming pots on a fire. Nurses came to get water from the barrel with a dented metal dipper; one kid asked, "Ma'am, is he *really* shot in the stomach?"

I went over to Wayne's camp. In a chest in his tent he had a copy of "The Military Maxims of Napoleon." A young boy asked, "Do you have to spend the night in this tent?"

"No TV!" his mom grinned. "No Ninja Turtles! Ooh yuk."

"It's a lot of fun," said Wayne, putting on his spook-the-kid face, "when it's twenty below."

I asked him how people decided in the battle that they'd been shot.

He laughed. "We lie down and fake it when we're too tired and hot, mostly." Then he asked me what this book I was doing was all about, anyhow.

So I said how this was the heart of America here, and how people in Europe, and probably in New York and California too, thought it was merely big and flat and boring—but that I didn't think so myself, and I wanted to see how that heart beat.

"Hey Kevin, you hear that? You know what they think in Europe? They think Kansas is boring. They sure can't have been here."

Kevin grinned. "They probably have been."

Kevin was back recently from Montana; he'd been working as an extra on a Custer miniseries up there. Checking his gun he said suddenly, "Hot dang, I still got a round in here. I could still be fighting."

"No, you couldn't," Wayne laughed. "You died."

You can mock up a battle, pretend to die, then get up and walk away afterwards. If a tornado, on the other hand, has your name written on the wind—there's no walking away from that.

The first known photograph of a tornado was taken in 1884. At the top of the black central column, two pointy little funnels drop down from the main cloud to either side of it: it looks like the devil with a goatee.

On average, tornadoes kill around a hundred people a year—but some years, obviously, are worse than others. The greatest single death toll occurred in the Tri-State Outbreak, on the afternoon of March 18, 1925. Along a 219-mile path through Missouri, Illinois, and Indiana, seven tornadoes killed 740 people.

It's possible that the Enigma Outbreak was worse, when sixty tornadoes struck Mississippi, Georgia, Alabama, Tennessee, Kentucky, and the Carolinas on February 19, 1884. The official death toll is 420—but the figure ranges in the literature as high as 1,200.

The Enigma Outbreak also involved the third largest number of tornadoes touching down in one session. The largest number of strikes, however, occurred during an event whose scale is staggering even by the habitually savage standards of American weather—an event called simply the Super Outbreak.

In 1974, from noon on April 3, through to the following morning, 148 tornadoes touched down in thirteen states from Illinois to Virginia, from Alabama to Michigan. They wrought damage in excess of six hundred million dollars—and killed 315 people. . . .

No one knows for sure how tornadoes happen. The conditions and the mechanics are well enough understood—but why one storm should produce a tornado, and another theoretically similar storm should not, continues to be a much-studied mystery.

For starters, however, you need a good juicy thunderstorm. Thunderstorms fire up, or "pop," in the local slang, when warm wet tropical air pushes up from the Gulf of Mexico, and meets either cold dry air coming down out of Canada, or warm dry air spilling eastward from the desert states off the Rockies. Where the air masses crash together, the warm moist air gets forced upward in a great tower of boiling cumulus;

aided by rising thermals off the earth at peak heating time in the late afternoon, these severe storm updrafts can hit 100 miles an hour. So you can literally stand and watch as crisp, glossy stacks of cloud surge majestically into the atmosphere, exploding into the jet stream.

Now up there you'll have a great spinning tube of wind lying flat over the storm—a tube set spinning by winds of, say, 90 miles an hour at 20,000 feet, shearing against winds of 150 miles an hour at 30,000 feet. And while the top of the storm cloud's being whisked off ahead by the upper-level winds—thus forming the anvil—that spinning tube gets buckled upwards in the middle by the rising surge of cumulus that you're presently watching.

So the back end of the tube tilts earthward. The speed of its rotation increases because, now it's been jolted off the horizontal, the winds acting on it are coming from different directions. Up high, the winds in the jet stream are westerly—but nearer the ground, the wind's still coming from the Gulf in the southeast. It's at this point that God's let his monster spinning top go.

Above all this, the cumulonimbus hits fifty thousand feet; chunks of ice condensing up there get big enough to beat the updraft, and start falling as large hail. The sky under the clouds where you're watching, by the way, may well be green by now—which is a thoroughly eerie thing to see.

Meanwhile, air's pouring in around the bottom of the storm, sucked in there by the tilted spin of what we must now call the mesocyclone— and the inrushing air further increases the speed of this upward whirl at the heart of the storm. The mesocyclone, accelerating, grows narrower and taller, until it stretches right through the full height of the system, blowing out a hole in the top of it, and hauling air up and inward at the base—and this too you can now see.

What you see is the wall cloud, the storm's suction pad, the dropping foot of the spinning tube. It's an ugly lowering clump of a thing, some-times brick-shaped, sometimes more conical, sliding down from the backside of the storm. . . .

Where the air masses have met, like the atmospheric equivalent of tectonic plates, the storm's gone grinding along the weather front, spit-ting lances of killer lightning from this great fault in the sky. But now, pushing out this sullen and threat-heavy wall cloud, it's attained to a full and stupendous maturity.

Because it's from this that your tornado slithers down to the earth—a windquake spawned by the massive collision of vapor and air. And, touching down with a roar like a freight train, it sets instantly to kicking unholy shit out of everything in its path.

Like I said, no one's quite sure how nature manages this last stage of the procedure, the actual birth of the tornado. But what we do know is that once the thing's born, if it pulls out all the stops, it's the most violent form of storm on this earth.

Tornado intensity is measured on the F Scale, so called after a Dr. Fujita at the University of Chicago. The scale starts at F0, "weak," with winds up to 72 miles an hour—so maybe you'll lose your chimney, and there'll be branches down off trees.

F1 is "moderate," the winds hitting 112 miles an hour. It'll push a mobile home off its foundations; it'll make a good stab at peeling off your roof, never mind the chimney.

F2 is "significant," and the winds now are topping 150 miles an hour. It won't just peel off your roof, it'll tear it clean away. It'll bring down big trees—and if you live in a mobile home, it'll explode that thing (so get out of there fast).

Then there's F3, and now we're talking "severe"—with winds over 200 miles an hour you won't lose just the roof, you'll lose the walls. This thing's turning trains over; it's snatching up pickup trucks, and tossing them every which way.

Next is F4, and that's "devastating"—that's 260 miles an hour. Forget worrying about the roof, you ain't got a house. All you got, once an F4's come by, is a shattered pile of matchsticks.

As for F5, they're "incredible"—they'll top 300 miles an hour. It's not like you haven't got a house anymore, it's worse—when one of those comes to town, you won't even find the pieces.

And F6? "Inconceivable."

Only 2 percent of tornadoes get to grow up and be big boys, F4 and F5—but those 2 percent are responsible for some 70 percent of the fatalities. These extreme tornadoes have an average path length and width of 26 miles and 425 yards, respectively—but they can last for hours, they can travel 100 miles, or much more (at speeds along the ground of up to 50 miles an hour), and they can be as fat as a whole mile wide. On April 9, 1947, the tornado that tore through Woodward, Oklahoma—killing around 100 people—was nearly 2 miles wide.

And as they go through a town they fill themselves greedily with a lethal churning cocktail of debris, branches, planks, bricks, tiles, nails, glass, tin, crockery, and hardware, all hurtling through the air at 250 miles an hour or faster—which is how come underground is the only place to be.

Otherwise, generally speaking, you can say that they mostly travel northeast along the weather front, they mostly happen late afternoon or early evening when the earth's good and cooked, and they mostly occur in April through June.

But they can also turn up at noon or in the middle of the night, they can turn up in August or in December—and they can travel any which way they please. If they feel like it, they can even go round in a circle and hit you twice. They can do, basically, whatever the hell they want—because they're sudden, they're arbitrary, they're just plain ornery unpredictable.

They're the index finger of the Lord, stabbing down at a bad and sin-busy world—and there's not a single damn thing you can do about it.

Tornadoes can occur pretty much anywhere east of the Rockies, clear on through to the Atlantic—and, very rarely, they turn up west of the Rockies too. But their favored zone is that great northeastward sweep of the heartland called Tornado Alley.

Over the vast expanse of prairie and farmland from Texas and Oklahoma, up through the Plains and the Midwest to Illinois and Indiana and the lake states, the air masses barge around unimpeded in the continent-sized sky and—as spring heats the earth—they start tossing out tornadoes with an alarming frequency.

Between 1953 and 1980, the National Weather Service calculated an average incidence of 734 tornadoes a year. Of these, 119 were in Texas, 53 in Oklahoma, and 43 in Kansas. Nebraska got 35; Missouri, Iowa, and Illinois—27 each. So pretty much every day through the springtime there's a good possibility that somebody, somewhere, is getting clobbered.

If Texas gets the most, of course, that's in part because Texas is simply so massive—at 267,339 square miles, you could fit Wales in there 33 times over. So on a different measure—the average incidence per 10,000 square miles—we find instead three areas of peak activity.

Two of these are relatively small, south of the Red River around Dallas, and between Lubbock and Amarillo in the Panhandle. The third and somewhat larger area, however, covers the entire central portion of Oklahoma around Oklahoma City—and if you want to see tornadoes, that's the likeliest place to go.

.  .  .

So bye-bye Coffeyville, where the long trains hoot and moan all the night and the day, and the grain elevator towers gleaming white against the shining blue sky, and the unpeopled stores quietly slumber downtown, and the marriages come and go, and the good citizens keep on trying their best to get by ... with another fine haircut from Mike Wilson on 9th Street I hit 169 going south for the last time, with the radio tuned to country out of Tulsa, and the forecast promising 95 degrees.

Beyond Tulsa the turnpike was a straight rolling strip of pale Tarmac through the baking green, dotted as far as I could see with the dazzling glitter-dots of cars in the sun.

Then, in Oklahoma City, I found the Well Club.

David was from New Jersey, a computer man on assignment to OK City for the Federal Aviation Authority. He said, "Anyone comes from Wales to Oklahoma must be nuts. This is the ugliest, nastiest place in America."

Judi the barmaid told him, "We let you in, didn't we?"

The TV said in the west of the state it was hitting 99 degrees. I said back home we never had that—never.

"So 117 would really do it to you guys, right?"

Later, walking onto the lot from the cool dark of the bar, it was like being simultaneously blinded and flash-fried.

Judi asked me if I'd ever been shot at. She had—Stockton, California. "I was walking into the grocery store and I heard this *boom*, right back here [she gestured at the back of her thigh], and it just nicked me there. It was some woman found her old man was cheating on her, and I just happened to walk in between. Scared me shitless. I don't like guns. I got me a machete in my house, though. I can throw that sucker, sink it right deep in a tree. And it sleeps with me, right beside my bed."

David said he was out target shooting one time in Arizona, he had an M-11, a 9-mm machine pistol, 30-clip, and his buddy had a .357 revolver. "We're walking down the wash looking for a target and suddenly *wham*, the side of the wash just explodes—some guy's shooting a goddam shotgun at us. So we go down, and I stick the Mac up over the top and just fire off at random. Must have scared him off, we found some tracks and cartridges—but I wish I'd hit that mother."

Judi said she was from Manter, Kansas; I asked if that was west or east.

"Ummm . . . I dunno."

"Boy. She really remembers her childhood, right?"

"It's ten miles from the Colorado line. Our excitement out there was watching the trucks roll by. And everybody was a Jobe—my relatives. It took fifteen minutes to walk around the whole town. We had a post office, a hardware store, and my uncle's pool hall. It was a blast. I loved it."

"Man," said David, "am I glad I grew up in Atlantic City."

"I grew up alright."

"That's debatable."

"But I only lived there my little life—we moved to Midwest City when I was seven."

Midwest's a suburb of OK City. I asked Judi if the move was a jolt.

David said, "Not really. Going from nowhere to OK City ain't any kind of big jump."

And he really wanted me to go to the southwest, see some decent country.

Judi said, "Why should he? He's having fun right here."

"Boy. That's almost . . . *disgusting.* You know," he then said, as the Forester Sisters on the jukebox bemoaned the inadequacies of men, "this is Cro-Magnon man out here. Show these women a man who's got manners, that's like introducing them to some wondrous alien being."

"What," said Judi, "do women do with their assholes?"

Tell me.

"They fix them packed lunches and send them to work."

"Well why," said David, "does New Jersey have all the toxic waste, and California all the lawyers?"

Because New Jersey got first choice . . .

What's black and white and red and can't turn around in an elevator?

A nun with a spear in her forehead . . .

Why hasn't Texas fallen into the sea?

Because Oklahoma sucks . . .

Judi told me how when she was a kid she lived on 18th and Midwest Boulevard, and a tornado went past down 29th. "There were car lots out there and it was fun, seeing all those new cars go flying around. We were always safe, though, we had this old Indian man lived across the street— and we never went down the cellar unless he did. But if he went down, you knew it was trouble—'cause they're masters. They're really masters."

On KWTV 9, Gary England was doing the six o'clock forecast. Gary England, they said, was the man I should go see.

.  .  .

Next morning I roamed the OK City freeways in a bleached and glaring light. The place looked like fragments of the future dumped incoherently on a bomb site. There was a woman on the radio whose dog could say, "Hammer," and did. The show's host gave her a cassette, and told her he'd give her something bigger if she came back and the dog could say, "Can't touch it."

KWTV 9 was out on the city's north side, a low building flanked by the Doppler radar golfball, satellite dishes, and a field of transmission aerials—and Gary England turned out to be a quick-witted little guy, fired on a boyish passion for the stacked banks of costly equipment he works with. He's been chief meteorologist at the station for over fifteen years—and, simply, the man loves weather.

He works in a cramped space folded behind curtains and soundproofing around the back of the news studio. It's like being on the bridge of a small and somewhat ramshackle ship; on a kind of makeshift console of narrow desks and shelves, I counted nineteen different radar and computer screens. Talking fast as he gestured round the different tools of his trade, he ran me through a bewildering babel of technospeak. "This is the FTT system to manipulate the Doppler data . . ."

What I understood was that they could see out any distance up to 225 kilometers. They could look into a cross-section of a storm 7,500 feet tall, breaking it down into 10 separate segments, starting as high or as low as they wanted. (Though at a distance—out in western Oklahoma, say—they couldn't see under 7 or 8,000 feet). Then they could analyze the storm's reflectivity, i.e., how much rain the thing was dumping; they could measure the wind speed and direction—and they could assess the velocity, both of the storm itself along the ground, and of the rotation within it. I gawped at the winking screens, and the laser-printed charts. England hit keys and buttons and dials, and made his magic boxes play their informative and maybe lifesaving tricks.

TV 9's had Doppler radar since 1981—a system developed, at a cost of three hundred thousand dollars, in conjunction with another station up in Minneapolis; with a serial number 0001, it was the first Doppler in the world used to give warnings to the general public. "But it was just a big old box back then," said England, "with a power lever on the side. And we have more tornadoes per square mile than any place in the world, so we have to keep getting better at this. With three TV stations and the Weather Service all competing, we do, too."

So how, I asked, had things been going this spring?

"We've had some horrendously large tornadoes this year—fortunately, not in populated areas. But the big ones, you can see them coming, you can get thirty minutes or an hour's warning before they're down. The one that went by Woodward the other day, we saw that an hour and a quarter ahead. The problem is the little ones, your babies fifty or a hundred yards across—you're going to miss them sometimes."

He said that Fujita in Chicago had proposed a theory of migration—that there was a cycle whereby the heaviest activity would rotate over the years through different regions, from the Midwest through the Old Northwest (Minnesota, Wisconsin, Michigan), then down through the South, the Deep South, and back around to the heartland again. England didn't know if this was true or not—but according to Fujita it was the heartland's turn just now and, sure enough, up in Kansas they had eighty last year, with the spring of '91 looking hyperactive too.

Then he looked at all his silently toiling electro-kit, and at an aerial photograph of a massive gleaming thunderhead, the anvil shearing off the crisp main tower, and he said, referring to these great American storms, "They're gorgeous. They're architecture in the sky. You don't like what they do—but they're gorgeous." He said a guy at another station got in trouble the other day for calling a storm beautiful on air, which of course wasn't too wise. But beautiful, in their terrible way, is exactly what they are.

He said, "We live our lives to deal with these things."

He showed me a program they'd made about that violent pack of storms back on April 26.

"KWTV 9, working to keep you safe."

The program showed England and his staff at action stations in the Forecast Center, a severe weather alert in force.

I asked if, at times like those, the weather became the station's primary function.

"Absolutely. This is a weather-driven market. In severe weather, 90 percent of our resources go to covering it. We need information from the field, we need warnings on the air, we need damage reports and interviews. So I don't care if they're microwaving a public execution—if there's a tornado warning out, we pull the trucks and we go."

He said he'd promised the camera crews a case of beer for each tornado they filmed, then grinned. "They've got ten or fifteen this year already—they're going to break me."

The program showed the forecasters hunched busily over the popping radar screens. "Oh look at this," said one of them, "major, major circulation—I can't believe this."

There was footage from the crews in the field, of black storms marching across the landscape, with breathless voices on the soundtrack. "Cars are pulling off like crazy here. We're going to try and get a little closer, get better shots . . ."

"That one," said England, "measured 287 miles an hour. When a tornado like that one's finished with your car, there's no space left for you in it."

Then the program cut to two extraordinary pieces of tape caught by crews up in Kansas that day. One, filmed by someone cowering either in or around the side of a building, showed a tornado chewing its way across McConnell Air Force Base near Wichita, a fat, black, swirling vortex of dirt and debris, furniture and appliances, roofs and cars. High-pitched and gasping voices on the soundtrack exuded the purest terror. A guy who'd hid in a culvert there said, "If a tornado had eyes, you'd be looking into the eyes of hell."

The *Kansas City Star* reported, "The scene looked as if a three-square-mile area of the base had been packed into a blender and spit across the landscape. The base hospital looked as if it had been bombed. Five cars were stuffed into the entrance like sausages in a sandwich."

The next slice of tape was even more outlandish. The crew's coming back down a highway toward Wichita from one strike, when they see another tornado behind them in a field. At first, they're filming it from the back of the car—then they're just trying to get away from it. They get to an underpass with other people who've also now left their cars; the camera jolts about as they scramble up the bank, getting close underneath where the bridge meets the earth. Behind them, a pale whirling mayhem of dust and wind's now jumped onto the highway, and it's bearing down straight for them. Out of the frame, a child's screaming. In the base of the funnel, something briefly bounces and spins like a scrap of paper . . .

England stopped the tape, and pointed at this vaulting tossed speck in the grainy frozen frame. "That," he said, "is a pickup truck."

Then the twister storms right over these people where they're hiding with an unearthly, howling rage of wind, the grass flattened all about them, dust and dirt darkening the air.

England said, "That's not a real big one, either—100, 120 miles an hour. If that had been a maxi, they'd have been sucked right out of there." Then he said that with all the divorces in Oklahoma—a thing he put down in part to the oil boom of the early eighties, "crazy times, gold buckles, gold rings, divorces everywhere"—there'd be a lot of kids at home alone after school in the afternoons.

"So in bad weather we'll do cut-ins and talk to those kids, we'll tell them what to do—get in the closet, get in the bath under blankets. We did it at three one time; then", he grinned, "at seven we got a call saying we'd forgot to tell them to come back out."

"We do intercepts with our cars, and the helicopter, 'cause it's competition. Who's going to get to it first?"

A Priority One would mean three ground crews, two live trucks, and the chopper all streaming out to chase the storm. That afternoon, it was Priority Three—crews on standby.

England ran his fingers over charts, helping me see how the weather system worked. Out west on the dryline, strong dry winds were coming in off New Mexico to meet a big and unstable moist mass from the Gulf. Upper level winds were shearing off nicely. "It looks like it could get real ugly. If this thing tilts . . . I'd be real surprised if it doesn't happen."

England's colleague Allen Mitchell said it looked, in the Texas and Oklahoma Panhandles, like there'd be enough forcing of the atmosphere to "bust the cap"—enough heat and collision to send things climbing and firing. . . . In Kansas City, the National Severe Storms Forecast Center issued a Tornado Watch for the Panhandles, valid to 11 P.M.

A Watch is issued when conditions favor tornadic storm development. Then a Tornado Warning (issued by the Weather Service locally, because no one's waiting on Kansas City by then) means that either the radar, or someone on the ground, has actually spotted one—and you're into a potential emergency situation.

Nationwide, this was Tornado Watch Number 428 for the year. Word came from Amarillo of storms building three hundred miles out west, along the New Mexico line. Mitchell said that wasn't in their area of responsibility—and they'd not want to piss the crews off by sending them all the way out there, when they'd be five, six, seven hours out chasing these things as it was, even when the weather was closer. Which, tomorrow, it very likely would be.

England said I'd picked myself a good time to visit—so I asked then if I could go out on the road with his storm chasers. And—like Red Nose Sam, like countless other unendingly helpful people across the heart of America—he said without hesitation I should come back tomorrow, and he'd fix me up.

It was a twenty-five-minute drive back into the city to the place where I was staying. In among the bars and the body shops, the malls and the marts, the fast-food joints and the gas stations and the tatty homes, I counted twenty-one churches, in those twenty-five minutes. In the phone directory, the church listings fill twelve pages.

But with weather like this, who wouldn't be praying?

Since the first recorded tornado struck Oklahoma City in 1893, nearly forty more have come through there. England said it was only a matter of time before an F5, a maxi, tore right through the heart of the place. It might be this year, or ten years in the future. But, he said, it would happen.

At the Well Club they thought it was really neat that I'd seen this guy; they liked him because he was "one of us." He comes from Seiling, a little place one hundred miles northwest where his parents had—debate raged on this point—either a grocery store, or a pig farm. (They had a store.) And, of course, they liked him because he tells them about the weather.

When he came on *Newsline 9* that evening one of the girls said, "That's where I watch, if there's storms or something—it's accurate. And it's not like a once-an-hour report; if there's any changes, they come right back on. I don't want, if there's a tornado somewhere, for them to tell me it's there, and then not come back and tell me where."

On the TV England said, "We promised folks there'd be a few things going bump in the night." Tornadoes were reported out by Amarillo.

I woke at six to a last edge of thunder passing away outside. Rain fell from heavy grey skies. It was forecast to clear, temperatures hitting high 80s by the afternoon, with scattered thunderstorms round the metro area.

A few calls in the morning got me sorted, the sky clearing all the while to a burning blue specked with baby clumps of puffy white cloud.

I learnt that I couldn't go out with station staff, like a camera crew—the risk of the insurance liability against TV 9 if I got pulped was too great. So instead, England got me in touch with a guy called Val Castor.

When I arrived at the station at lunchtime, England was talking with his news boss. This guy said to me, "You going out with Val? Well, he'll get you a tornado if anybody will—because he's aggressive, man, he's one *aggressive* storm chaser. He's like a dog after a bone with them things."

England said conditions today were, "Very favorable. What we classify as a high risk of severe thunderstorms and tornadoes. The surface features, the upper air, the turning of the wind—it's all there. And it's going pretty early, so Val needs to hurry—you got maybe two hours to get out there."

He said, "We're on Priority One. We've got a live truck out to Erick, that's two vehicles, three people—and a second vehicle with a live truck's somewhere west of town right now, maybe an hour and a half from Clinton. Once they get there, we'll decide to turn them north or south—and then a third crew'll go accordingly. Now the actual movement's from the southwest, but I figure at some point it'll turn more easterly—it's all in this box of western Oklahoma, anyhow. And there's a storm out by Erick . . ."

Alan Mitchell was peering in the radar. "Hell," he said, "look at that."

"Before we had radar, we just tied Mitchell to the top of the mast outside. Worked pretty good, didn't it, Alan?"

He said they'd not told the public yet. "We'll probably tell them there's that storm moving in now—tell them it's a crawl situation, slow northeast, could be a threat . . . but we'll wait on Kansas City to put a watch out first."

Then he muttered to himself, "Come on, Val, where are you? We got some urgency here."

Val arrived. "What's the vector?"

"Two hundred and thirty. Should be turning east. You guys be careful."

As we left he said, "Good hunting."

"When you go tornado chasing," said Val Castor, "you'll not see something three times out of four. But I've seen seven this year already—hell of a year—and it's looking real good today."

He was twenty-nine, a wiry, good-looking little guy just graduated from the Oklahoma School of Meteorology at the university down in Norman. He'd been taught there by Howard Bluestein, "The king of tornado chasing—definitely the king."

Bluestein and his team developed a thing called (what else?) TOTO—the Totable Tornado Observatory. They drive around trying to set it down in the path of tornadoes . . .

"I'll tell you something he did last month, April 26—see, he's been working on a project, portable Doppler, only one in the world far as I know—and he got within three quarters of a mile of this tornado, measured wind speeds in there at 287 miles an hour. That's the strongest wind speed ever measured on the face of the earth. That's not saying it's the strongest we've ever had . . . but I got pictures one and a half miles from that one and it was a big, big tornado, three quarters of a mile wide. I tell you, that'll pluck a chicken bare. It hopped over some guy's house, he had one hundred cattle in his back pasture—and afterwards, he found twenty of them best part of a mile away. And there were others still alive, but with pieces of hay or grass driven right through their knees, in between the bones and out the other side. It was stripping all the grass from the ditches, clean down to bare dirt. I've seen trees debarked . . . Here's one for you. Back in '79 in Lawton, a bank got hit. Four days later, a lady in North Carolina found a cancelled check in her front yard that was written to a lady in Lawton—been sucked clear into the jet stream, fell one thousand miles away."

Val drove a black '85 Silverado, with extra lights on a silver roll bar behind the cab; in the cab he had a radar detector, a cellular phone, a Weatheradio, CB, and still and video cameras. Doing seventy, we shot west out of the city on I40—and I asked what it was like, as red earth and green pasture opened wide all about us, to live in that country out there.

He said, "People say it's boring, but it ain't, no way—there's a lot of things I like to do out here. I can go fishing, get bass, catfish, I can go hunting. . . . Northwest Oklahoma, that's the best quail-hunting in the world out there. And then, I chase tornadoes. That," he said, "ain't boring at all."

At 1:50, he called in to the studio. It was muggy, the sky filled over with low grey cloud. "Did the dryline hit Amarillo yet?"

Word from England was that reflectivity on the storm by Erick had hit level five, which is as strong as it comes—but then it weakened, and fell back to two.

"So," said Val, "there's nothing out there that's real strong just yet—but that's good, 'cause we're not out there yet either. And he says the dryline's punched past Lubbock and Amarillo, it's making a push eastward, and that's real good—that's what we need."

He switched on the Weatheradio. It's a little hand-sized affair locked to three frequencies on one of which, wherever you are, you should be able to pick up a local branch of NOAA, the National Oceanic & Atmospheric Administration. A crackly voice offered us the Oklahoma thunderstorm outlook; it confirmed what we knew, and talked also about a low pressure trough in the upper levels over the four corners area where Arizona, New Mexico, Colorado, and Utah meet. That buckled trough was also headed our way.

"Vertical wind shear," said Val. With that, and the low winds southeasterly, and higher winds from the southwest, we had everything we needed.

2:10. NOAA said, "Thunderstorms are expected to develop in mid-afternoon, and rapidly intensify. Atmosphere and wind profiles support the possibility of supercell thunderstorms, and the possibility of tornadoes."

How did that make Val feel?

"Makes me feel damn good. That's what we thrive on. And if they put out a Tornado Watch, I'll be feeling a whole lot better yet."

2:15. "If we get out here a little further and the cloud clears off a bit, that's good—lets the sun heat the earth." We crossed into Caddo County, past the Anadarko turn-off.

2:20. Val called TV 9, then told me, "Nothing's changed. The dryline's across the east Texas Panhandle; behind it at Lubbock and Big Spring they've got mid-90s, there's some real good heat out there. The storm they saw originally, that's shut down to level one—but the sky's clearing off. Temperature should rise now. I got an outside thermometer, see—it's 86.4 out there. Pretty warm."

At 2:30, it was 88.

Val chewed tobacco, spitting out black juice in a tin. I asked him what it was like, to see a tornado.

"Awesome. You can see pictures of them, but it's not like being there. So much incredible energy. And if you get close enough, you can hear the roar—they make a roar like a jet plane. The big one on April 26, when it set down east of Enid I watched it for maybe ten minutes on the ground, and it had this really low roar—and when it first came down it was totally black. Then the way the sun was on it as it moved, it turned white—unbelievable. It's like having sex."

2:50. England said a new level five just popped, fifteen miles northwest of Elk City. We were into Custer County, nearing Clinton; we had to decide when we got there whether to stay on I40 southwest, or head straight west for Carpenter on 73. Val figured the latter. Then, suddenly, NOAA gave out a long, high-pitched beep. It was the Tornado Watch signal: "A potentially dangerous weather situation."

3:00. Val: "You can begin to see the top of the storm now. Those sheets of high white smooth stuff."

NOAA: "Spotter networks and all emergency management agencies are urged to maintain a high level of readiness."

The radio whined out the piercing signal again; we cut off the interstate onto 73. "There is a Tornado Watch in effect for portions of western Oklahoma and the Oklahoma Panhandle." The Watch area ran from eighty-five miles southeast of Lubbock, to fifty miles north-northeast of Gage. We were arriving in the northern piece of it.

"Make preliminary plans for getting to safe shelter."

Val: "We're in business."

Again, the radio shrieked. Val said, "I bet that's a warning on this storm right here."

A severe thunderstorm was reported twenty miles southeast of Cheyenne, moving northeast at twenty-five miles an hour.

"That's our baby."

"Remain calm, but be alert to rapidly changing weather conditions."

3:10. "See those towers—there's another one going up."

"Remember—severe thunderstorms can and do produce tornadoes with little or no advance warning."

At 3:15 we were south of Foss Lake on 73. The western horizon was a glowering fog of grey, the storm a bulk, a mass, a rising wall flanked by shining blue to either side. High above it, the anvil stretched out bright and white to the north. I asked Val how he felt.

"Excited. Anxious. I want to get there. I want to get there fast. Wish I had a truck'd run 150 miles an hour."

3:20, and he called England again. "We're starting to see a fuzzy base. I can see the rain core. Right now it doesn't look *too* impressive. . . . Is it still level five?"

Another tower was going up farther south, and another anvil spreading. Val fretted, "We're still a long ways away—ten, fifteen miles." He sat forward, driving and staring, chewing and spitting. We whipped across the bumpy rolling grassland, past scooped hollows of red dirt. This far west, there were very few trees.

"This is rapidly looking good." We hit a T-junction and spun north onto 34 towards Hammon, so the storm was now closing diagonally upon us. The trick's to aim for the southeast flank, and then run alongside it. We were right on the button.

"If I didn't know any better, man, that looks like a wall cloud to me. It's far enough away that it might just be scud, but it looks good, it's got good lowering on it, and it's in back of the rain shaft . . . Gary says this storm looks like it might be weakening on the radar, but it looks good to me."

Rain began to spatter on the windshield.

"Hell. It's fading."

3:30, and another call to Gary England. "How's this baby looking? It's died? That's what I thought. You're coming in real fuzzy, let me try to find a hill."

He put down the phone and said, "He says it's down to level two. It's pooped out on us. They're firing up along the dryline, in the eastern Panhandle round Memphis—but this one's breaking up. Looks like shit now—just rain, no base. But there you go—happens all the time when you're chasing."

We pulled up. The storm, sloppy-backed, wandered away north. Val turned around south, aiming to get back on I40 at Elk City. Due west, two small towers rose against the blue, but he said they were too thin, "They haven't got a chance."

And for a minute I thought it was like he wanted them to grow, to spawn their demon babies; most people do say, storm chasers are crazy. When we stopped for gas we told the woman what we were doing, and she said we were nuts. "I want to get *away* from them things."

But—quite apart from their contribution to a warning system that means the fatality rate is now extraordinarily low—it isn't really that spotters like Val are running round heartlessly praying for tornadoes to happen. After all, with the possible exception of the actual victims, these guys know better than anyone what a tornado can do.

I think it is, instead, that they know tornadoes do happen—that you can't change that—and when they happen, they just want to be there to see it. Because like he said, as an event it's that electric, it's like having sex.

So I guess what happened to us was coitus interruptus.

Val said beside tornadoes, he'd had his house flooded twice, in '76 and '84—three to four feet deep each time. "That second flood killed fourteen people in Tulsa—so I'm interested in the weather. Besides, people say I'm crazy, but who likes boring weather?"

In pursuit of excitement, we must have driven near four hundred miles that day. Along the way he introduced me to a new intransitive verb, "to tornado"—as in, "I'm real pissed that thing didn't tornado."

We cruised about under weather that, by 4:00, had gone normal again. Mitchell in the studio reported storms in Texas between Clarendon and

Silverton—but all there was where we were was just the unbending wind of the Plains. The woman in the gas station said when both doors were open, she needed an anchor. I asked Val if we'd lost it.

"No. I'd say there's still a good chance of tornadoes today."

At 5:03 we crossed the state line, and stopped soon afterwards in the lot of Mitchell's Family Restaurant in Shamrock, Texas. A rusty iron sign clanked and creaked in the quick and gusting wind. There were three storms visible. One was way north, at least fifty miles, "You'd be after that for an age—pointless." Another in the southeast covered a big area, "but it's not high, it looks strange, unorganized." Then there was a third in the southwest that might come our way. "Right now, I think we should just stop and wait. How much patience d'you have?"

Due west, there was nothing, just a vast shimmering flatness under cloudless blue. "That's dry air."

At 5:40 Alan Mitchell told us the three storms were level three. The short wave trough was coming over Lubbock; England could see it on the satellite. "They still expect it to pop. That short wave's like a pocket of energy, a little ripple traveling along the main flow of the jet stream . . . but it all looks pretty wimpy from here."

So we ate—and when we went back outside everything was gone, the world was blank and blue. Val called the studio and told me, "They still think it's going to happen when the short wave comes over, but that'll be nighttime stuff now—and you don't go hunting tornadoes in the dark. You can do it, if you know where you're at, and you can video the tornado off the lightning—but you can also get yourself in a whole world of shit real fast."

He was pretty low. Why did nothing happen? "It's a chicken-and-egg thing. Maybe the short wave held off, so there wasn't enough upper-level energy to fire things up. Gary said they've got watches here, in Kansas, in Nebraska—and nothing's happened anywhere."

We set off back east, past Elk City, home of Susan Powell, Miss America 1981, past the Cherokee Trading Post 24-Hour Restaurant, past fields of golden-red dirt, and the infinite green lines of the horizon. Val said, "It took me four or five years at college to understand all this stuff. It's physics, it's mathematics—a lot of math, I mean, I'm talking algebra here, calculus one, two, and three, engineering math, thermodynamics . . . Basically we have to go through the same stuff an engineer goes through."

It's a study worth making. Like England, he said OK City was overdue for an F5: "And it'll be catastrophic—it'll kill one hundred people, more, easy. If it's rush hour, if you got people in their cars . . . an F5'll carry a car a mile in the air, it'll wad it up like a piece of tin foil, just crumple it. A car is not the place to be in a tornado."

He gave me an automotive version of the F scale. An F1 will push you off the road. An F2 will flip you around, most likely roll you too. An F3 will pick you up, roll you a hundred yards—while an F4 will carry you a quarter of a mile in the air. "An F4 is absolute death."

So an F5?

"The bodies'll be unrecognizable."

F5s are rare—only three in the eighties in the whole USA. But like the San Andreas fault, they're out there . . .

8:45. We closed on the city sitting glittery and neon, smack dab in the heart of Tornado Alley; the sky ran its sunset opera all about us. Fluffs and ruffles of pink and indigo fell eastward out of the roof of orange overhead; the sun was gone, but still a slo-mo bleed continued, seeping through this dangerous sky.

In the studio England said he'd had three crews strung out between Hollis and Woodward, a live truck in Watonga, and a satellite uplink truck in Elk City. "So I'm going to commit suicide on the ten o'clock news." It was a good few thousand dollars down the drain—but then, he said, "You're damned if you do. But you're *really* damned if you don't."

He and Mitchell sat trying to figure it out. "The dryline never really moved. It had twenty-five knots from the southwest, mid-90s behind it, it should have shoved—it always shoves when that happens."

"The day of the Woodward tornado, we didn't have those kinds of winds."

"I'll go burn my forecast."

Goddam weather.


*The Medicine Wheel*


I went west from Gillette in the Wyoming dawn, mauve cloud scudding so low you could almost reach up and touch it. I was the only soul on the road. Then, barely after six, I was out from under the cloud into crystal blue again, over a rise—and there on the horizon ahead were the Big Horn Mountains, a line of white shadow on the pale far rim of the world.

A big buck mule deer loped moronically across the four lanes. I hit the brakes; he cantered close across the front of the truck, then away again into the massive wreckage of the empty landscape. Scrubby grass barely covered the cracked, red-brown jumble of knolls and gullies. Slowly the mountains rose—and the last gasp of the High Plains all about became a crumbling moonscape of worn castles and pyramids, a frozen ocean of crests and troughs sculpted in blown dirt.

I had breakfast at Bozeman's Restaurant in Buffalo. The back of the menu had a history of the Bozeman trail to the Montana gold fields, of Forts Reno, Phillip Kearney, and C. F. Smith established along it in 1866, then abandoned under the Fort Laramie treaty with the Sioux two years later. The last paragraph began, "The wall decor is representative of the Sioux Indian culture."

Plastic masks?

"Wall decor is for sale."

I climbed into the mountains on 14, taking 14A from Burgess Junction. Sheets of dirtied snow still lay about on the tops. Where wide, hazy views began opening onto the Big Horn Basin and the Rockies beyond, I turned off up three miles of vertiginous wet dirt to find the Medicine Wheel.

A design of small stones on the ground seventy-four feet in diameter with twenty-eight spokes, the Wheel's a mystery ten thousand feet above the world. The Crow, who migrated into the basin in about 1776, say it was up there when they came . . . Today, the shabby barbed wire fence around it is bedecked with offerings, fronds of pine, bundles of herbs and burnt tobacco, bones and bandanas and swatches of cloth.

The Crow were cleared from the basin barely a century after they arrived; within five years after that, the biggest rancher of the day had twenty-five thousand head of cattle in there instead. And the Indian has a lot more praying yet to do . . .

The Wheel stares blindly over tourism now. I drove through the bleached yellow-grey shimmer of the basin to Cody, and on into Yellowstone—and it wasn't nature up there, it was gridlock. It felt like I saw more vehicles in an afternoon than I'd seen in five weeks on the Plains—so I drove straight through, past the ungainly morass of people "camping" in their hooked-up RVs, with their microwaves and televisions.

Jackson after sundown was no better, a Bijou West of swarming strollers and gift stores, every motel full. I slept in the truck in the Green Acres Campground; the green acres in question were a gravel lot behind a gas station.

In the morning I wrote notes on how this book might end, then left Jackson heading south. I had everything I needed—but the thing with America is, you just always want *more* . . .

# 3.

# No Man's Land

Some folks, like the weather, are terrifically confused.

At the Well Club they were amazed I hadn't caught any good storms; they said there'd been watches up and buzzing all afternoon and evening. But there you go—and the conversation shunted round to other matters American, like Rusty and his guns.

"I got six. I got a .25 Beretta by the bed, and a 9-mm before you get to the bedroom door. I got a shotgun in the entry hall, and a machine gun by the back door. Then I got a .357 Colt, and a .380 Beretta."

Why?

"Because I like guns."

But why six?

"Home protection."

"A .25," said one of the girls, "won't stop anybody."

"Well I don't want to kill anybody in the bedroom, do I?"

But really, I pressed, why six?

"Hell, I had twenty at one time."

"And all I have," said the girl, "is a switchblade."

"Let me tell you," Rusty told her, "you are undermanned in this age. When I was a kid," he said, "I could go down to the creek, do what I like—but right now, I would no more let my kid play on his own in the backyard than I would fly."

And then out it all comes—here, and over and over throughout the trip—a litany of betrayed and angry grievance against unseen armies of welfare bums, and their kids growing up knowing nothing better than the green check every month, and the politicians pandering for votes to this teeming host of idlers, and how the honest working white man in this sea of indolence was the last American minority—and mixed in with that, the rage and paranoia against criminality and dope—and then, to cap it all, the gloom over "Them," somewhere out there, trying to control a free man and his guns.

Rusty said if he was president, he'd know how to change things. "Sure, I want every man to get a free and fair trial. But once the jury finds a man guilty, that should be that. You should go out and string him right up. I guarantee you," he said, "crime would fall off 70 percent there and then."

So does he sound like a bloodthirsty redneck? He was, in fact, a strutting, cocky sort of guy, but essentially amiable; eager that I should have a good time, and see the best of a country of which, stubbornly and paradoxically, he remained fiercely proud. He wanted me to go down and see "little Dixie," southeastern Oklahoma—and why?

Because it was *poor* down there, and *crazy*, and awash with dope and gangsters . . . He related a barbarous tale in which a policeman there gives a man a speeding ticket—and next thing he knows his house is burnt down, his wife and kids are murdered, *for a speeding ticket*, said Rusty, in awe at the demented glamour of this violence . . . when all the time he's worried about crime in his backyard.

Some folks, like the weather, are terrifically confused.

Anyhow, I wasn't going southeast. I was going the opposite way entirely, to the Oklahoma Panhandle—No Man's Land. Val Castor said, "You'll flip—you can see the curvature of the earth out there." It was time to get on the High Plains.

In the morning, the National Weather Service in Norman said it'd continue warm and humid through the day and the night, with a chance for thunderstorms just about anywhere in the state, most likely in the west. And—after putting a total of twenty-one counties under Tornado Watches yesterday—they explained how a cap of dry western air had prevented the expected storm development. They said, "It was like putting a lid on a boiling pot." But still, conditions remained potentially . . . I called Gary England.

"Summer Central."

He said he wasn't sending any crews out. "Doesn't look like anything's going to happen. So it probably will."

I bought a Weatheradio for $26.67 at a Radio Shack on North Meridian, then left town on the North-West Expressway. On the way, I passed England smiling chirpily from a TV 9 billboard, OKLAHOMA'S #1. In storm country, the weatherman shares top billing with the news anchors.

I stopped at Okarche for gas. Under grey blankets of hot cloud, wind whipped through the wheat, and raised up veils of red dust. It was Highway 3 all the way, over creeks running a rich blood-brown.

After Seiling the sky cleared to blue, scattered with sweeping processions of low-level cumulus. I passed Woodward, and the land became bare bumpy flats of pale green tussock grass. A sign warned HITCH-HIKERS MAY BE ESCAPING INMATES. And then—190 miles out of Oklahoma City—there came a magic moment.

On the 100th meridian where Harper County stops, and Beaver County and the Panhandle begin, I pulled over at a historical marker. YOU ARE NOW ENTERING NO MAN'S LAND.

And getting out of the truck I realized—boy, you are on the High Plains now. There were no trees—just sky, grass, and wind, a whole lot of tugging, buffeting wind. Come to that, a whole lot of sky and grass too ... The grass all leaned permanently northeast as, ever so rarely, cars hissed past like ghosts in the gusty and whispering void.

Oklahoma—the word means "red people"—started out as Indian Territory, the end of the Trail of Tears, the dumping ground for over sixty nations shoveled off their lands elsewhere. But then the white man decided he wanted Oklahoma, too—so it was opened up to settlement in 1889, and joined the union as the forty-sixth state in 1907.

The Panhandle, however, that thin stick of three counties wedged out west between Texas and Kansas, is a historical anomaly that didn't fit in with this process. Originally Spanish and then Mexican, the land became part of Texas after 1836. But when Texas joined the union in 1850, the new state relinquished it—the Panhandle lies north of the 36.30 parallel—so as to remain a slave state under the Missouri Compromise. Meanwhile, the Cherokee Outlet's western border in Indian Territory was established on the 100th meridian, and New Mexico's eastern boundary was fixed at the 103rd. So when the Territory of Kansas had its southern border drawn along the 37th parallel in 1854, that left a strip of land 34 miles wide and 167 miles long that didn't belong to anybody—a "Public Land Strip" that was, effectively, ungoverned, until it fell into Oklahoma's statehood more or less by default.

So No Man's Land is a historical glitch, a pucker in the middle of the quilt, a place that's not naturally Oklahoman at all. Sloping gradually up westward from two thousand feet above sea level at the Beaver County line to nearly five thousand feet on the top of Black Mesa, the Panhandle has 8 percent of the state's land, but less than 1 percent of its population. Or, putting it another way, Oklahoma overall has forty-four people per square mile; but out in the Panhandle's plains and mesa country, Texas County has only nine people per square mile, Beaver County four, and Cimarron County at the western end less than two.

Those numbers, already tiny, are shrinking even further: the population of the three counties has fallen in the past decade by nearly 10 percent. And as I drove from the marker thirty miles west to Elmwood, then north another fourteen to Beaver, a guy sang on the radio about the farms disappearing and the skies turning black, about baby boom America as a nation of takers who never give anything back . . .

And I guessed Rusty might go along with that.

A mile out of Beaver I had a beer at the Cow Chip Lounge. It was a white, tin-clad shack with a Bud sign in one window, and a Lite Beer sign in the other. Inside, it was a low-ceilinged, cement-floored little barn of a place—and at 7:30 on a Friday evening, I was the only guy there. The barmaid put music on the jukebox; the song said the world was running short of honest rednecks.

I downed my beer, and watched from the doorway an anvil spreading in the southwest over a crisp white storm tower. The sun dropped away, a glaring, yellow-white disc in the empty blue; the wind picked up, streaking over the plain, whining on the telegraph wire, bumping against the truck on the bar's gravel lot.

I couldn't get anything clear on the Weatheradio, just crackle and hiss. I drove north through town to Beaver State Park, and walked to the top of the rust-colored dunes on the north side of Beaver River there, a weird little micro-desert of sand sage and skunkbrush. The storm now filled the south-central horizon; the first high cloud was arriving overhead. In the humidity—the temperature was still low 80s—the wind had a sinister, turgid push to it. I guessed any action would pass to the east—but that thing building, all the same, it looked frankly . . . *nuclear*.

At 8:50 the southern horizon was a soaring wall of indigo. I went into town, and called Gary England.

"Search and rescue."

He said at a guesstimate it was thirty knots southwest, weak just yet, but all updrafts, building to 32,000 feet now. It was a bit far out for him to see it real clear, "But it should go by—unless it turns. Then you might be a news story. 'Cause it may be big, if we can see it at 180 knots."

He said to call back at 9:40, collect. When I did, the sky all across the south was a grey-black mass. He asked of the storm, "Got you an eighteen-wheeler? Where you staying?"

State campsite.

"Should be an interesting night."

I told him the Weatheradio wasn't getting anything, and he said, "Well, you're way out there. No people, right? Did you go through Seiling? You should have looked up my ma."

I was calling from the Hillcrest Motel. When we were done the lady there told me, "I've never seen so much bad weather in so many places across the country in all my life. It's everywhere." The Weather Channel was reporting Severe Thunderstorm Watches from Kansas to the Great Lakes.

I went back to the campsite with a couple more beers, and a microwaved Italian sub. The wind was busy in the trees, but not fierce— just a constant, straining seethe and sigh.

On the truck radio, I found two guys broadcasting a minor league baseball game from Liberal, Kansas. The commentators remarked on the game's progress occasionally, but mostly it was a mild and articulate meandering of memories and stats—the fiftieth anniversary, for example, of Joe DiMaggio's fifty-six game hitting streak. It was pleasant, listening to the slow murmur on the radio of the summer game, sitting there in the blowing dark with the cab light on, a cold Busch and a greasy, mustard-smothered sub . . .

So pleasant, you could almost forget there was a storm out there.

I woke before six in a torrent of birdsong, had a shower, then sat for a while by the lake. Frogs grumbled; ants were busy in tiny tunnels like bullet holes in the sandy red earth.

The sky was a pale grey morass. The station across the line up in Liberal—thirty miles northwest—said the storm watch was still operative until nine. I drove into town, got gas and cigarettes, then settled down in the diner for sausage, hash browns, and two eggs over easy.

In the short time that took, the sky filled with a dense, lowering mass of marbled dark grey. In the diner it was like night fell over breakfast, sullen and gloomy; then the rain began, pinging off car hoods and roofs.

One guy said, "That sure come in in a hurry."

The thunder cracked and rolled.

In the doorway of the diner, there were photos of four local boys gone to war in the Gulf.

I drove west on a local blacktop that started by the John Deere dealer just south of town, and soon became dirt. The sky behind me was a lilac and cream jumble of sunlit scud, as the last storm broke up; up ahead lay the beginnings of another one, a luminous sheet on the horizon of deep grey-blue. At 9:54 the first lightning spit down from it, as I headed on in.

I pulled over to take a picture, waiting for a pickup coming the other way to get out of the frame. But the guy slowed and asked, "Y'all don't need any help, do you?"

They look out for their neighbors, in that storm country there.

By 10:20 the lightning was getting frequent, both single and multiple bursts, some white, some livid yellow, across the whole span of the Southwest. In the storm's core the cloud was crushed into a dense mass, a distinct, mushroom-shaped lid dropping low from the sky, pouring blue-black walls of rain. Steadily it advanced over the wide pale grass-land, a flattened cone of raw energy—you could see clearly the roiling disc, the rotating mass of its solid heart. Higher cloud pushed in ultramarine circles ahead and around it; lightning tumbled from the leading northern edge.

The local road hit 83; I turned north three miles, then west again on another paved local. Lightning was falling all about within a few miles now; the narrow band of sky compressed between storm and prairie turned a dense and turbulent green, like the bottom of some poisoned sea. At 10:50 it was almost upon me; the storm's core became three bruised, purple-black rolls of circular sky-muscle in the thick and humid air.

Gary England's last words when I'd left? "Be careful."

I was in the rain now. The sky behind me, unbelievably, was *red*—like the sun was setting in the morning on the wrong side of the world. The road turned south, bang into this thing—but what the hell, it was bang on top of me anyhow. And there was lightning horizontal in there, cloud to cloud; while the rain smashed down, a glowing grey mass marching over fields and over me, throwing lances of fire on all quarters until I was into some dark and alien waterland, lit by these furious bolts of jagged white through a dim, sodden mess of grey-green, submarine shadow.... It was no longer possible to drive; the windshield streamed sheets of viscous water, the metal roof of the cab drumming and singing.

So I pulled up at a farm, and a kind old boy said, "Oh, it doesn't really look too bad. Mind you," he added cautiously, "there's no absolutes."

It looked pretty absolute to me. All I could see, looking out from his screen door, was a whole world of water hammering steadily down now in a kind of numinous, crystalline, sourceless pale light. I said it was awesome—beautiful, in its way.

He said, "Well, I guess you might look at it that way. But we get a little apprehensive too."

Then it seemed to ease a tad, and, still half-blind in the downpour, I backed the rear right wheel of my truck into the farmer's ditch.

He was way quicker than me—by the time I'd got back to his door, he was already steering a tractor the size of a locomotive from his barn to haul me out.

I got down on my knees in inches of liquid red mud, wrapped the tow-chain round the front axle, and, feeling small before the storms and the people who live with them, I got set to rights on the road again.

Red Nose said for a community you needed air, water, money. And Coffeyville may be short on the money—but out in the Panhandle, and on the High Plains in general, the water's short too.

Across much of the windblown, semi-arid vastness west of the 100th meridian, in the rain shadow of the Rockies, fifteen inches of rain counts as a good year—when in the Midwest they'd expect twice that at least. Moreover, if half your fifteen inches falls from spring storms in a fortnight, that can do you more damage than good. In some parts of Kansas just then, for example, they couldn't get the wheat in, because the fields were turned to bogs of clogging gumbo not fit for any combine to enter.

But storms apart, it's more likely it won't rain than it will—so after the eco-horror of the dust bowl, they set to solving things with irrigation. By then, however, the water system was suffering already.

A herd law in 1906 obliged ranchers to fence their cattle. Without the freedom to drink where they pleased, the cattle trampled the banks at waterholes, turning the grassy riversides bare—so any good rain eroded those places, washing sand and mud into the stream beds. The dust storms in the thirties then dumped mightily more soil off overcultivated uplands into the river courses; after which, a series of floods from '39 to '41 then filled and widened those courses, finally turning narrow, clear flows into a mess of shallow, sluggish, sandbarred meanderings. Now, start sucking water off of that for irrigation . . . When you drive the Plains today, the creek and river beds are mostly parched and empty gullies.

Worse, however, is the fact that much irrigation water comes not from on the land, but from under it, from wells tapping the Ogalalla Aquifer. In the early sixties in the Panhandle, there were about four hundred ground water wells; by 1981, there were over two thousand six hundred.

Since 1956, some wells have shown a corresponding drop in water levels of up to one hundred feet.

The aquifer's been estimated to have a volume equivalent to that of Lake Huron. It's also estimated to have been depleted by anything between a quarter, and a third.

So what do you do? Dam the Beaver and the Cimarron? Transfer surplus water from the east? Carry on with ever more crude and hungry adjustments to this delicate, marginal, much messed-up environment? But you'd be turning your face in the process against reality—against the steady, tornadic march of economics and ecology across the landscape, a march as devastating and inexorable in its way as any wind ever spawned in the storm country sky.

After the dust bowl, in other words, it was irrigate, or die. It may soon, however, be irrigate—and die anyway.

I drove west to Boise City which, in Oklahoma, is pretty much the end of the line. I was after the Lil' Hombre Rodeo—but when I got to the rodeo ground, it looked like I'd missed it. There were just a few kids lolloping round the fenced dirt arena on their horses, and a couple of guys in cowboy hats watching. A big guy twirling a lasso reeled in the rope, then came over with his hand out to greet me, firm and friendly.

"Hi, I'm Doug Cherry, how you doing?"

After the introductions he said I'd been lucky—I hadn't missed any rodeo. "It started to rain, and the ladies' makeup went all to running, so we figured we'd hold off till tomorrow. About the first rain we've had in five years—I guess folks wanted to stay home and enjoy it."

Another guy said, "People didn't know what it was. Figure they was scared to go out in it."

They said they'd be starting up by lunchtime; I said I'd be there, and went back into town. The day was getting on, so I bought a cooler for $3.99 at Love's Country Store, filled it with ice and sandwiches and a six-pack, then drove twenty-five miles farther west to Black Mesa State Park. Next stop, New Mexico . . . and along the way, there was a historical marker where the Cimarron Cut-Off of the Santa Fe Trail used to pass. According to local historian Norma Gene Butterbaugh Young,

probably the first trader from the United States to make the journey to Santa Fe successfully was a French Creole, Baptiste La Lande. In 1804, the year after the Louisiana Purchase, a well-to-do merchant in Kaskaskia, Illinois,

William Morrison, sent La Lande off to Santa Fe with a stock of goods that Morrison thought would make all of them wealthy. But Morrison miscalculated slightly. La Lande's mama didn't raise any idiots, and he recognized a good thing when it fell in his lap. When he got to Santa Fe he sold the goods, purchased land, eventually married one of those beautiful little dark-eyed gals and raised a big family. The only thing that Morrison ever got from him was word that yes indeed, he had reached Santa Fe safely. Period.

La Lande and those who followed him took a northerly route via what's now Garden City, Kansas, and La Junta, Colorado. Then, in 1823, William Becknell struck out more directly southwest across No Man's Land—and came close to dying of thirst in the attempt. They had to cut the ears off their mules and drink the blood . . . they didn't, back then, call it desert for no reason.

Surveyed in 1826–27, the trail saw its heaviest traffic during the '49 Gold Rush, then died when the Santa Fe Railroad was completed in 1880. So for a few short decades, this was the southern frontier's freeway—a lea line of American history born, and just as quickly swallowed up again, on the blank and intimidating High Plains.

The wind pulled at my hair and my clothes, and rocked the truck behind me. It seemed never to stop, day after day, until eventually it seemed the very voice of the earth, potent, unforgiving, supremely indifferent. In the bright and sweeping vacancy of the prairie, I tried to imagine the jolting wagons—but to be honest, I couldn't. When they say in America, 'You're history,' that's exactly what they mean—that you've been, and you've gone.

Marble- to golfball-sized hail was reported all along the front range in Colorado, with funnel clouds and tornadoes. But here, the sky was purest blue—and the wide land swept away until, standing in the wind, I felt small like dust.

Why do they call it God's country?

Because *he can see you out there* . . .

In the morning I left the campground at 7:40, and stopped on a rise overlooking Lake Etling. Dead trees stood like bones out of the still water; a pair of mule deer trotted away above the dirt road, crunching lightly over dry grass and broken stone.

The mesa country's a shattered wilderness of piñon and juniper, cholla cactus and scrub oak and hackberry; it's movie terrain, barren valleys flung down between abrupt scarps and bluffs. I went as far as

Kenton, then turned back for Boise City, rodeo-bound. Coming off the mesa, I rounded a turn to find the flat plain smothered again under low masses of cloud. Rain began ticking on the roof, and thunder rolled. Miserable knots of cows stood lined with their faces to the fence, backs to the southwest where the weather was coming from. It was Sunday; I had some preacher raving against false prophets on the radio.

"There *is* a hell!"

But that's okay, there's a heaven too. It's called Sheen's Country Kitchen—winner of my award for Best Breakfast In The Heart Of America.

Feeling fat and happy, I went to the kids' rodeo. The Lil' Hombre's for children thirteen and under—and I mean all the way under, right down to five, four, even three . . . Cheryl Gayler, one of the organizers, said, "Everybody round here knows how to ride a horse. And today the kids have their day—they get to rodeo today like the big people do."

So there'd be pole bending, goat tying, steer daubing, barrel circuits, calf and steer riding . . . Maybe twenty-five kids turned and trotted round the arena, warming up, all looking easy like they were born in the saddle, like they came out of the womb wearing boots. Hooves tossed up flurries of thick sandy dirt. Pickups and trailers stood parked in ranks against the fence, and then packed back across the open patch of land towards the first street on the edge of town. Fine tall horses huffed and whinnied all about; the men all wore cowboy hats. Cheryl asked one of them, "Did you get that rain this morning?"

"Hell, I'd take some rain."

"Every one of those horses out there," said the announcer, "is worth a million dollars to those kids."

His name was Dan, he had a ranch out by Kenton, and he said he pretty much started this thing back in '69. He turned back to the microphone, starting to hustle the contestants to get going in case the weather dropped more rain again. "We want a good rain—but not before we're done."

So after all the kids had ridden round the arena for the grand entry, two of them, a girl with the Stars and Stripes, and a boy with the flag of Oklahoma, went galloping out to post the colors. The Stars and Stripes had a yellow ribbon attached. The boy held his horse stock still in the center of the ring; the girl tore around and around him, hooves pounding and thudding in the dirt, the flag batting and whipping against the wind, as another girl with a sweet clear voice sang "The Star-Spangled Banner" over the speaker system. Everyone stood.

"Almighty and most merciful God, we come to you today in our rushed and hurrying moments to do our best in the sport of rodeo. We don't ask any special privileges, but just to do as good as we can . . ."

The children streamed on their thundering horses through the flying dirt—and as they'd hung on to their history at the Caney Mayfest, so here they were hanging on to their way of life, in a hard terrain. Because it may not rain, prices may be down, government many miles away might not give a flying cuss—and Boise City may have lost one in seven of its population in the last ten years . . . but the ones who stick it out have a steely determination, and want their kids to be the same.

Cheryl Gayler said calmly, "We can still afford to do it; we still get our donators. We're keeping going."

The pole bending's a slalom against the clock. First out was Stormy Nettles, a twelve-year-old from Liberal. Dan announced, "I've called this cowboy's name . . . well, I was going to say a million times, but I ain't *that* old."

Stormy span and weaved the horse through the poles like a seamstress threading a button, fast and easy. Then came Jackie Cherry, Pake Mayness, Cheyenne Osborn, Nichole Pate. Nichole was a sharp, striking eleven-year-old wearing shades, and a red bandana in her tawny hair. "Nichole won the egg race out at my place last week. You still got that egg, Nichole?"

She smiled, a little dazzle of light under the sun, and nodded at the booth as she passed.

Twelfth out of the gate was another heartbreaker, Stassi Walker, wildly pretty in a light purple T-shirt and jeans, with a purple saddlepad and purple leggings on her horse. "Guess you folks know what Stassi's favorite color is."

Doug Cherry came over. "This is where the West begins," he said, "and the pavement ends. The people here are outgoing, they're just wonderful people; they're down home, neighbors help neighbors, we stick together. The crime rate's really down—you see our kids, they just run around, we turn 'em loose."

A kid fell off his horse, and got straight back up. "Good cowboy," called Dan. "I tell you, folks, that cowboy's tougher'n an old woodman's axe."

"But I will say," Doug said, "the last few years have been a struggle. We've lost businesses; you look around town, there's shops been closed. Mostly it's no rain, and the grain prices."

They had five-year-olds doing the pole bending now. "Kimberly, I'm real sorry, but you broke the pattern there, so you got a no-time. But don't you worry, you done good and I'm real proud of you. Folks, some of these kids, it's their first or second time out there, so sometimes they have a little problem. But they'll get it right, I guarantee you."

Doug said, "Cattle's been doing good. But it makes you nervous—that could change any time too."

The goat ribbon race involved getting your horse to the far end of the ring, getting down, yanking a ribbon off the tail of the goat, then running back with it across a line where the judges were, all against the clock. Jake Colletti and Shancee Howell both did this one—they'd come 150 miles from Tribune, Kansas, to do it, they were riding regular horses just like everyone else, and they were three years old.

Jake didn't want to let go of his horse; when he'd got the ribbon he tried to tow it with him back across the judging line, stumbling and tugging in soft earth up to his knees. Shancee got off hers by hanging down from the saddle as far as she'd go, then just flipping out and falling away into the dirt on her back. A great surge of pride and encouragement welled up off the people on the stand all about me. "Will you *look* at that little kid?"

Then came the steer daubing, the best event yet. The steer gets released from a pen, and you're in a gate beside it; you have to pelt out after it the minute it's loosed, and chase it close enough to whack it with a yellow-chalked wad of cloth wrapped on the end of a stick. A cowboy in shades, denim shirt, and black-frilled chaps sat astride the pen, letting the steers bolt out. The kids went tearing out one after the other in jingling drumrolls of hooves and earth.

The steer has to get past a barrel—you're not allowed to whup it before it's got at least a taste of a headstart—and the judge on that was the local cop, a stout man named Bob in a livid orange shirt that drew a good deal of ribbing comment.

"Bob," said Dan, "you make a perfect barrel."

Kids charged round the ring after the twisting, bucking steers, leaning way out of the saddle until the chalk dust flew from a successful strike.

I took a break about four, and drove idly down dirt roads west of town. Each great irrigation wheel stood like a long thin trellis in one vast field after another; under a blazing sun, the wind whipped and howled. It felt as if you really could, like Val Castor said, see the curvature of the earth.

The radio said that if the world's population continues to grow at the present trend, then the world's farmers will have to grow as much food in the first two decades of the next century as they grew in the past ten thousand years.

And if the water's running out—then how?

"Wheat ain't been worth a shit for three, four years. And if there ain't no farmers, the town shuts down."

Larry Taylor was twenty-four, and worked for a vet; his buddy Eric Warner ran a feedlot. Eric said of cattle that it had been good for a while, but now the market was too high. "You can't afford to buy 'em—you pay five, six hundred dollars a calf now, by the time you're through paying trucking, feed, labor, you're gonna sell it for less or the same than what you bought it for. Gonna be some sumbitches go broke this year, I tell you. Used to be you'd buy a calf for three, four hundred dollars—but it just keeps going up, them sumbitches in the ring just keep jacking it up, them order buyers . . ."

You watch the prices every day?

"You bet. Last week they were selling fats [cattle going to slaughter] eighty-two dollars a hundredweight. Now they're down to seventy-two dollars, seventy-five dollars—still a pretty good price, but you can see it going down. So what it cost you to raise 'em to that . . . This year'll break some people."

Larry said the trucks helped keep Boise City going. "In the winter you get a snowstorm, there'll be a hundred, hundred-fifty rigs parked up in this town."

Boise City's a five-state junction, nearer to the capitals of New Mexico and Colorado than it is to the capital of Oklahoma. Highways 3, 56, 64, 287, and 385 all rumble round the courthouse square, carrying road freight back and forth from Texas to Denver, Kansas to Santa Fe.

Eric said, "I'd hate to think how many rigs you'd count in twenty-four hours. But all they keep in business is the Kwik-Store."

I'd gone back to the rodeo, and bumped into these two by Larry's pickup. When I told them what I was doing, Larry pointed in his flatbed, and said I'd have to learn what the essential cowboy carries these days.

"You got to have your horse tack—bridle, halter, brushes. Then you got a couple of ropes, roping glove, calf bottle, a few old empty beer cans, fenceposts, spare tire and jack, pliers—anything that squeezes."

"Baling wire," said Eric.

"Baling wire," said Larry, and rummaged. "Hell, Eric—I'm not a complete man."

"No doubt. If you break down, you're up shit creek. How you gonna tie that engine back together without you got some baling wire?"

"Beer cans," said Larry, still rummaging. "I got those."

"Hammer—you got to have a hammer to beat things with."

Larry gave up hunting baling wire. He grinned and said, "Nine times out of ten if you got enough beer, you won't need no baling wire. And that there's the inventory," he concluded, "of your typical Oklahoma cowboy's pickup truck."

I asked them then whether it was typical that there hadn't been good rain for so long.

"Rain?" asked Eric. "I run a feedlot, don't mean shit to me. But some people, they sit and bitch all year long 'cause it's dry. Then planting time, it rains and washes 'em all out—and they sit and bitch, 'Too much rain, too much rain.' See, out here, you just never can tell."

I said how over east in Coffeyville, OB Johnson had told me that fifty years ago, a man could make a living there with forty acres and two horses. Now, he'd said, in southeast Kansas you needed one thousand acres minimum, and a quarter million to spend on it.

"A thousand acres? You ain't gonna make a living off one thousand acres out here, no way. The land's not good enough. This land, this should be in a different state—'cause this country's all sand, hell, it ain't shit. This should be New Mexico, or Colorado. If you ain't big out here, you're broke. But it's still good country—'cause you got to think bigger, and work harder. Take me, I got an '87 pickup—that thing's got 225,000 miles on it. My dad, he got a new one last August, ain't seen a year yet, and it's got sixty thousand miles—and that's just in Cimarron County."

Another guy rolled up then and asked, "You writing a book? Put my name in it, would you?"

Gary Kincannon.

"He's the town drunk."

"No, don't put that—I'm a pillar of the community."

So where does a man get a beer around here?

"There's the Branding Iron and the VFW, they're both out of town. Then on Main Street there's Tumbleweeds, which is just strictly Mexican—you're up the creek if you go in there, 'cause hardly anybody speaks English. And there's the Friendly Tavern, now we call that one the Knife & Gun Club. Four, five years ago there's this local boy shooting pool with some roughnecks, and one of them goes out to his truck and gets his pistol and shoots him—over a two-dollar pool game. And he done three years in the penitentiary, and now he's back in town working. 'Cause what you'll find in this town is, money walks, bullshit talks."

So I went for a beer with Larry in the Friendly Tavern. It was a dark wooden tunnel of a place, vaguely visible behind the dust kicked by passing trucks off the roadworks on Main Street. It's changed hands since that shooting Larry talked about—and was now tended by a scrawny, dark-skinned, empty-eyed little woman named Barb.

"Larry Taylor," she said. "Where's your wife at?"

"She farted and flew out the window, Barb."

Barb looked at me—and bear in mind, I'm eight years older than Larry here. She looked back at Larry and asked him, "This your son?"

As Barb slowly fetched us cold Buds, Larry whispered, "She's loco. Done too much drugs in her younger days, and now she don't know where she's at."

She asked me, "Where you from?"

Great Britain.

"I don't know where that's at."

Larry said, "She's dumber'n a box of rocks."

We drained the beers, then went for a tour round the town—and on the way back to the rodeo ground, passing a clutch of modest brick bungalows, Larry Taylor said this.

"This here's your basic low-income housing, we call it Taco Villas. The Mexicans got it made in this town; you got the girls with green cards, the wetbacks come up and marry them, before you know it they've popped four kids. And the wetbacks are out cutting our throats on the jobs, and the girls are on the welfare getting money for the kids, and food stamps too—it's a cutthroat situation, I tell you."

He said, "They ought to slit all their throats and stick 'em on a plane to Tijuana and chuck 'em out. Government needs to pull its head out of its ass. Poor country fucks like me just busting our balls to make a dollar, and then these other people . . ."

Family values, community virtues—honesty, hard work, hospitality, looking out for your neighbor—person after person in town after town extolled these merits in the heart of America. And very plainly they did exist there, resilient and stubborn in the face of the pressures—in the face of the tornadic march of history sweeping the prairie clean of its people again.

But every now and then I'd be brought up short by the paranoia those pressures are also enhancing. It would be suddenly and ruthlessly made clear that for some people, those values and virtues existed in a box—and the only people in the box were white.

No Mexicans.

No blacks.

No Indians.

In Austin, Texas, I went to the Laff Spot, a comedy club, and a Texican comedian said, "You know, there's half a million Mexicans got into this country illegally already this year. They can't catch them, right?

"And what I want to know is, why don't they catch them when they're counting them?"

Back at the rodeo as the warm evening settled, the seven- to nine-year-olds were riding calves, and the kids ten and over riding steers. A calf would be three to four hundred pounds, a steer five hundred. Stout Bob the cop in his radiant shirt had the clipboard and stopwatch; other men clambered up the pens, swinging high round the fence rails to settle the kids down on their rides, making sure the gloved hand was tucked in tight to the rope-hold on the animal's back. Three men waited on horseback to shoo each calf or steer away to another pen, when the ride was done.

When the pen was flung open the ride came bucking out into the dirt, jumping and heaving until the kid was tossed. A few of them lasted the time, and got themselves off of the animal intact—but most landed with a rough thump every which way, as the animal sooner or later abruptly got clear of them.

Skylar Howell, eight years old from Tribune, Kansas, looking fine in his big hat and his sky blue chaps with the silver frills, got stomped—but he got up grimacing and gasping, determined to walk away on his own.

Another kid made it nearly all the way across the width of the arena, his dad chasing over behind him, throwing his hat exultantly in the air. When the kid was on his feet his dad put out his hand—and the kid whacked his own hand down into Daddy's palm.

"Way to go, kid."

Then a terrified wail rose up from the narrow pen where the calves did their confined and angry jolting, as the kids were settled down on their backs.

"I don't want to. I don't *want* to . . ."

The boy was three years old. He screamed and screamed, as the pen burst open; his dad ran out beside the kicking calf, holding the kid in big hands round the ribs as the animal leapt and twisted—then after a few seconds he picked him off its back, and set him down quivering and shocked on the dirt.

*Danged* if my boy ain't riding that calf . . .

Among the many good reasons Norma Gene Butterbaugh Young would have us believe that Cimarron County is unique, is the bizarre fact that Boise City's the only town in the continental United States to be bombed during World War II.

On July 5, 1943, a B-17 from Dalhart Army Air Base in Texas mistook the lights round the courthouse for a target from which it was thirty miles astray—and proceeded to drop six bombs on the place. Happily, no one was hurt. They put up a notice at the base afterwards saying REMEMBER THE ALAMO, REMEMBER PEARL HARBOR, AND FOR GOD'S SAKE—REMEMBER BOISE CITY!

Boise City was thirty-five years old then; it was established by three charlatans called Stanley, Kline, and Douglas in 1908. In a splendid booklet called "Not a Stoplight in the County" Young writes, "The men platted the town and sold about 3,000 lots for $45 each to people, mostly in Illinois, Indiana and Missouri . . . so that prospective buyers were not likely to come to the area, and see that the brochures they were circulating were mostly fabrications. These showed rivers, paved streets, many trees, dozens of houses and businesses, and numerous sidewalks. Actually, a windmill stood in the center of the townsite, there was one concrete block building, and a strip of cement sidewalk about half a block long."

It turned out that the three men didn't even own the lots they were selling . . . Douglas died of TB; the other two were sentenced to two years in jail.

Word gets round quick, when there's a stranger in town. Barbara Tapp introduced herself in the bank, and invited me to visit with her. She and her husband Bob lived at the French place, a two-story house past the hospital—and I was barely through the door, before the proud history came spilling out.

It was like, *people should know about this* . . . before it vanishes forever.

Barbara's grandparents were Hugh and Mollie French, descended from French Huguenots from Virginia, via Scotland. Hugh French sold an eighty-acre farm in Lincoln County, Oklahoma—where Barbara's father Robert was born, 350 miles east—for $750, in the fall of 1906. Then in the spring of '07 they traveled west, the trip taking seventeen days, until they settled 2½ miles northwest of where Boise City is now.

Barbara's mother was Ruby Opal Munson from Oronogo, Missouri; she and Robert were married in Guymon, Oklahoma, on August 8, 1916. Barbara said, "Daddy was the first man to introduce irrigation into this county—'course, it was ditch irrigation then. But he loved to see the country improve, and grow—and he worked till the day he died, nearly—he had leukemia."

It must have been hard . . .

"Oh listen, it took courage. Now Bob, he says he'd have liked to live in those days, but me, I don't know . . . Well, I guess I could, I was born to this country—I was born in this house. And I'll tell you, I couldn't go to your country, I'd near to drown in all that rain. I need to see the sun every day, I need to see the dust. I think I'd die, if you took me out of this country."

They had eight thousand acres in the family, out north by the Cimarron River. I asked how it went up there and she said, "It's getting dry right now. We've had a quarter inch here and there—but we need an inch, an inch and a half to soak in. Then in the summer when it's real hot, you get those hit 'n' miss thunderstorms . . ."

And tornadoes?

"Our tornadoes, usually you can see them and get away from them out here—it's not like cities. We're out on the fringe of that, anyhow. But we get big storms—the lightning, ooh, it cracks and pops round here, I just get down on my knees and ask the Lord to protect us . . . But as to tornadoes, well, we had one when our son was a child come right over the house one night, sounded like a freight train, I'll never forget that sound, getting louder and louder—and you couldn't breathe, the air was so heavy—I was going to the crib to get my son, and I never did make it. And Bob was going to light a cigarette, and he never did either."

There are other threats too. "Fiddlers, they used to call them barn spiders, they'll make you deadly sick—they'll kill a kid. Down in Amarillo they had a kid got bit, and the doctors said he didn't have a chance—but they had it on the Christian Broadcasting, on the Pat Robertson show, people prayed and he lived, and they considered it a miracle . . . I'll tell you, spiders, they scare me more than snakes. I'll kill a rattler; some people use a chain but Im scared it'll come back at me, I'll use a long shovel—got to be long, else those things'll jump. And don't go barefoot by those streams, there's water moccasins out there. . . . One child I knew got bit, and his mother just cut a chicken right in half, put one half in the stove, put the other half straight to the bite, feathers and all—and when she took it away it was green, it drew that poison out. Then she put the foot in kerosene, and it worked."

Of the country here she said, "You know we almost got taken into Texas? They should have had us too—we'd have been an advantage to them."

She and Bob had been ranching down in Texas, near the Mexico border. "We ran three, four thousand goats down there—and when we bought them, the herd came with dogs, mongrel dogs that they'd raised from pups with their eyes shut suckling on a nanny. So when they opened their eyes that nanny was their mother, and they never would leave that herd. If some other dog came along, they'd beat the tar out of it."

They had goats by the house now, and sheep too; Barbara said, "I really like sheep. With sheep you won't starve to death, and you won't freeze to death neither. But they're dumb dumb dumb dumb dumb. Mind you, I got eleven orphans, and they're smart, 'cause I educated them. But the herd—where one of them goes, they all got to go. Dumb. And sheep are beginning to come back now, 'cause they got this farm program where they're getting everybody to put the land back to grass. 'Course fifteen, twenty years from now they'll have everybody plowing it up again—that's how smart governments are."

I got the feeling she'd have gone on forever, and I wouldn't have minded. I met several fine women like Barbara Tapp in this disregarded and shrinking piece of America, who only wanted what they and their people had done to be remembered—and it seems to me that it should be too, as the land empties, and the world congeals into cities, and history gets remodeled into movies and theme parks . . .

But at the rodeo I'd made an appointment to go visit with a rancher name of Alan Shields, so I had to leave—and Barbara was still telling me stories even as I got in the truck, with her vigorous urgency that these things be recorded.

"Bob's grandfather was a sheriff," she said, "and he had his horse shot from under him by Jesse James. So he went to Jesse's mama's place and he said, 'You owe me a horse.'

" 'Over my dead body,' she says."

"Now Jesse's mama was meaner'n a snake. But Bob's grandpa just said, 'Well that may be—but you owe me a horse.' So he took one too—and you know, Jesse never did a thing about it. Because he knew he *did* owe that man a horse."

The Shields place was on a dirt road way out by Black Mesa. They had twelve thousand acres there for cattle, and then four thousand more across the line into Texas growing wheat, corn, and milo. Alan's father Jim, who'd just turned sixty, and his brother Steve, twenty-eight, ran the grain; Alan lived alone up here, and took care of the ranching. He was thirty-one; neither brother was married. "You need to get Mom in there too," he said, "she does all the bill paying, the bookkeeping. We couldn't make it without her."

Jim and Steve were up from Texas that afternoon, helping stack hay in a barn. Steve said of the ranch, "For out here, it's not very big."

Alan said, "We've got one hired man. It's strictly a family deal—that's still common out here."

So I asked about corporate farming, the agri-industrial outfits—bankers, accountants, lawyers, men in suits working the price support systems, and swallowing up the little man.

"They've tried it out here—and nearly every corporate farm in the Panhandle went bust."

Steve said dismissively, "They're in it for the money."

Jim said, "The management gets too far away from the work."

"They leveraged themselves way too high," said Alan, "borrowed way too much money, that's my opinion. And then they had set plans—we don't have a set plan, we try to change as the market changes, and the rain—but they didn't do that, and they got caught."

"They're like a pyramid," said Jim. "There's too many of them want a piece of it—and out here, there ain't too many pieces."

Alan told me, "We've been in beef here four years. Before that it was strictly grain farming—but we wanted to diversify, because the way our business is running right now, our grain is just barely breaking even, and all our profit's been in cattle. What we do, we're yearling men—we buy steers at four, five hundred pounds, grow them to seven-fifty, eight hundred, then sell them to the feedlots."

We were driving now in his pickup through a sparsely grassed little canyon of broken red and yellow stone along Carrizo Creek; Alan said it ran right through the ranch, and about a third of their land was sand and malpais like this. The rest was better grass up flat on the prairie round about, buffalo grass, with blue grama mixed in. It was, I said, good country.

"I wish it'd rain though. Because it's not how much, a lot of times, it's when—sometimes, if you can get two and a half, three inches in ten days, you could go forty-five days then without another rain. For the cattle, that is. And right now, that'd be ideal—'cause the buffalo grass don't grow too long. But our annual is seventeen inches, and that's enough. Usually. If we get it."

The track was a jolting, indistinct mess of ruts and stones through the bare dry land. I told Alan what OB had said, about how in eastern Kansas you'd need one thousand acres, and a quarter million to get it going. He said, "I'd say out here you'd need close to ten thousand acres before you'd make a decent living—on strictly cattle, that is. You wouldn't need so much investment, though."

Just land . . . Dan at the rodeo said it took forty-five acres to run one cow and a calf. And that they'd had one and a half inches of rain this year.

But there was more than rain bothering Alan. He said, like Eric had too, "This year we're having to give more than we ever have to buy cattle—and when it comes to selling in the fall, looking at the futures market now . . . it's going to be a break-even situation."

Farming, I said, had been no fun in the eighties.

"It's been tough—but it's weeded out the bad managers. If you was a good manager, you'll have expanded. What is bad," he said, "is when the businesses in town fold. That affects us. In Boise City now there's just one car dealer, one tractor dealer—there used to be more. But when you got fewer people farming bigger farms, the town shrinks. It isn't bad for us out here, exactly—but it affects you."

We went past piñon and juniper on the shadowed low bluffs; the ground was scattered with yucca, Adam's needle, Spanish bayonet—called soapweed here, because the old-timers made soap from the roots. Looking at the land Alan said, "I've been other places, and I wouldn't trade this for any place. I went out to Long Beach, California, once—it was a National Young Farmers' & Ranchers' Convention. I went with the Oklahoma Young Farmers—and we tried to get people to wave at us, the way you'll see people do here when you pass them on the road. And they just all looked at us like, shoot, they're crazy. First car we did it, they gave us the finger. You couldn't *make* me live out there."

We came out onto the flat top land. A hazy blue rim of mountains rose on the horizon by Des Moines, New Mexico, sixty miles west. Alan said occasionally you'd see a bald or a golden eagle. He said there were bobcat and coyote, deer and antelope—and then, wondrously, where the Shields land ended at a wire fence running straight and arbitrary over the featureless dry green, there stood a dozen buffalo.

"These buffalo, the guy that owns them, he's not here right now. He's a custom wheat harvester, he's got combines and he follows the wheat— he's already started cutting down at Hobart—but he keeps these as a hobby, and sells the kids every year. And I claim they're mine, 'cause I see them."

We stopped in the middle of the massive earth. The air—near four thousand feet and a million miles from any place—was dry and clean. Under the cloudless sky Black Mesa ran like a dark jetty into the ocean of land to the north; two peaks, the Rabbit Ears, jutted pale against the horizon thirty miles southwest. The buffalo were four hundred yards off; we got out of the truck, and Alan said to look at the ground.

We were stopped in the four-lane ruts of the Santa Fe Trail. You could see them sweeping away over the next low rise, miles of the faint indentations of history still marked on the land. "In the fall," said Alan, "you can see it real good—the grass is different in the depressions, it has a different tint to it then."

There was nothing else there—just two windmills, a dozen buffalo, and the long straight line of America's past on the move across the earth.

We drove up to the fence, and stood face to face with the buffalo. They were shaggy, losing the last of their winter coats; the adults moved big and slow, with three calves starting and trotting excitably among them. There was a vast bull, shoulders way taller off the ground than the top of my head—and his own black-haired head had more bulk than my torso, and his breath was a thundery whisper in my face. I tried to take pictures—but the way the fence line ran, the buffalo were right against the sun.

Alan, seeing this—this amiable man in his denims and seed cap with his disarming, goofy laugh—hopped over the fence, and shooed them into a better light for the camera. He waved his leather chaps at them saying quietly, Hyah! Hyah! The calves jumped and turned; the adults faced him, the great bull half a length out ahead of the rest idly pawing the dry earth, barely two yards off him.

And everything you read says you don't walk with buffalo, that they're ornery and fierce. But I figured what the hell, Alan Shields knows his land and what's on it—so I jumped the fence too. I walked— somewhat tentatively—among the buffalo.

The sound of their breathing, basso snuffles and grunts; the faint crackle and thud of their slow, heavy hooves dully impacting on the dirt and thin grass; the sound of my heart racing, in the heart of America . . .

There were eighty million of these things once. They used their bones for hard core and fertilizer, and their hides for buffing rags.

There were academics in New Jersey who'd come up with an idea that settlement out here was a mistake, and that the land should go back to being "buffalo commons." I asked Alan about that.

He said, "I think they're crazy. If they did that the whole world would feel the effects of it. Besides, there's not a better conservationist than the farmers and ranchers themselves. Water, soil, wildlife—if we don't take care of those things, we don't make a living."

But the water was running out . . .

"We haven't had no run-off water last year, and very little the year before that—that's from a real hard rain, from three inches—we've had none of that. This pasture we just came through, it's got a pond in it that's the only water there, and it'll be dry in a week. The old-timers tell me they ain't never seen it dry. So I got to do something . . ."

Was it drying out, year on year?

"It's a weather cycle, is what I say it is."

Greenhouse effect?

"No, I don't believe in that. We had droughts before they thought of the greenhouse effect."

So was this a drought now?

"Close to it. If it hadn't rained that bit last week it would be—but it's close to it. And if I don't get any rain this summer my cattle won't gain, and then I'll lose money. That's what it boils down to. And so many people say that for farmers and ranchers to survive they've got to diversify—into what? You get up in the corn belt where they've got rain, they can change—but not here. All you can do here is cattle. For this area, cattle is it."

So I asked him if it was worth it—close to a drought here now, with his life hanging on the rain and the market every year—and the answer was immediate.

"I've got a college degree in accounting, and I did that for two years. I put on a suit and tie every day for two years; people don't believe it, but I did. Then I told them it wasn't what I wanted to do."

He said, "This is what I want to do. And I want to do it right here." In No Man's Land.


## The Last Outpost

I drove south through Wyoming, taking 191 from Jackson into the Green River Basin. Cattle stood like specks of bright dirt on the parched sheet of the prairie; the Wind River Mountains were a snowcapped line of grey rock in the east. Crossing from Sublette into Sweetwater County, the road ran along the rim of a low sandy butte; below and beyond it the west reached out shimmering forever, planet-sized to the ruler-lined horizon.

I stopped in Farson for gas. It was searing hot, burning blue through a skeined featherbed of cirrus. A Farson postcard announced: "Shortest route from Interstate 80 to the fabulous Bridger Wilderness, Jackson Hole and Yellowstone Park. Oregon Trail Cafe, Hotel, General Store, Service Station, Petrified Wood Bar, Laundermat, Natural Soft Water. Wyoming's best antelope, deer and sage grouse hunting. Historical Monument. Petrified Wood & Fossil Area. Overnite Park." It didn't leave much room for your news.

The next place was called Eden. I guess they must have everything you could possibly want there too.

Then came thirty-six more empty miles, past Pilot Butte into Rock Springs—a town veiled in wind-whipped dust, tooth-clogging, eye-scouring whorls of yellow grit dancing through the barren lots and forecourts. I stopped to check my tires. In back of the station a ragged man with a huge, bobbling lower lip stood on tiptoe by the dumpster, sifting aimlessly through the trash. The wind whisked dirt past our heads, and the stale smell of garbage. I couldn't check the air; someone had liberated the gauge.

I turned west on I80 to Evanston, past a place called Little America that consisted solely of a motel and truckstop. I wondered if that was what the future would be, as the little towns fade out—just wilderness, dotted with gas pumps and motels . . .

In Evanston I went to the Last Outpost Bar. I told a shifty kid with a patchy blond beard and round tinted shades I was going on tomorrow to Salt Lake City, for the Square Dance Convention. He said I'd made a good choice. "When they dance the women go around and their skirts go up, and you can see their panties."

I told Rusty Fife I'd driven 922 miles in the last 48 hours.

He grinned and asked, "What took you so long?"

And I talked to a girl named Belinda. She said she was from upstate New York, but she'd cut out with her kids after nine years of marriage; she'd put up with the guy punching holes in the walls, but then he started punching holes in the kids too. She'd lived, if I recall correctly, in a whole welter of places after that, Florida, California, New Mexico—and now she was here.

She was a right-to-lifer. . . .

She said no one had the right to take the life of an unborn child. But she also said murderers, rapists, Charles Manson, the Son of Sam, these people should all be hanged. Into the chair, out with the gas, lethal injection, whatever it took—those people weren't people, they were "worth nothing."

I drank foul, sweet-tasting bar whiskey. Belinda referred randomly to the Old Testament and the New, and railed in a terrible ecstasy of paranoia against the nation of knife-wielding rapists out there. She said she didn't have a gun but she wished she did have, 'cause she was a protective mother to her kids, and if she saw some bad man coming up the path she had the right to shoot him right there—that bad man wasn't no way getting in her house near her kids.

What if she made a mistake? What if she was drunk and shot the postman? Because certainly, she was drunk just then—on long drinks early in the evening, and now shot glasses of some evil-looking schnapps, laced with Bailey's off the back of a spoon.

I had a flash of light through my whiskey. Where, I asked, are your kids right now?

"They're at my friend's place."

And what are you doing in here?

"I'm unstressing."

So you're going to pick them up later?

"Sure I am."

In your car?

"Sure."

I stumbled into the garish splashes of neon and white strip light along the road outside, and went to bed in the Vagabond Motel across the street.

# 4.

# Lucky in Liberal

I drove from the Shields place up to Liberal, Kansas. Along the way I got lost on dirt roads in the Cimarron National Grassland, the truck kicking dust across drifting rolls of bleached green, God's lawn, lit all over by the pale yellow blooms of the yucca. A vein of trees followed the course of the Cimarron through the prairie—but the river was dry. Away from the irrigation wheels, there was no sign or sense of water anywhere under the torched and remorseless sky.

Liberal got its name from the kindness of an early settler named Rogers. It was customary at that time for homesteaders to charge travelers on the plains for the precious water from their wells—but when travelers had water from the Rogers well and then asked what they owed he'd tell them, "No charge. Water's always free here."

To which they replied, "That's mighty liberal of you."

So when they picked his house for the post office, it seemed only natural to call it Liberal. . . .

I got a room in the Tumbleweed Motel; when I parked in front of it, I checked the meter on the truck. I'd been on the road a week, I'd put on 1,148 miles—and all I'd done was pop in and out of Oklahoma.

I sat in the lot as evening came down, and felt America stretch away from me . . . then I walked down the scattered neon of 54 along the south side of town, and found a low wooden box called Rumors.

I shot pool there with a skinny, lank-haired young guy named Richard. Richard's wife'd left him, he said, 'cause he was running three whole separate Dungeons and Dragons games all at once; and he had a two-year college diploma in art & design, but could he get a job? Could he shit. So now he was working in a meat-packing plant. "But I'll make it," he said. "You watch me. I'll make it."

He was from Beaver. He said, "You went to the Cow Chip? Well hell,

I went back there just a weekend or two back, with this friend of mine. And the thing of it is, he's a real sticky fingers, right? And I'm just drawing on the napkins at the bar there, and this big old boy comes and says, 'You seen a ten-dollar bill?' And I say, 'Hell no,' 'cause I don't know what he's talking about. And I'm wearing this big old duster of my grandpa's, got pockets deeper'n a well, so I pull out all the shit in there and lay it on the bar, and the last thing out's my big old hunting knife. And I say, 'You see anything there that's yours?' And he says . . . Nope. Categorical, like. Only then I see it in my friend's eyes—he's took that ten. And I think, You fuckhead. So we walked out. We walked out of there, 'cause otherwise we'd have got us carried out. And the thing of it is—that big old boy used to date my mom."

Then I talked to a guy named Stacey. Hearing what I was doing, he asked had I seen the corn growing east of here, twelve, fifteen feet tall? Best in the country.

Where's the water come from, that's good enough for corn?

"Underground."

And wasn't that drying up?

"Some places, yeah."

And then?

"Then this is all just gone, man. Gone." He stared in his beer.

I said I'd been storm chasing.

"Hell, you don't want to chase those things—they'll come chase *you*. Then you'll be . . ."

Gone. All just gone.

History.


In Wal-Mart I bought a pair of shoes, but when I went to pay with my Visa card, the authorization line was down. The checkout girl said, "Usually when that happens it means there's hail or lightning some-where. It was awful when we had our storms here—nobody could pay with anything."

The weather even fouls up your shopping.

It was oven-hot and cloudless, the forecast promising low 90s. I went to Dorothy's House, where you can sponsor a yellow brick. On the wall was a picture of three women honored as Munchkins in 1985. One of them was named Fern Formica.

An old lady told a kid, "Remember you were in Dorothy's House. It's all imaginary, but you were here."

The kid said sharply, "But *she's* not here. She's gone in the tornado, right?"

In the Coronado Museum next door there were quilts and Indian blankets, bullets and barbed wire, branding irons and horse tack, an outstanding collection of old postcards, Mrs. Lee Larrabee's wedding dress, December 6, 1905—and, in the hallway, a small case of items connected to the first European in Kansas.

In 1929, in Horse Thief Cave to the northeast of Liberal, a man named Bryan White found two rusted buckles, and a bridle bit. They'd been left there—as of 1929—388 years earlier.

In 1540, Don Francisco Vasquez de Coronado was governor of the province of New Galicia in New Spain, now Mexico. In February that year, about thirty years old, he set off north in search of the fabled wealth of the Seven Cities of Cibola, and the fantastical empire of Quivira. By summer he arrived at the Seven Cities, which turned out to be the pueblos of New Mexico, and goldless. So he wintered with the Indians, then went on for Quivira with thirty-six of his men. They got as far as central Kansas, finding plains Indians living in dome-shaped grass huts—but still no gold.

Coronado reported that after leaving the pueblos, "I traveled for forty-two days . . . living all the while solely on the flesh of the bulls and cows which we killed . . . going many days without water, and cooking the food with cow dung, because there is no other kind of wood in all these plains, away from the gullies and rivers, which are few."

After strangling his mendacious Indian guide, "The Turk," he concluded, "These provinces are a very small affair . . . there is not any gold, nor any metal at all in that country."

Central Kansas was more promising. The land, he wrote, "is the best I have seen for producing all the products of Spain, for besides the land itself being very fat and black, and being well watered by the rivulets and springs and rivers, I found prunes like those of Spain, and nuts, and very sweet grapes and mulberries."

He stayed twenty-five days, eventually getting back to New Spain with less than a hundred of his original three hundred men. He was stripped of his rank, and died soon afterwards—but he had introduced the horse to the Plains, and ushered in by doing so the high flourishing of the Indian Plains culture.

· · ·

According to the Kansas Guide written in the 1930s by the Writers' Project of the Works Progress Administration, the state's principal indigent Indian tribes were the Kansa, the Osage, and the Pawnee. There were also the Wichita, and wandering tribes of Cheyenne, Arapaho, Kiowa, and Comanche. Some hunted the buffalo; some grew maize, beans, and squash, living in semi-permanent earth lodges.

In 1835, the Kansa population was estimated at around one thousand six hundred. By 1859, they were penned in a reservation nine miles long, by fourteen wide. By 1872—thanks to liquor and smallpox, and the rest of the panoply of European diseases—they were down to barely two hundred people. The following year, they were moved into Indian Territory.

As for the Pawnee, these were a great nation one of whose four bands, the Tapage or Noisy Pawnee, lived in the Smoky Hills of north-central Kansas. The others lived on the Platte, Loup, and Republican rivers of Nebraska—but the smallpox got the Pawnee too. An Indian agent reported that they were, "dying so fast . . . they had ceased to bury their dead, and bodies were to be seen in every direction, lying in the river, lodged on the sand bars, in the weeds around their villages, and in their old corn caches."

Those who survived gave up what was left to them in Kansas in 1876, and were moved to Indian Territory too. By 1880, virtually all Indian titles in Kansas had been extinguished.

Apart from Coronado, and three other equally fruitless Spanish gold treks in the next 150 years, the first whites into the area were French traders descending the Mississippi from Wisconsin. Traders from Canada were doing business among the Osage and Missouri tribes by 1694; the Spanish tried to turf them out with an expedition from Santa Fe in 1720, but failed, and lost control of the territory to the French until 1762. The French got it back again in 1801—then sold it to Jefferson.

Captain Zebulon Pike's expedition came through the prairie in 1806. He reported, "These vast plains of the western hemisphere may become in time as celebrated as the sandy deserts of Africa; for I saw in my route, in various places, tracts of many leagues where the wind had thrown up the sand in all the fanciful forms of the ocean's rolling wave, on which not a speck of vegetable matter existed."

Daniel Webster asked in Congress, "What do we want with this vast and worthless area, this region of savages and wild beasts, of deserts, of shifting sands and whirlwinds, of dust, of cactus and prairie dogs; to what use could we ever hope to put these great deserts, or those endless mountain ranges, impenetrable and covered to their very base with eternal snow? . . . Mr. President, I will never vote one cent from the public treasury to place the Pacific Coast one inch nearer Boston than it is now."

Indian tribes from the east were pushed westward towards this "worthless area." The Delaware came in 1829, and then the Kickapoo, Pottawatomie, Kaskaskia, Peoria, Wea, and Piankeshaw in 1832. The Sauk, Fox, and Iowa arrived in 1835, the Miami in 1840, and the Wyandotte in 1843. But they all got moved on again, in the end, from Kansas into Indian Territory—because the white man was running onto the new land right beside them.

Daniel Boone's son, Daniel Morgan Boone, got to what's now Jefferson County in the northeast of the state in 1827; his son Napoleon, born August 22 the following year, was the first white child born in Kansas.

Even so, in 1854, when the Missouri Compromise was repealed so that the Kansas and Nebraska territories could decide for themselves whether they wished to become slave states or not—and although thousands of emigrants were pouring west by then along the Oregon Trail—the resident white population of the nascent state of Kansas was still only 1,500.

Missouri, on the other hand, had a population of some 80,000, and 12,000 slaves. So now the settlers poured in, free staters from the North and the East, slavers from Missouri and the South—and set busily about prolonged, often barbaric guerrilla war. It was Jayhawkers for the Union, against Bushwhackers for the Confederacy; it was "bleeding Kansas," messy and unpleasant, and there was drought, famine, and grasshopper plagues thrown in.

And yet, by 1870, the population of the state had risen in sixteen years from 1,500, to 362,000.

The last Indian raid in Kansas, the last flicker of native resistance in the state's far west, was in 1878. Ten years later the state's last county, Greeley, was organized on the Colorado line.

Greeley's county seat is Tribune—from where, 103 years later, Skylar Howell and Jake Colletti and Shancee Howell went to rodeo in Boise City.

Liberal, meanwhile, is the seat of Seward County, organized in 1886. The mid-1880s saw a huge immigration into the "worthless area" of western Kansas; in just two years, the population of the western third of the state increased by a quarter of a million. Among them were many German-Russian Mennonites, bringing the hardy Turkey Red wheat that could survive and grow out there. Phil Bernhart, back in Coffeyville, said his grandma could remember swimming in the Volga when she was a child.

There was, naturally, a turmoil of land speculation set swirling by this massive influx—and a good piece of it centered round which settlement would get to be the county seat. In Seward County, the principal rivals were the towns of Fargo Springs, and Springfield; Liberal, to begin with, wasn't even in it.

In a history course paper dated January 1, 1943, Ella Blanche Kennedy notes acerbically, "The pride and loyalty of the inhabitants of these pioneer towns continued so long as that town had a chance for success; then these ambitious people moved on to where the opportunities were brighter."

The Fargo Springs boosters, certainly, went at it with a vengeance, chief among them the proud and loyal Abe Stoufer, proprietor of the *Fargo Springs News*. It was a town, he wrote, "not ten months old, with 700 people," and it had, "one bank, no sinners, one bakery, three hotels, four doctors, one minister, three lawyers, one feed store, one seed store, two laundries, two restaurants, one billiard hall, four drug stores, one jewelry store, two watchmakers, one harness shop, one meat market, two barber shops, two lumber yards, three feed stables, one furniture store, one milliner store, five grocery stores, a good stone quarry, one first class dairy, plenty of good water, two hardware stores, one blacksmith shop, three daily stage lines, one boot and shoe store, several real estate firms, one church and school house, two contracting and building firms, two newspapers, two boot and shoe manufacturies, and one millinery and dressmaking establishment."

Stoufer called Fargo Springs, "The new Chicago."

The hated rival, of course, wasn't seen in the same gloriously prospering light. A joke of the time went that a Springfield man dies, goes to Heaven, and is refused admittance. So he goes to Hell—and they won't let him in there either. "Oh Lord," he moans, "will I have to go back to Springfield then?"

Come polling day, the election to determine who'd win the county seat prize was purest chaos. A Springfieldite lavishly named J. Malcombed Johnsing gave a speech off the back of a wagon "that would put the Chicago anarchist leaders to shame"; large numbers of people were "walking arsenals." The Springfieldites eventually refused to vote at the polling station at all (when they found they couldn't storm it) and voted separately in a private ballot box of their own. They won, too—though only after the outcome had been further contested on a long march through the law courts.

In Fargo Springs, Abe Stoufer was undeterred by this electoral reverse. After all, a vote counted for nothing beside the import of where the railroads chose to go—and he confidently expected the Rock Island, the Missouri Pacific, and the Santa Fe all to be coming to his town. Fargo Springs was, he wrote, "building rapidly, and is conceded to be one of the most promising towns in the south-west."

In 1887 his paper announced that Fargo was "as sure to get them [the railroads] and make a large city, as Springfield is to turn up its toes to the daisies and moulder away and die in its frog pond."

In 1888—seeing which way the railroad tracks were laying, and that it wasn't in the way of Fargo Springs after all—Stoufer moved his newspaper with abrupt and casual treachery to the settlement of Arkalon.

G. S. Smith moved out too, but not to Arkalon; he took his drug store to Liberal instead. (In 1943, writes Kennedy, it was still there—with the telephone number 1.) Because while Fargo and Springfield slugged it out, Liberal had been quietly starting up in the meantime, its settlers sending their local news to Stoufer's paper under such *noms de plume* as "Stroller's Best Girl," "Crank," and "Rip Van Winkle." Now word spread that the Rock Island would go through Liberal . . .

"Liberal is attracting large crowds of people, and even now before the (railroad) company is ready to sell lots, the whole prairie is covered with waiting capitalists and mechanics."

The plat of Liberal was opened on April 13, 1888. Within twenty-four hours, lots had been sold to the value of $180,000—a third of that paid in cash. Mrs. Myra E. McDermott Stevenson later recalled, in a Golden Jubilee edition of the *South-West Daily Times,* "We paid $1,000 for ten acres in the quarter where old Liberal and the well that gave the place its name were located—and a few years later bought the other 150 acres for $35. We always spoke of it as 'our thousand and thirty-five dollar quarter' . . . many later land transactions were as wild-sounding as this one. By staying there until the country overcame the handicap of its sudden and unreasonable growth, we managed to come out a little more than even on this land business."

There were no houses on the land newly sold on that April 13. The following day, three shacks were up—and by the end of a week, eighty-three plank houses.

By 1892, people were saying the county seat should be in Liberal. Stoufer moved his paper there from Arkalon because, as he shamelessly admitted in his final Arkalon edition, "It is in the personal financial interest of its editor to do so."

The Liberal paper meanwhile carried a headline memorably announcing, LIBERAL PEOPLE FEEL GOOD.

Kennedy writes that by 1943, despite dust bowl, Depression, and a tornado strike ten years earlier, Liberal still had over four thousand people, while Fargo Springs and Springfield were ghost towns. Fargo, "the new Chicago," was, "a pile of brick on the Kneeland ranch"; Springfield was a filling station on Highway 83.

They were gone, all just gone.

They were history.

In the thirties, the WPA Guide listed Coffeyville as the state's sixth biggest city. Liberal didn't rate a listing—but today, it's grown to be a little bigger than that other gas town now languishing to the east.

David White told me, "We're never booming as much as some when it's good, but we're never as bad when it's bad. We're a little more diversified—besides the farming we've got the oil, and the natural gas too—so it balances out."

Liberal is the only town of its size for ten counties around in southwest Kansas and No Man's Land. It's a distribution center, with eleven truck lines and the railroad—"We can't ride the rails no more, but the wheat still can"—and it's an energy center too. The Hugoton Gas Field is one of the largest reserves in the world—and Liberal's on the eastern end of it.

White, a small, polite man, careful in his speech, was the boss at Bruce Well Servicing; more important for the town's self-image, he was also president of the Liberal BJ's.

The BJ's are a semi-pro baseball club in the Jayhawk League. College kids hoping to make it to the majors come to play here through the summer; since the club's first season in 1955, nearly fifty have gone on to play pro. Calvin Schiraldi, Greg Swindell, and Randy Velarde are among their present alumni in the big time.

The BJ's have also won three national championships, and been runners-up six times—the kind of thing that does a small town good.

White said semi-pro was just an old name that stuck. "Really this is summer collegiate baseball—these guys aren't paid. But they're twenty, twenty-two, they want to play pro ball, and this is one of the best leagues in the nation—scouts come to watch here, and look at their stats—so we get kids from southern California, Houston, Florida, and we find them jobs. Usually we'll work about four of them on the field, raking, picking trash, mowing the grass, cleaning the locker rooms—then the rest are in grocery stores, retail stores, filling stations, oil and gas companies . . . and people are glad to hire them, but they do have to work. If they don't get out of bed in the morning, they get fired, just like anybody else."

When the working day's done, they go down in the evening to Fairgrounds Park. It was June 4, only the fifth game of the season, and fifteen of the BJ's roster hadn't yet arrived; seven were playing at Wichita in the College World Series. Tonight was the second of a three-game series between the BJ's and the St. Joseph Cardinals from Missouri. The BJ's had been beaten 14–11 by St. Joe the night before.

There was one small bleacher, and a crowd of twenty-two. The guy sitting next to me said, "This is wild. I saw the posters saying there's forty-some made it to the majors out of here so I expected, you know . . . a stadium or something. I've played softball in front of bigger crowds than this."

There was no score in the first, as the crowd grew to thirty-seven in the light and pleasant evening. The BJ's pitcher was a beanpole blond from Lamar, Colorado, name of Scott Brochial; others on the team were from Indiana, Nevada, Texas. There were three local boys.

The guy next to me was from Enid, Oklahoma, an accountant for the state. He'd been in Guymon doing the Texas County accounts—"it's real down"—and he'd driven forty miles from there for a decent meal and a ballgame.

In the second inning, the BJ's scored three times; St. Joe got one back in the fourth.

The accountant said he had two hundred acres of wheat, "just enough to do it on the side. But it's been real dry, hurt it real bad. It's down . . . oh, forty percent, I guess."

The BJ's made it 4–1 in the fifth.

"Then last Thursday or Friday we had four inches in one and a half hours. People had started to cut, and now the ground's too wet to get across it."

An elderly lady had it in for the umpire. When he called an obviously low pitch a strike, she yelled, "We're not playing golf." The lights came on, as dusk settled down. Now and then a foul ball flew back and landed with a clang on the old tin roof of the stand. The crowd was up to sixty—kids scampering about, winsome teens, old couples with cushions and picnics.

In the sixth, the BJ's got three more: 7–1.

"Pizzas are now on sale at the concession stand for just a dollar-fifty, hey, that's a buy—so if the hungry pains are there . . ."

The BJ's won 9–2, and tied the series 1–1.

The old lady hooted, "That's the ballgame."

David White said the club had a budget of seventy thousand dollars. "We get sponsors locally, we sell ads, we do the concession stands—we'll go door to door, if that's what it takes."

By the looks of the program, he'd doorstopped every business in town—banks, meat firms, medical companies, car dealers, radio stations, lumber yards, builders, jewelers, oilmen and gas men, Arby's and Wendy's and McDonald's: "It's not whether you win or lose, but how well you eat after the game."

The assistant coach was Trip Couch from Louisiana. He said, "Come on a weekend late in a good season—you'll have eight, nine hundred here then. There's a lot of history here, thirty-six years—this is one of the most famous summer ball teams in America. A lot of them come and go, come and go—but not the BJ's."

Like David White said of his town, "We're never booming as much as some when it's good, but we're never as bad when it's bad . . . so it balances out." Then he said, "And that's good for the club. We can plan for the future here."

The sprinklers were running under the lights as I left. They threw up a delicious, ozone freshness into the green air of the ballpark.

Precious water. . . .

In the morning I drove to David White's office off of 54, and he took me into the country to look at some wells. We threw trails of dust off the dirt roads, past pump jacks and slender rigs standing solitary in the wide wheat fields and pasture. It was hot again, hot and dry.

David said, "We got six rigs just now, and twenty-three men. We work on oil and gas wells both; we don't drill them, we work on them after they're in. It's maintenance work, pump changes, or fishing jobs—fishing jobs is pulling out the rods when they break, we do a lot of that."

He guessed oil and gas would be half or more of the Liberal economy.

Himself, he'd been there thirteen years, but he'd always been in oil. "I'm from the Texas Panhandle, little town called Lefors—it's an oilfield town, that's all there is. I was raised in the oilfield."

As to the local farming he said, "I don't get involved in this, but the farmers and the oil people bicker back and forth, the farmers think the oil people get all the breaks and vice versa, the oil people think the farmers are getting rich . . . but me, I got to feel sorry for the farmers. Everything's in Mother Nature's hands for them. Us, at least we have a bit of control."

Not, he admitted, that it was always controlled as best as it might be. The Enid accountant had said of the oil boom, "Ten years ago it was crazy, money no object, motels all full, guys on the rigs living in tents in the parks with their pockets stuffed full, people flying to Vegas for the day, Mercedes everywhere—so people got mortgaged up over their heads. And then it ended."

David agreed. "A lot of waste, a real lot of waste. I'm a conservative guy, I really wish I'd been in on it—I'd have had something left. But oil's okay now—I don't watch it as much as I did during the war, but I look maybe twice a week and it's about twenty-one dollars, we can live with that. We can live with it at eighteen dollars—but it can drop so fast, people aren't comfortable if it doesn't stay still for a few months.

"But then," he said, "that's just oil. My dad was in the oil patch from the early fifties and it's always been the same, up and down, up and down. It's going to get better, and it's going to get worse."

So the oil was okay—but not the gas. "It's all domestic. And what you need for a good gas market is real bad winters; we've had two real mild ones, so that's real down. We watch the weather all winter, not just here but all over—because we've got pipelines going north, west, east, every place."

We passed a tractor with its plow wings wide, so we had to hit the shoulder to get around it. And he'd said he felt sorry for the farm people, in the hands of Mother Nature—but I couldn't see, in the end, how the energy people could say they had any greater control. If you need hard winters to pump the gas price, like you need fair rain to pump the wheat—then what's the difference?

The market, connected intimately to the weather, is as capricious a master to them all. And with masters like these, it seemed to me that whichever of these commodities you were getting from the ground, you had to be stubborn as hell to keep at it out there.

. . .

We pulled off the track into empty pasture; the rig stood against the sky, spindly and stark. David had a crew, three men—operator, floor hand, derrick hand—doing a "frac job." I put on my hard hat, and smelled the sour, rotten-egg tang of the gas.

The company man was there, the guy whose well it actually was; he drew me diagrams, and explained what was up. In essence, they'd punched holes through the pipe casing three thousand feet down, and were preparing to run in acid now to clean those holes out—to "fracture the perforations"—and let the gas come through. The company man said, "We'd anticipate five hundred thousand cubic feet per day—and that's small. This is an edge well, this is the upper pay zone. In the heart of the field they could get six, seven million c.f.d.—but that's over by Hugoton, that's the gas capital of the world over there."

David, satisfied things were running okay, walked back to the truck; as we went, he pointed to a little cabin on wheels sticking out of the prairie under the vast blue sky. "That's the doghouse. Got a cooker, a change of clothes—and it's a place to keep out of the weather if there's lightning. Derricks," he said casually, "attract lightning."

Then he told me, on our way to the next rig, that his crew on this one were all Mexican. "We probably have fifty percent Mexicans work for us, and most of them are good, good people. They're hard workers, they want to make money and keep their jobs, and a lot of them are real good at saving money too. A regular hand, if they work the full year and stay busy, they'll make eighteen thousand dollars, twenty-five thousand dollars. Then the operator'll make a lot more—and we have three operators that are Mexican too. But they live on a little bit of nothing here, and send the rest all back home, and I admire them for that. For most of them, the dream's to get home and buy land. Not to stay here."

So I told him what Larry Taylor had said in Boise City about slitting Mexican throats, and lobbing the carcasses off the plane over Tijuana.

David just shook his head. "We need them. If they all went back home, I'd be in a bind—because most people don't like to do this kind of work, it's too hard, and it's dirty. But," he said, "it's good money, and there's a future in it. Take this operator where we're going now, he's been with us eleven years; we finally talked him into being an operator two months ago. He didn't want the responsibility—but he's got it now. He's got to communicate with the company man, run the whole show— he's doing good too, getting better every day."

.   .   .

We went off down the dirt tracks to Moscow for lunch.

David said contentedly, "I just love driving, I love being out here—I could be out here all day. A lot of people don't like it, I know—no water, no trees—but I love it. And the kids who come out here from California to play ball, they think when they come it's no people, no beach, it's flat and the wind blows—but most of them go home with a different idea. They wouldn't want to live here, but they learn to respect it. We had a coach from there, he came back and brought his kids, 'cause he thought this was the way it ought to be—people get up and go to work and they're friendly. And he wanted his kids to know there's different places to California."

So I said, okay, but when it came to living here—not just visiting for the summer to play ball—what about the exposure, the harsh vagaries of the weather and the market?

"Yeah—but if you tell people to look back twenty years and think of all the bad things that happened to them, it ain't so many. People have a pretty good life here. A lot of people might disagree—but these Mexican guys that work for us, if people want to see a tough life, they should go down there. People don't realize how good they have it—but I guess some people, they ain't happy if they ain't complaining."

I asked then, with no particular intuition or inspiration, if David White was religious.

He said quietly, "I read the Bible every morning, I pray every morning—it's just part of my life. I don't go round bragging about it, I don't get on a soapbox—it's just a way I get comfort. And it's so beautiful here; I see a beautiful sunset and I want to go on my knees and thank God. You want to give credit. Because you can feel His presence."

But aside from fine sunsets, I suggested, He also sends you down tornadoes.

"I've been in a tornado, at Lefors; it was at night, I didn't see it, but I felt it hit my house. I was working the evening shift and I got in late, and it was lightning all around. Have you ever been in a lightning storm? God, it's beautiful. Anyhow, I got in bed, my wife and son were already asleep, and I'd been in bed ten minutes, the wind was getting louder and louder and the house was like . . . it was like a tuning fork. Then, real sudden, it quit—just like that. I just kind of opened my eyes and thought, well—storm's over. And I could see red flashing lights go by the window, it was one in the morning; then somebody knocked on the door. It was my little brother and he hollered at me, David, there's been a tornado. I didn't believe it, I thought he'd been out partying, drinking—then I heard my mother hollering, There he is, there he is.

"So I looked outside, and my garage was completely gone. It was flat, all four walls just on top of my car, and the car was wrecked. And part of my roof was gone—that got my attention then, I tell you. My sister, her family lived about a hundred yards from us, so we went to check—their whole house was gone. They'd gone next door in their neighbor's cellar, so for a minute there we were real scared . . . It was an experience I'll never forget.

"But the thing I'll remember most was all the people from all the surrounding area coming to help—bringing clothing, food—we didn't have electricity or water for a good while after, it wiped out half the town, and all these people just came in and helped."

You learned then, he said, to respect God in those people. And—of course—to respect Him in nature . . .

This was no fanatic speaking in tongues. This was a regular guy, cadging a sneaky cigarette or two because his wife thinks he's given up, but he can get away with it today because he's got Smoky Joe from Great Britain here riding in his truck.

This was a regular guy who talked about how, when he was a college kid, him and his friends planned to go to his parents' trailer at Lake Green Belt one weekend with girls, and—he paused—"have a good time."

Then that weekend a storm came up, and they didn't go—except for just the one girl, whose grandparents had the trailer next door.

And a tornado went through the trailer park, killed a bunch of people including the girl's grandparents, and the girl lost a leg.

So call it God, Nature, whatever you want—but you got to respect something out there, because you sure as hell can't control it.

And in the meantime, you just get up and go to work and you're friendly. . . .

David White was the boss of his own company, and the president of the ball club. But that night, during the deciding game of the three-way series with St. Joe, he was also the guy taking ticket money at the gate.

I got to Fairgrounds Park about five-thirty, and watched the players working out. It may not have been a stadium—but it was a neat little ground, tidy and well-tended, with a low bare wall around it, and a modest line of local company billboards behind the outfield facing the one simple stand. The gauze-green safety net hung from the tin roof, shifting in a dry warm wind under the empty blue sky.

The assistant coach Trip Couch was twenty-four, light-framed, dark-haired and easy-going; his regular job was coaching at Southwest Louisiana State. He said after tonight they were on a road trip to the Nevada Griffons in Missouri, and the Wichita Broncos. "We got our own bus—the furthest we go is the Clarinda A's and the Red Oak Red Sox up in Iowa, that's twelve hours. A lot of these guys, at college they'll be used to flying—but the bus is the way it is in the summer leagues, and it gives them a taste of how it might be, if they get into the minors. 'Cause there's gonna be a day when that bus breaks down. Or there's gonna be a day when the air breaks down, and you're all sitting in your underwear sweating."

Trip's boss, Matt Stine, was thirty-two, come to Liberal for the summer from Chapman College in Orange, California; he called the team into the locker room for the road trip rules and a pep talk. Amid a soft thwacking of leather and a clacking rustle of studs on the concrete floor, the players settled down on the benches. Stine stood in the center of the room, and laid down the law.

"The bus leaves tomorrow at twelve—be here. I'll not wait for you. Curfew is two hours after the game ends: game ends eleven-thirty, so be back at one-thirty. If you're not, you don't get your meal money. And if it starts becoming a habit—I'm not making threats, I'm just laying it on the line—but if it starts becoming a habit, you'll be going home.

"Now I don't much mind what you do in the day, but I don't want too much laying by the pool, it gets hot out here. It'll be four to a room, with the phones turned off—you want to make personal calls, you make them yourselves. Otherwise, no alcohol on the bus, no alcohol in the rooms, and no women in the rooms—that's BJ rules. I know what some people think about road trips, they want to dance with every woman they can, fuck every woman they can—don't do it. You guys are all adults. You know how it is.

"Now these guys, St. Joe—they're a horseshit ball club. They're horseshit physically, they're horseshit ability—no class. So don't fall into what they want to do, You suck and all that—don't get into that, that's all I'm telling you. You can bury them, so don't let up. That's all."

He sent them back out, and we went into the spartan box they had for a coaches' room.

"Coors Lite okay with you?"

Stine fished me a beer from the fridge behind his desk—he had a Coke himself—and he was friendly, but taut already with wanting to win. He said he'd have the rest of the roster in by the middle of next week, a full complement was twenty-five, "but we'll lose a few guys to the pros—have to make up for that."

I asked about discipline and Trip said, "It'll arise. Someone's gonna do something before the summer's over. It'll get out of hand with someone, somewhere—but if you get control at the start, you're okay."

"A lot of people," said Stine, "think the manager just comes in, makes a lineup, then they go out and play. But we've got to handle going on the road, all the arrangements, be like a baby-sitter. Summer baseball's looser than it is at college—but there's still that fine line of control. I'm not going to jump on their ass—if a kid doesn't execute a play, I'm not going to get all over him about it—because these guys, they have the tools already, they have the ability, and we don't change anything, we just work those fundamentals. But they're here to maintain that ability, and to learn something from being around different people—and to do that, there's a line you don't cross. At school, that line's just closer to you."

But besides what people might learn, you're still here to win . . .

"They hire me to win. This is their life, the board members here, you know how small this town is—they put up a lot of money, they work hard, so it matters here. And they could fire me any time they want—but I have a good relationship with the board, so I'd hope that wouldn't happen. Because they give me pretty good money too, one of the best-paying teams in the nation—and there's incentives. If we win the championship, myself and the staff split a percentage of the take."

Then he said, "There's another incentive. I don't want to go back to California too soon."

Because he liked to coach ball, and win games, in the wide summer spaces of western Kansas.

"Be a low crowd tonight," said Mike Barlow the trainer, "Wednesday's church night." I'd heard the bells ringing earlier. "You're in the Bible Belt now, man—they go to church all the time here."

Players ate pizza in the dugout; a few were on the field, raking and chalking.

Around 7:30, after the national anthem played on the tiny speakers, the home team went into a brief huddle, bust out of it with a small communal grunt of "BJ's!"—then scattered onto the field in their sky-blue uniforms under the summer evening sky.

Looking out the back of the little wooden box of the dugout, from the bench littered with paper cups and leather gloves, I noticed how in that summer sky to the south and west, a wall of grey cloud was building against the blue.

Tony Costa was pitching for the BJ's, a kid from Lemoore, California. He struck out the first hitter.

"Attaboy."

But then he walked the next man, who promptly stole second, then third.

"Settle down out there now," Trip yelled.

But Costa walked a second hitter. He kept pitching low, and he started getting hit. St. Joe scored two runs. Costa looked anxious on the mound.

Stine fretted over him. "He fights himself so much. Doesn't make any adjustment."

St. Joe scored a third.

"I'm taking him out," Stine said. "I've seen enough."

Three and o down already, top of the first; the little crowd was silent.

Trip took Tony Costa aside behind the dugout, talking fast and quiet, close in his ear.

The new pitcher was David Duncan from Lynnville, Indiana; he picked a man off first, then got a quick out to retire the side.

Stine told them, "Down by three now, let's get this thing rolling."

Jeff Boydston from Texas got a base hit for the BJ's.

Stine called, "Got to be aggressive early here now."

One man out, and Boydston on second.

Behind us the sky was getting heavier, and the wind picking up.

The next batter walked; there were runners on first and second.

"Be aggressive early for me now, here we go."

Spitting tobacco juice, Stine stood with his right foot on an overturned ball bucket, lightly touching a finger to his knee, his chest, the peak of his cap; the signals went out with an abrupt, abbreviated, flickering urgency.

The runners advanced on a ground out. Two down, men on second and third. Local kid Eric Armstrong went to the plate.

Barlow said, "Boy, you know it's dead when they don't even clap for Eric."

Stine was letting out little spurts of words to himself that I couldn't catch at all, tense, chewed, accented little oaths and entreaties.

Armstrong walked to load the bases. Dan Madsen the outfielder went to the plate.

"Be aggressive early in the count. Early in the count."

Madsen whacked the first pitch right up the middle—and here's where baseball's beautiful, the sudden whirling welter of action every which way round the field as the runners spill through the bases, red grit kicking up under studs, fielders darting as the first man comes home, two men still running . . . the outfielder fumbles it, three runs scored.

People were on their feet around the dugout—but they were pissed too, because this was scrappy baseball.

"Three–three ballgame in the first. Shit."

"With a tornado," said someone, pointing at the cloud-murk growing steadily broader and taller to the southwest.

"I knew it was going to be a freak night," said Barlow, "when that ball hit the sprinkler standpipe." Water was still hissing from the leak onto the grass where the ball had cannoned into the joint.

The next hitter struck out; it was 3–3 at the bottom of the first.

The far storm rising helped nightfall spread darkness through the sky.

There was no score in the second.

I said to Stine he looked wound up; he'd not sat down once, and we were barely into the game.

"Yeah, I'm wound up. You'll see me move more and more—because this is baseball. This is great."

I asked Trip if he was wound up too.

"Oh man," said Stine, "he's an absolute mess."

"I'm just quiet during the ballgame," Trip said. "Until I get angry."

There was no score in the third.

The wind was getting stronger, and the clouds were over us now; the last light was a turquoise strip of sky left dying in the east. The players on the field gleamed in their uniforms under the floodlights, the ball whipping away from the pitchers in a white blurred flash. It was like being in a bright and magic cell, a forcefield sealed against the night—a place of regular, sweet, geometric action under the great mess of the dark sky.

At the bottom of the fourth Shawn Hensley, another local boy, doubled down the line. The next batter hit a little dribbler down to first, but the first baseman slipped trying to make the play, and Hensley got home. Four–three BJ's, with a man on second.

A couple more hits, and now it was 5–3. The crowd permitted itself a broken scatter of cheering.

We went to the top of the fifth under the looming sky. St. Joe scored three. Stine sighed into the clouds. The sky was covered right over; a first flicker of far lightning flared deep on the horizon.

St. Joe got another man in, and went ahead 7–5.

The sky was jet black. In the bottom of the sixth, Stine exhorted his boys, "I'd like to get ahead here—so when it starts raining we can call the fucking game, okay?"

The BJ's quickly had runners on second and third, with one man out. The next man struck out.

"C'mon, Jesus," moaned Stine, "whatever it takes to get a man in."

But the next man grounded out. Two runners stranded . . . still 7–5.

Stine: "This ain't fucking happening to me."

Bottom of the seventh. Lightning ripped through the middle distance, balloons of white fire swelling and popping in the clouds. The BJ's first man went to the plate.

Stine said, "Let's go now, let's go—crush that fucking ball."

The batter flied out. The next man struck out on a 3–2 count.

Stine: "Goddam, I can't stand this shit."

The third batter grounded out. Still 7–5 down—and St. Joe to bat at the top of the eighth.

Coach Stine was—in case you hadn't gathered—upset. He told me, "This team's real bad, talent-wise, the way they handle themselves, the way they act—we should be beating them. Their pitcher's okay, he's throwing a good game—no hitting, that's our problem. We're relying on a couple of guys, and they're just not doing it."

He'd sent out Peter Coleman to pitch, a guy he coached at Chapman. And he got two men out. . . .

"Finish it strong now."

Two strikes.

"Nice job, Peter, finish it right here."

Third strike and out.

"Attaboy."

Bottom of the eighth, still 7–5 down.

"Just gimme three runs. Just gimme three fucking runs, that's all I want."

Trip said, "Let's go now, this team's *not* very good."

"You're *letting* them beat your ass, goddammit."

Madsen hit it long . . .

"Nice hack."

. . . but not long enough. It was caught at the fence. One man out.

Then Dan Trump hit it long too—but this time the St. Joe outfielder misjudged it, and the ball ran away from him.

Stine was jubilant. "Oh look at that, you gutless son of a bitch, he's got no sack between his legs."

Trump pelted round to third.

"Know your infield, Danny."

Hensley got a base hit too, making it to first as Trump ran home. 7–6.

The dugout was on its feet again.

"Way to go."

Now Anthony Barron from Amarillo took his turn—and he flied out to centerfield. Two men out.

Pacing by the dugout through sprays in the grass of grit and sunflower seeds, Coach Stine made his twitching, urgent little signals.

Hensley stole second.

"Bat on the ball now."

The pitcher looked about him, pulled back his arm . . .

"Stay hot now, stay hot."

Dietrick hit the ball short, hustling down the line to first; Hensley went to third.

"Hey, what you say, pick 'em up now, home run."

The bat hung over the plate in the eerie stormlight. . . . Jason Shirey hit the ball through first base; Hensley ran home, and tied the game 7–7.

The scattered crowd was yelling and screaming; someone was playing a trumpet and howling, "Charge!"

There were men on first and third. With the game tied and two men out, the designated hitter, Brian Currier from Texas, now went to the plate.

St. Joe brought in a reliever.

"What d'you say, Brian, rip his tits."

Which means, smash the mother right back in his chest . . .

Strike one.

Strike two.

Base hit, man home, BJ's lead 8–7 . . .

There was a brief surge of ecstasy, players jumping and whooping—then a steadying and an intent rushing out into the field to do it one more time.

Top of the ninth—Stine brought in his closer Brian Currier. The first two batters grounded out.

"Two in the wagon, one dragging, let's go."

Currier struck out the third man.

8–7 BJ's.

The players ran together in a leaping pack under the lights, slapping backs and hands—Stine walked among them saying, "Great job tonight, guys, great job."

Lightning burned in the west.

Turning to the electric sky one player joshed another, "Hey, you—go stand on the mound with a rake or something."

I said it was good, that I'd get to write a win.

"Oh, you're luck," said Coach Stine, "you got to stay with us now."

Back in his office Stine looked like he'd just run a marathon, laying back in his chair and breathing deep—and it was gone ten-thirty, but he hadn't stopped working yet. David White was in and out; Stine was organizing ten dollars per kid per day for the road trip, fixing uniforms for the new players joining up, shuffling room arrangements on scraps of paper—like getting the bus driver to room with the starting pitcher, so he'd get some rest. And all the while, he was talking to the local reporter from the *South-West Daily Times.*

This guy had the stats for the first five games. Stine told him not to get on Barron's back, "His average looks terrible—but he walks a lot, 'cause he's short."

And he effortlessly offered an instant mediaspeak analysis of the game. "Obviously a great comeback, they hung in there—it's what we need to carry us onto the road right now."

He said he was, "Pumped, really exhausted and pumped—and excited. Those kind of games take a lot out of you."

A new pitcher turned up.

"You ready to throw tomorrow?"

He wasn't.

I asked about Scott Brochial.

"He threw one hundred pitches yesterday. He'll need three or four days' rest."

And Costa?

Trip looked wide-eyed.

Stine sighed. "If somebody could learn to get inside his head . . . He's a good-looking kid, he's big. If only we could get in his head."

Eventually it calmed down and there was just the three of us left, in a bare breezeblock office at the ballpark in a little town in western Kansas.

So we got a beer from the fridge, and I asked them what it was really all about.

Turned out Trip Couch and Matt Stine had both left girls behind, girls they were serious about. "And it's real hard, we're out here all summer—but we're all in that boat, and we chose to come anyhow. Because we want to do well here."

Trip said, "I'd like to be a college head coach. My coach at Louisiana was assistant coach here when they won the championship in '85, that's where he got noticed. So it's career—but then, you know *Field of Dreams*, the movie? These kids coming in here, and us as well—this is dreams for us out here, baseball in the summer in Kansas and Iowa, that's dreams. When you hear guys around here say, 'Signed'—that's pro ball. And that's what you dream of."

Stine said, "I know in about three weeks' time I'm going to start getting tired of calling the local radio live at seven-thirty in the morning to talk about last night's game, it's going to get old on me. But I just bought a camera—and I'm not big on that normally, but I'm going to take pictures of all the ballparks. People will tease me about that—but I want pictures of these places. And I'll send them home to my mom, and my girlfriend . . ."

"Because," said Trip, "this is the most exciting part of America. We come from California, Louisiana—tourists go there. But this is America."

"For me," said Stine, "there's no people more friendly than the people out here. I'm from Houston, originally—but there's no people who'll go out of their way to help you more than these people right here.

"And then," he went on, "you got to understand this is baseball. We went years and years doing this and not getting paid for it—because we love the game. Take Ed, he's the local high school coach—he comes to coach first base here, and he doesn't get paid for that. But you just love the game, you love the game so much since you were a little kid . . . People say you're going to Kansas, ugh, Iowa, ugh—but we want to see these places, *'cause it's baseball.*"

He said, "You take where we're going to now, Nevada, Missouri— that's an all-dirt infield. Yuk. Or here—this must be the only ballpark in the universe with a racetrack around it. You saw the players taking the signs down in back of the outfield after the game tonight—that's so the race drivers can see where they're going tomorrow. And we tell the players when they come—they come from nicely manicured college places, so they come here and they say, How about this place! It's inside of a racetrack!—but we tell them when they come, this is home. And soon they get a lot of pride, a real lot of pride, because this is their home field—it's not the best, *but it's home.*"

"My friends," Trip said, "they're lawyers, accountants—they look down, they say, You're coaching? But they can't understand. It's like falling in love, it's like there's one right girl out there—and that's the way you love baseball."

"Nine-to-fivers . . . huh. They say we don't work. They don't realize we're on the phone from eight till twelve, we're out on the field from twelve till four or five, then we go out and watch games till eleven or twelve at night, scouting, recruiting—and they're frustrated. But we're not. We're happy."

Stine said, "I'll be walking back and forth by the dugout, and Trip'll be silent there. And we'll be happy."

Outside the park, and driving back to the Tumbleweed, the clouds were bursting and firing with the raw, fierce energy of lightning that seemed, somehow, to be in every quarter but here. The radio in the truck was impossible—fizzing and crackling at every burst in the black sky, seen or unseen. Voices came and went in the static seething of the ether.

I parked outside my room, and walked across 54 to the Super Convenience for a Busch and a chicken sandwich. The cashier wasn't supposed to sell me beer after midnight—but she sold me one anyhow, on the grounds I was British.

I was lucky in Liberal.

And the cashier said a really weird thing.

She said, "I made a little chimneysweep once. He was British. He was real cute."

Made? Did she mean she . . . surely not.

Maybe she said "met," and it got tangled in the accent—but I don't think so. It didn't seem a whole lot more likely anyhow.

We stared at each other, grinning foolishly like true friends from distant planets, which I suppose was about the size of it.

So I thanked her, and told her not to worry about the beer. "No one will ever know. I'm going to Garden City tomorrow."

"If it's still there," she said. "They got storms up there."

"You got storms down here. You can see lightning right outside."

"I don't mind seeing it," she said, "so long as it doesn't come in my store."

I walked back to bed in the beginnings of the rain, as the Lord's sound and light show came marching our way across the great and empty High Plains.


## Rascals

From Evanston I crossed the line into Utah. The interstate was speckled with burst tires and roadkill, mostly deer and raccoon. The land became a splendid parade of rough-layered red cliff face jutting from parched green mountains. I passed three brilliant yellow Union Pacific engines hauling one of the monster railfreight caravans, a hundred, maybe a hundred-fifty cars—but out in this landscape, it looked like the toy train in your attic that you had when you were small.

Rain fell as the road dropped off the mountains. In back of the city behind the shower, drenched hills glowed gold in the fresh new light.

"In the last forty years," said a man on the radio, "I have drunk the juice of over a million carrots."

The van from Wisconsin in front of me had a bumper sticker: HAPPINESS IS SQUARE DANCING.

They came from every place, from California to Connecticut; the massive Salt Palace Convention Center was thronged with literally thousands of them. And I fast got to wondering about the predilections of that shifty young lecher back in the Last Outpost Bar—because it seemed the average age of the square dancers was in the region of ninety . . . and who wants to gawp the panties of a legion of wizened lizards?

A few days later I heard on the radio that a man was still unconscious in a Salt Lake hospital, after getting beaten to a pulp by an enraged square dancer who'd caught him peeking up his partner's twirling skirts.

But maybe the angry dancer was crazed on liquid vitamins. I'd heard about this festival of the folkloric bizarre from an old goat named Otto in Oklahoma City. Otto sold a "sublingual" Vitamin B complex to square dancers—an energy juice that you took under your tongue, direct into the bloodstream, for an instant body-battery charge.

So now I roamed the streets of Salt Lake City among the hordes of these bespectacled and leathery reptiles in their preposterous costumes—it was like they'd raided Snow White's place and turned the drapes and tableclothes into blouses and skirts, it was an orgy of white frill and gingham—and I wondered if all the manic smiling going on here was some kind of mass collective vitamin high. . . .

I went back east on I80, then south and east on 40 through Heber City and Fruitland, across the head of Starvation Reservoir toward Duchesne and Roosevelt. The Utah landscape was red rubble and yellow dirt; the sky to the north was lemon and pale cherry as the sun fell through bands of cream cloud into the Uinta Mountains.

Roosevelt's a border town in among the scraps and pieces of the Uintah & Ouray Indian Reservation. I came in at sunset, down the wide empty street to the Frontier Motel. A bunch of Mexicans sat across the road on the shadowed porch of a closed store. They seemed the only souls around.

The Frontier cost too much; I asked if the Regal down the road was any cheaper.

"Oh yeah," said the old woman, "they rent monthly, they rent to Indians—they rent to anybody."

And the ugliness raised its head again.

"I don't rent to Indians," she said. "They're too hard on the rooms. Those Indians . . . I like to get along with anybody, but those Indians are rascals."

The sky burnt fire-red outside.

I went over to the Regal. And I'm not surprised they rent to anybody—they'd rent to Godzilla if he could write down his name. I'm talking a comedy double act of congenital idiots here, a short and shapeless mother and daughter, both lank of hair, slack of lip, stale of odor. . . . I took the registration form and under Name, I wrote Davies.

The daughter looked at me; in a voice like a dentist's drill through the temple she said, "Is that yurr whoooooole naaaaaaame?"

Indian kids were letting off cheap fireworks on the fire escape outside. Wafts of acrid smoke drifted through the darkening evening.

I went to bed, with 218 more miles under my belt—but that was nothing. I needed badly to do a lot more driving; I needed badly to get some place nice again.

# 5.

# The Forces of Erosion

Rain, rain, rain, soft steady grey rain . . .

I had breakfast at Mr. Breakfast—"Our food is so good we eat it ourselves"—then drove north out of Liberal on 83.

The fields were sodden, flooded in the corners. When they'd needed it, it hadn't rained; now they didn't need it, it was raining.

Sixty miles north, I kept going through Garden City. Liberal had been big enough, but Garden was bigger—eighteen thousand—and I didn't feel like big places anymore. I wanted to get out, instead, to where it doesn't come any smaller. I wanted to find the vanishing point where if it comes any smaller it's gone, all just gone. . . .

The rain grew heavier. I was driving forty-five or less, the air a watery fog, the sky just grey slop on the fields. Passing roadfreight threw up storms of blinding spray; it was nasty driving, the truck slipping and sliding in sheets of water on the road. I stopped at the Pizza Hut in Scott City, and waited for the weather to go away over a Supreme Thin 'n' Crispy.

Eight miles north when it cleared, I cut west into Scott County State Park. There's a ruin there called El Cuartelejo—just a floor plan in a meadow really, the walls reconstructed to a foot off the ground so you can see how the rooms would have been. It was an Apache pueblo, dated to the 1660s; after the early 1700s, the Comanche forced them southwest. And history went on storming by, until now there's just this chalk-pale layout restored by diligent archaeologists, given markers and plaques, and left marooned between the low rises by a wooded inlet off a reservoir . . . another Little House on the Prairie.

From human wreckage, to geological wreckage . . . I drove northwest on dirt to Chalk Bluffs. Amid flat wastes of sandy pasture maybe twenty-five miles from Scott City, these last sediment remnants of marine life and ocean floor, two hundred million years old, stand in a clump of yellow, bulky chalk stacks, grey-skirted, maybe fifty feet tall—and slowly they wear away under the weather.

It's an eerie place—a dot of time in slow motion on the blank sheet of the plain, an arresting reminder of how much fossil and bone, how much soil and sand, how much of the turning world already has been washed and blown away in this desolate and lovely place. In the vast silence of the prairie out there, you hear the ticking of the millennia, and the slow scrape and grind of the blind forces of erosion in the wind and sun and rain. It's a sound like heartbeat, the slow pumping through the years of the earth's ancient blood; you stand in the dust hearing it, watching grasshoppers ping through the scrawny grass, and the wind tugs and whispers—and in the spirit-rich silence your soul melts away, bleeds off into the sky and land until you're nothing but sand and grass yourself, a speck tossed in rustling voids of eternity through the heart of America . . .

It couldn't have been more than fifteen miles farther to Russell Springs, but I took two hours over it—lost on dirt roads, steering vaguely by the sun, riding my whale-truck through the ocean of land. Often I'd stop, and listen intently to the singing emptiness. The land was green, yellow, bleached and infinite; the sky was clear blue, and infinite too. I rode the low sandy wave of a scarp, and found prairie running away from me in an unbroken sameness to the cloud-spattered horizon. Birds popped off the ocher tracks, or sang on fence posts, or flew point in little V-shaped squadrons just ahead and on my flank as I drove; dragonflies and butterflies flashed briefly in the luminous air. Untended tractors stood in part-baled fields like ships laid up and waiting in the deep sea for instructions from afar.

The V8 rumbled steady and low; I sailed stunned and smiling through the vastness of an unpeopled space and time—until I did, eventually, come to Russell Springs, population fifty-two.

Russell Springs, Kansas, was named after a cattleman, William D. Russell, who watered his herd there; it's on the Smoky Hill River, bang in the middle of Logan County.

Given that central location, the town was chosen in September 1887 to be the county seat—but it turned out, in the end, that this accident of being bang in the middle was about the only thing the place had going for it.

If David A. Butterfield had been a more successful pioneer of the

American transport business, Russell Springs might have got off on a firmer footing, as a trade route way station. Born in Maine in 1834, Butterfield went to Kansas in 1856, and to Denver in 1862; from there, he mapped a route back down the Smoky Hill that shaved 100 miles off the more northerly route then used by Ben Holladay along the Platte.

After raising nearly $6,000,000 back east, Butterfield returned to inaugurate the Butterfield Overland Dispatch. Drawn by 1,200 mules and carrying 150,000 pounds of freight, the first wagon train left Atchison for Denver, 592 miles west, in June 1865. In July another caravan set off up the Smoky Hill, this one carrying seventeen steam boilers for the Colorado gold fields; a third train left in August, for Salt Lake City.

The Cheyenne, however, were hardly pleased with these sizable intrusions on their buffalo grounds, and without an army escort, the journey very soon became too perilous. After a year, and $1,000,000 poorer, Butterfield sold out to Ben Holladay.

He died in 1873, shot in a quarrel with an employee of his horse-drawn streetcar system in Hot Springs, Arkansas.

Russell Springs didn't get lucky with the railroad, either. The Leavenworth Pawnee & Western, later the Kansas Pacific, was incorporated in 1855; construction commenced in 1863. In 1868 the tracks went through Logan County, reaching Denver two years later, passing fifteen miles north of Russell Springs.

When the line was going through, Buffalo Bill Cody was hired—at $125 a month, with board—to shoot buffalo to feed the laborers. He killed, according to one account, 4,280 in seventeen months. So much for the Cheyenne hunting grounds.

Meanwhile, the first settlers came—mostly Scandinavians, Germans, German-Russians, and Canadians—but somewhat less hymned were the black settlers who also came during and after the Civil War.

Writing in the 1930s, Ruth M. Tinsley said she didn't know which generation of her people came from Africa, but she knew how. A mother and a son, the boy about sixteen, went on board a ship to sell eggs, were captured—and that was that.

With the aid of white sympathizers in the underground railroad, Tinsley's great-grandmother Rachel escaped out of slavery in Missouri in 1862 with two sons and three daughters. They nearly didn't make it: a new master, Mr. Bernard, was coming to get them off their old master Mr. Briggs . . .

Hastily they gathered together their few things. The two white men who had accompanied them urged them to make haste, for the rumble of Bernard's wheels could be heard in the distance. Quickly they climbed into the wagon and had started off, when one looked back and saw they had left Grandmother Caroline, a little girl about four years old, sitting in a swing in the yard. The rumble of Bernard's wheels was growing closer and closer. One of the white men who was on horseback rushed back and snatched the child up on his horse. They had gone about a mile when they got stuck in the mud. A man who was logging in the timber by the road saw them and shouted, 'Briggs' niggers are running away.' He probably would have said more had not the white man stuck his musket in his ribs and said, 'Hitch on here, or I'll blow a daylight hole through you.' So the man hitched on and pulled them out of the mud hole . . . by nightfall they were in Kansas.

Tinsley proudly notes how her grandmother Caroline grew up to become the first black woman in the state to get a teacher's certificate.

"She always taught her students never to give up, although the path seemed hard, for some day they might have the privilege of doing some great thing for this world."

But you don't see many blacks in western Kansas now.

The Reverend and Mrs. J. F. Clark settled in Logan County in 1876. Mrs. Clark said the grasshoppers were so bad, they ate the clothes right off her line . . . but the settlers said to themselves, "If the buffalo can live here, so can I."

Russell Springs, at first aborted after its ill fortune with the B.O.D. and the railroad, was settled again in the 1880s, with the great new influx of people into western Kansas that decade. After it was proclaimed the county seat in 1887, over a hundred houses were built there that autumn, as well as a hotel, two churches, restaurants, a bank, and several stores. The population was nearly three hundred.

But after a drought, and with no sign that a railroad spur would come down to them, many people left the very next year; many of the houses were simply put on wheels and hauled off elsewhere. Lots that had sold for $300 were given away for 10¢. The population by 1901 was 43.

There was a second brief boom after that, with good crops in the early years of the century, and a railroad spur finally coming in 1911. But the train ran for only six years.

The place hung on as the county seat. County government was run from an imposing two-story brick courthouse, a fine pile built in that first flush of 1887 enthusiasm—until, in 1963, the county seat was moved to Oakley.

Two years later, the courthouse became the Butterfield Trail Museum. The curator said of the town's first hopes, "They were going to have it like an oasis"—and it would have been beautiful too, on its rise over the Smoky Hill, with its long views south across the prairie . . . except that the Smoky Hill, like the Arkansas through Garden City, was now dry.

I drove thirty miles to Oakley through Page City and Monument, unincorporated hamlets huddled round the grain elevators. In Page City a sign warned: CAUTION—WIND CURRENTS.

The guy in the Oakley Best Western said I could sleep in his parking lot. I sat in the back of the truck there, eating cold Supreme Thin 'n' Crispy from the doggy bag—and wondered what the hell I was doing, gnawing congealed pizza in a parking lot in west Kansas.

The wind whipped across the junction of 40 and 83; I walked up the street toward the town and the rail tracks. After two hundred yards I came on the Scotts Bluff Private Club, with a bunch of pickups parked among the puddles in the dirt out front. To get in, you signed a guest book. There was baseball on TV, and a monstrous guy at the bar saying, "I'm outta here"—but it seemed he'd been saying that the past two hours. Someone told him he shouldn't drive.

He said, "Hell, I *got* to drive. I can't walk."

The morning was cold and grey again. On the Weatheradio, NOAA was tracking showers and strong storms to the east, between Oberlin and Quinter. There were flood warnings along the Solomon and Prairie Dog creeks; there was a 40 percent chance of showers and storms throughout the area in the evening.

I went to Oakley's big attraction, the Fick Fossil & History Museum. The Ficks lived on a ranch down by Monument Rocks, a bigger version of Chalk Bluffs; Ernest Fick collected thousands of fossils around their home, and his wife Vi used them to make "fossil art." Her work, in all its delirious eccentricity, was given to the city in 1972, and you can spend hours with it, I tell you, because what Vi Fick created makes the brain spin.

I counted 116 pieces. She used fish bones, vertebrae, clam shells, shark teeth, crinoid—an animal called "lily of the sea"—all mixed up in livid and lumpy oil paints to make pictures of an outlandish, throbbing, eye-warping fecundity. In lurid cerise and saccharine turquoise, pulsing indigo and screaming vermilion, there were still lifes and landscapes, deer and bears, cowboys and fall scenes. My favorite was *God Making the Beginning of the Cretaceous.*

There were piles of other stuff too: pterodactyl wings, huge fish skulls, mammoth bones, a complete Portheus Molossus skeleton, a great submarine brute of a thing, along with barbed wire, telegraph insulators, and a collection of wildflowers: Slender Showy Goldenrod, Curlycup Gumweed, Jack-in-the-Pulpit, Roughseed Clammyweed, Narrow-leaved Four O'Clock, Whitetop Peppergrass, Missouri Loco, Black-eyed Susan . . .

There was a display of photographs entitled "Hardships Endured Through the Years." The pictures showed fires, floods, blizzards, tornadoes, dust storms, grain elevator collapses, and jackrabbit drives. In the dry thirties the rabbits were eating every blade of grass left, and the cattle were starving—so they'd drive the rabbits into horseshoe-shaped wire fence enclosures, and club them to death.

There was a replica of the original 1886 railroad depot.

The last passenger train ran in May 1971.

The population of Oakley is around two thousand, and falling.


"We don't have anything to keep our young people here," said the old lady minding the museum. "I'm sorry to say it's getting very serious. We've lost our jewelry store, we had two grocery stores and one of them's gone . . . The economy's been pretty bad, what, ten, fifteen years. They say everybody on the coasts are prospering, but it never reaches here. Wheat right now is the price I can remember it was years ago, I can remember it was two dollars in the sixties. And the further you are from Kansas City or Denver, the less you get for it, on account of transportation; so being midway, we're worst off. But then another reason wheat's so low is so many of them got greedy: They were going out and breaking up the pastures, and I don't like to see that. We had a man in from Nebraska saying they didn't have so many pheasants anymore, there's no cover, no place for them to lay their eggs."

Here in Oakley, she said, "We need some manufacturing, and they've been trying, but we haven't succeeded yet. I first looked for a house here twelve years ago, I've been a widow fourteen—and at that time Monfort's, the meat packing people, they thought they was coming to have a plant here, and prices were sky high. So I waited and bought about eight years ago; they hadn't come and prices fell, and I thought I was getting a bargain. And prices are a lot lower right now ... though a lot of people say it's good Monfort's didn't come. They'd have made some jobs, but they'd have brought a lot of outsiders in, foreigners—and crime's gone up very badly in Garden City and Liberal since those plants went in there. I had two kids went to Garden City to college back in the seventies, and it was a quiet town then. But it isn't any more. Lot of murders."

I asked, what foreigners?

She fumbled for the name. "Vit ... veep ... veem ... vest," she said, befuddled over the alien word.

Vietnamese?

That was them ... funny. You fight a war with people fifteen years, and still you don't know how to say their name.

Logan County's had thirty-one newspapers in its time, starting with the *Oakley Opinion* in 1885. There was the *Scout* in Gopher, the *Courier* and the *Obelisk* in Monument, the *Page City Messenger*, the *Winona Clipper* and the *Elkader Journal*—but only two remain. There's the *Oakley Graphic* (since 1895), and the *Winona Leader* (since 1957).

I talked to Barb Glover at the *Graphic*. She said, "Whenever we graduate a class of students they go to college, and they don't come back. The North-West Kansas Educational Service Center was relocated here from Colby—that runs special programs in 21 counties, and it's 150 jobs, obviously not all of them here—but we don't have the size of town to attract industry."

And the farming?

"Wheat's down seventy cents from this time last year; last year was abundant, but this year's not going to be that good. To break even, they need forty-five bushels an acre; some will, some won't. The average is thirty-nine, but the county agent reckons it'll be forty-five this year. Some people had sixty-bushel wheat last year, the elevators were full, they were pouring it on the ground to store it. But this year, some of the farmers didn't fertilize—they've cut their chance of yields by twenty percent or more, to save that money—because it's hard to raise wheat, when you only get two dollars a bushel."

So what about those professors in New Jersey, and their buffalo commons?

"We've taken offense to that. There's a pride here. This is not going to be a barren plain again. It'll be tough, but there'll always be farmers."

. . .

She said I'd picked a good year for the weather. "This spring has been more active than I can remember. We've had tornadoes down at Leoti, baseball-sized hail at Grinnell . . ."

While we talked, rain fell for five minutes outside, five minutes of hammering cascade that stopped as bluntly, as abruptly as it began.

NOAA said a storm system was anchored over eastern Colorado and northwest Kansas, spawning showers and isolated thunderstorms. "With the ground already saturated, creek and low-level flooding is likely, and those with livestock in flood-prone areas should take the necessary precautions."

I drove south to Monument Rocks under livid, mauve-orange skies. The Rocks are taller than the stacks at Chalk Bluffs, and more spindly; weathered, cream-grey pillars and turrets of ancient chalk, they jut from the scrubby prairie with the millennia written through them in clear layer upon layer. It's a temple, a cloister of past time stranded in the moonscape.

Grasshoppers popped and zinged around my feet; tumbleweed scuffled over the dirt. In one quarter of the horizon the sky dumped rain; in another it threw down lances through the clouds of dusty, soupy light. I kicked about a bit, hoping for fossils. No luck.

So I went back on the dirt to 83, past the abandoned dots of a crumbling plank farmhouse or two—and past the Pyramid View Cemetery, lost and left behind in the void out there, dead as the chalk rocks.

NOAA announced a Severe Thunderstorm Watch.

As I checked into the Annie Oakley Motel towards the north end of town, there was rain and thunder coming in on a black western sky, and the beginnings of lightning. Just as I got into my room, the heaviest rain I'd seen yet came smashing down, cannoning off the roof of the truck outside in violent explosions of spray. The parking lot was awash with inches of running water in seconds.

Great. Just when you realize all you've eaten all day is a doughnut and your last cold slice of Thin 'n' Crispy, the Scotts Bluff Bar is ten minutes' walk away through *that*.

But it didn't last long. When I walked out the storm, still lightning-packed and rolling with thunder, was sliding away up the northwest side of town, a low black mass hanging heavy over the soaking land. Water ran a yard wide in the gutters, pouring away in torrents into the drains. Cars hissed by, spraying curtains of water off their wheels. Crossing the railroad tracks between the elevators, the low band of sky in the west under the purply-black tail of the storm was a bilious red. In the bar, the lights were flickering dimmer, then up again, at irregular but still frequent intervals.

I ate breadcrumbed bulls' balls, made a note that the Scotts Bluff was a prime candidate for Best Bar in the Heart of America, and talked with a guy named Mark Robinson that I'd met the night before, and his buddy Steve Boyd, about Monument Rocks. They asked if I'd seen Old Chief Smoky. "It was just like an Indian chief's head, headdress and all—a pillar maybe fifty, sixty feet tall—but the back of the head eroded away till the neck was real thin. And then sometime in the eighties, the wind just took that thing over."

The forces of erosion, taking the rocks, the Indians, the small towns all away . . .

Mark said, "There was a hole I used to scramble through when I was a kid, I used to have to duck—I'll bet that hole wasn't two feet round back in the late sixties. It was a pretty hard climb, too, kept a kid busy a good hour and a half—but it's probably seven feet wide by fifteen now."

There was another hole Steve used to ride bikes through, the handlebars just fitted—that was '76, '77. "You could park three bikes side by side in there now. But see, there's a lot of sand in that country; the wind blows it around, and it just eats away all the time. That does more damage than rain and wind and heat and cold all together. Another hundred years, I'll bet all that'll be down there is just a pile of rocks."

"Won't even be that," said Mark. "The wind'll blow and the dust'll cover it, and all it'll be is a mound."

He said Stan Moorhouse and Katie Lehman got married down there. "We dug a pit and had a big old roast. That firepit must have been cooking two days—the hole's eight deep, fifteen long, six across, and you burn enough wood in there till there's embers and coals three feet deep. Then you throw some steel grating in there, wrap the pigs up in screens—like off screen doors, you know?—then just throw them in and bury it. And I tell you, when we went back and picked them out, that was *tender* . . . cut the screen away, and that meat just fell right off in a pile. And we took a big old flatbed out there, had all the women serving potato salads and Jell-O and beans, we had a few kegs of beer, and everybody went down there in their good jeans—a few wore suits, not too many—and we lasted there, oh, I'd say from noon to about seven. Then everybody headed back into town for the dance."

On the TV, someone hit a home run.

"Boy—he had that one to eat."

Mark said his dad worked at the grain elevator in Monument, and his mom in a grocery store ... and he said the meat-packing plant wouldn't ever have come. The way he figured it, they just used Oakley as a ploy to get the concessions they wanted from the town they really wanted to be in, Nebraska someplace. Besides, he wasn't sure even if they'd been serious, whether the old people who ran the town really meant to let them in.

"You got to understand," he said, "you'd have to call this a bigoted town. They don't want no Koreans and Veem-tahnese running around in here. The way I see it, you got bad bunches in every banana patch—I know whites I'd cross the street to be away from—but there's older people don't see it that way."

The boss of the bar had his wife on the phone; it was 9:30, and his fifteen-year-old daughter was still out in mom's car. He said he'd have to go dragging Main Street.

He asked Mark, "Where do fifteen-year-old girls go on a Friday night in Oakley?"

"Where the sixteen-year-old boys are."

On the TV now there was some bizarre show from Barbados, "Swim-suit '90." Women wearing very little indeed paraded tanned and smiling in the faraway sun. Mark said, "You don't see many in Oakley wearing suits like that. Not unless they're in sixth grade. And you know to keep your hands off of that, 'less you want to get in jail."

Then he went back to explaining how the government paid guilt money towards the employment of Veem-tahnese, and how that was good business for the companies that employed them. "And people complain, people bitch, but when you've lived around a place like this, you maybe don't want to work in a slaughterhouse that bad. But these boys—they'll do it, they'll work. And the thing is, people forget this place was made by immigrants in the first place—but now while these boys are working you got others, Americans, just sitting in their rat holes, don't do nothing but fuck all day and get welfare for the kids they make at it. Hell, I work four months for the government every year—I wouldn't mind getting paid to lie about and fuck all day."

Welfare—another of the forces of erosion ...

Mark had been to Seattle, and liked it—never seen so much water in his life. And he'd been to Chicago, that was okay—though the food didn't thrill him. "You get a side plate's worth of food and they expect you to pay thirty dollars for it? And be happy? Back here I'll get a steak for twelve dollars so big, you'll need two plates to bring it in on."

And he'd been to Texas too; he knew people down there that still spoke German round the dinner table, and then English and Spanish on the street. He liked that. He'd done French three years in school, but he couldn't remember any. After I'd left the night before he'd sat at the bar till they threw him out, thinking about Europe.

But round here, he said, "I can count on one hand the people I know that's got a passport."

There is, of course, another way of getting abroad. On Main Street as I walked back to the Annie Oakley I noticed, in the window of Waddell & Reed, lawyers, twenty-six local names gone off to the Gulf. By the names a little sign said: IT'S NOT OVER UNTIL THEY'RE *ALL* HOME.

Still the lightning popped and flashed, north and east.

I drove to Oberlin the next day, sixty miles north. Along the way, the land began gently to buck and roll; still grassland, but spotted now with stubby stone outcrops, and even—occasionally—trees.

Oberlin itself was well shaded, neat and clean, the streets tidily paved with red brick—and on South Penn in this town, tucked behind a deceptively tiny old wooden porch front, there's the Decatur County Museum, known also as the Last Indian Raid in Kansas Museum.

After Custer and his men died at the Little Big Horn in Montana in 1876, over 1,000 Northern Cheyenne were sent down to Indian Territory, with promises they'd be fed—but they got only two days' worth of rations a week. When Little Wolf and Dull Knife made their last-ditch decision to brave all and go back north, there were only 246 women, children, and old people left to make the journey, with 92 warriors to fight for them.

In 1878, on an epic and desperate 1,500-mile trek home, they came through Decatur County; in northwest Kansas in all, thirty-nine settlers were killed.

Mostly, miraculously, they'd kept ahead of the pursuing soldiers, holding them off sometimes by setting prairie fires. There was violence around Decatur County, however, partly to do with getting food—and partly in revenge for the deaths of twenty-nine warriors killed there three years before.

But for the most part, unsurprisingly, the museum's about white people settling, rather than Indians resisting, and the Indian room's a meager affair, beside the overspilling cornucopia of America's advance.

There were fittings and furniture from the home of Otis Benton, a banker; the house was built in 1909 but, said my guide, pointing to an old photo, "They tore it down in the fifties to make a clinic. They should have kept it, it would have made a neat museum. His wife, she traveled a lot, she wrote a book called *Maud Abroad*. But they say a lot of people didn't like her, she was real pushy."

There was the Kiefer barber shop exactly as it had been in 1905, with the shoeshine chairs, and a mug for every man with his name on it, and the prices—a dime for a shave, a quarter for a haircut. "They had," said my guide, "the same prices in the Depression too."

There were Bill Petracek's beautiful old model carriages and horses, and his complete model farm set with all working parts—barns and windmills, hog sties and cattle pens and grain silos. "One woman came in here the other day and said it's not exactly right, there's no cow poop on the ground . . . but he even used real grain, he just dripped melted wax on it to keep it hard in the feed troughs. And he made everything except for the black and white cows—they're plastic. He died in January; a couple of months before that he came in with two lady friends from the home, and he told us to tell everybody his wife didn't help him one bit, excepting only the curtains. But I think he was just trying to impress those women."

There were twelve portrait photos of old-timers, but only three were still alive. Eleven of the twelve were women. "Must have been rougher on the men back then."

There was the general store, "the Wal-Mart of the 1880s, they had everything imaginable. Wire-rimmed spectacles . . . it's real interesting, how things come back. Well, I doubt swimming suits like *that* will come back . . ."

A sign said SHOOT OUR BARTENDER IF YOU LIKE, BUT PLEASE SPARE OUR MIRROR. IT'S THE BIGGEST AND FINEST IN TOWN.

There was Dr. F. E. Gierhart's dentist office, with a foot-operated drill, and a cogged grinder to roll the gold for caps and crowns.

There were telephone exchanges. "I had a telephone operator in the other day used to run one of these things. He said everybody'd listen to everybody else's calls—and if someone was out for the day, they'd come in and call him to find out what they missed. News traveled fast back then."

There was a piano, the first musical instrument in the county, brought in because the woman who played it said she'd not marry her man if he didn't bring it when they settled. So he did, and he had to build a second sod house by their first one to store it.

There was a replica sod house built in 1958 for the museum when it opened; inside there were pictures made from dried flowers, and tatted human hair. The bottom mattress was stuffed with corn shucks; the top, if they were lucky, would be feathers. "A girl would keep feathers from when she was real small—so when she was married her contribution would be a feather mattress."

They used cow pies and corncobs for heating. They baked once a week, and stored what they'd baked in a pie safe with a tin punch door.

There was the tack room, a huge pile of tools and junk: corn shellers, apple corers, cherry pitters, mangles, washing machines, blade sharpeners, blacksmiths' bellows, stoves, fly nets for the horses, stagecoach seats, an ancient toaster, Ward's Dependable Incubator.

And back inside, there was the library and a schoolroom.

My guide said, "These rooms are probably used the most. When people come back for the alumni banquets in May, on Memorial Day, you get a lot come in here then. They look for photos of their parents, and their classes.

"Most all of them move away when they graduate," she added. "There's very few that come back."

I drove 138 more miles that day, with no particular notion where I was headed. I crossed the Nebraska line on 83, turned east on 23 through Curtis, then north again on 47—until, in the slow settling down of a pale pink evening, I came in Custer County to the little town of Arnold.

After Curtis the shift in the landscape, already hinted at before Oberlin and more so beyond McCook, became definite. It wasn't the Sand Hills proper, as yet—but the land was buckled and scooped out now into rolling wave forms that you swept and dipped through, as if sailing on a long and gentle ocean swell.

There was another difference too. The Republican River at McCook had water in it, as did the Platte at Gothenburg, and the South Loup at Arnold. The land everywhere was green—a bright, dense, singing green.

I slept in the truck at Lake Arnold State Recreation Area; at sunset, kids gathered fireflies in glass jars by the fire-red lake.

Then I went in the morning for breakfast at the Model Cafe, and discovered why the rivers were running, and the land so green. The

*Omaha Sunday World Herald* reported that—in stark contrast to No Man's Land—Nebraska had been getting rain ten percent over the average all this spring and early summer.

It was great for the cow-calf business, greening up the Sand Hills into a grass-rich blanket speckled with wild daisy, bluebell, and sweet pea; a rancher commented happily that, "They'd rather brand in the rain than in a dust storm."

Otherwise, however, this rain was very far from all good. In Nebraska, half a million acres of crops had been damaged; in Iowa, half of that state's north and central corn land remained unplanted. The first five months of 1991 were the fourth wettest in Iowa history; Ed Swanson near Galt said, "If it rains again this weekend, I won't wind up with anything. This is a lot worse than a drought to us."

Normally puny rivers were flowing fast and deep—sometimes, too fast and deep for comfort. At Crawford in northwest Nebraska, the flooding White River picked up seventy-three-year-old Virlyn Norgard's truck "as though it were a toothpick." He got out on the roof of the cab, grabbed a phone pole, and was left stuck there for nine hours. He said, "The water was deafening as it went by under me—like a tornado. I said a couple of prayers."

Matthew Scott Boggs climbed a tree, and the water ripped it right out from under him. He drowned, one of fourteen to drown in Nebraska and Iowa since May 11. The latest drowning was in Howells, in eastern Nebraska; there was hail there, high winds, and tornado funnels. Main Street had mud and water running five feet high; 12 public buildings, 34 businesses, and 247 homes got hit, with the damage put at $25,000,000. Fire Chief Gary Baumert said, "I thought I was in Baghdad."

Meanwhile, in southern Oklahoma, five inches of rain washed cars off the road, flooded homes, and, in one county, closed every highway they had. Lone Grove Fire Chief Leo Potts laconically remarked, "We get any more rain, we're going to be in trouble here."

Between January and May, these storms had also spawned around one thousand tornadoes. It was the most tornadoes for these five months in recorded U.S. history. With all this apocalypse going on, it seemed a good time on Sunday morning to seek out a man of God.

Arnold has five churches, Catholic, Baptist, Lutheran, Methodist, and Nazarene. Picking one at random, I pulled up at eleven that morning outside the United Methodist Church on North Walnut, a substantial pale brick structure whose ministry dated back to 1914. People were coming out from the service in their Sunday best—and I began to notice that a few among them were crying.

In the foyer I found the congregation embracing the pastor one by one. And they were tearful because—after seven and a half years of his ministry in Arnold—Pastor Jerry Schwarz had just preached his last service. He was moving ninety miles south to Arapahoe.

They were going to have a picnic for him and—being in the heart of America here—I found myself invited within minutes to join them. Pastor Schwarz, however, had the kindness to give me some of his time before that, so we sat together on a pew in his empty church, and talked about the little town he'd served these last years.

He was a well-built, dark-haired, and handsome man who chose his words carefully, seeking hard for the positive. But we'd not been talking long before he was looking away from me, and falling silent—because the population of Arnold, it emerged, had dropped in ten years from a little over 800, to around 600 today. A loss of one in four . . .

Schwarz said, "It's younger families that can't make a livelihood here, so the community has a lot of older folks. The women's group do a special meal every year for everyone over seventy-five, and out of the community they usually come up with eighty or a hundred people of that age. We have a lady of one hundred here . . . We find people retire here, and a community like this then becomes a large family—people respond in so many ways of helping other people. Within our own church we have a tape ministry—the worship is taped, and twenty copies are put in a box for delivery round the town; then we have someone who reads the entire newspaper onto tape for the sixteen here who can't see well enough to read. We also have cheer baskets at Christmas—fifty or sixty boxes of homemade bread, jellies, canned fruit, food for the shut-ins. And the Baptists do it on Valentine's, and the Lutherans on Thanksgiving . . . Then we have a food pantry serving people who need food around a twenty-five-mile radius—that's over 250 families. All they need to do is show us they're not making adequate income. Now this is all volunteers . . ."

But, I said, it wasn't saving the town.

"I've worked with our volunteers as to how we maintain this. The more we involve younger people in this ministry, the better they feel about being here . . . but we have to provide fun for them too. We're working very diligently to provide recreation. The Rotary Club built a sandlot volleyball court, they hauled a hundred truckloads of dirt; then we have baseball, tennis—and the Masons have donated their building to the community for a civic center which can be a theater, a playhouse so the kids can do some acting, and the older folks can come along and get tickled. We just did a dinner theater for four dollars at the school, and we had to turn people away."

I felt bad pressing him, as he stared away across the airy church on his last day of preaching there—but, I said, it still wasn't saving the town.

He paused a while, then said, "It's a real struggle. Because there's no industry." Again he paused, and apologized; he said he wanted to get it right.

"I'm trying to think of something the community's trying to do to bring in younger couples . . . it's a real struggle. I'll be quite frank with you, I'm hesitating, because I'm frustrated—I'm frustrated because I've lost many members of my church, they've gone to the bigger cities . . ."

Again he fell quiet, looking away across the hushed space of the church whispering with the quiet echo of his words—and I realized there were tears now, silently running from his eyes.

"The faces are coming to my mind who've gone away. . . . There are those who stay, who are willing not to have the finer things in life, because they sense the love that is here, and I praise God for that; but I make a list of the roster of those on my church, and the ones under thirty-five . . . I can count them on the fingers of one hand."

He said, "I've been here seven years, and I've been part of a group called Vision Volunteers, trying to dream some things we might do, some way we could make our community . . . some way we could keep our younger folks. But we're struggling. And I do not feel we've come up with the answers."

It was a small, tragic encounter. He seemed a kind man, sorrowfully helpless before the wind sweeping his people away. He quickly pulled himself together, and went to his picnic—but I didn't feel I should accept their invitation, and go along too. It seemed any grief or celebration should be theirs, and private.

I drove out of Arnold heading east, and thinking . . . anyone for buffalo commons?

I turned southeast on Highway 2 through Broken Bow for Berwyn. It was an entirely whimsical move—I live by the Berwyn Mountains in North Wales, and was merely wondering if the place had a Welsh founder. But whimsy, after the tears of Pastor Schwarz, seemed a pretty good motive to be moving along with just then.

Berwyn turned out to be a tiny place tucked away off the highway across the Burlington Northern. I crossed the tracks past the elevator, and drove up a small street past a row of abandoned businesses. Beyond these, a guy was leaning in the Sunday sun against a pickup in the road, idly chatting with the driver; I pulled up and walked over, and told them what I was hoping to learn.

Mary Tiff, they said, is the lady you want to see, a teacher—and they gave me directions to a house just back the way I'd come, down the lane opposite the cracked windows and boarded doors of the derelict stores.

I drove back there. In the garage by the house a thinnish, wiry man was plastering; he was of middle height, with glasses and a moustache. His name was Cliff Critchfield and he was a welder, self-employed—but he was cleaning the garage out, because he had plans to start an upholstery business soon. He said he came originally from Lincoln, but he was married to Mary Tiff, and this was his mother-in-law, Rosa Tiff's house.

He came out and stood blinking in the sun with his trowel, the last crumbs of soft plaster drying on his handboard. A freight train roared by, the slow, remorseless thunder and clank of a hundred or more cars of coal from Wyoming shaking the air—and I told him what I was doing, and how the things I was learning seemed sad.

Cliff wouldn't have it. "You got to understand," he said, "it has to be really drastic before people actually say, I quit. There's still a lot of pioneer spirit in the people out here, they're raised on that, and though people do recognize the writing on the wall, they'll go to the last effort to try and stay here. People here will absolutely try to work it out, because they love this country. So I think most people will stay if they possibly can."

But the young people go . . .

"Well, to keep the kids around here . . . gee, I don't know. If I had the answer it'd be great. Anyhow, did you eat yet? C'mon in and eat—we've got five daughters, so it's a zoo, but you're welcome."

*Five daughters* . . . next thing I know I'm in this whirlwind of femininity, Mary Tiff and her elder girls laying out a fine spread of chicken, biscuits, green beans, and potato; and the younger girls are popping questions, and giggling at my accent; and we're saying grace; and I'm feeling a bit like a Martian, to be honest, suddenly landed in here out of the long blue of the road . . . but a happy and well-fed Martian, too.

Cliff said the chicken was, "Reared three miles from here, and not a chemical in it."

Mary Tiff was a boost as good as the food, too; a short, stocky woman, adamant and determined.

"No," she said, "the small towns will never die. Because there are small-town people who believe in small-town values—like having your kids safe, and having your education system with some control still over what gets taught, and how. We've got our church yet in Berwyn here too, that's United Methodist. You could walk in there and feel at home, you'd be welcomed—and that's part of the Plains feeling. People are welcoming here, because we've always needed each other."

"But also," said Cliff, "because we don't have the big city problems. We know each other. We feel secure."

He said, all being well, he'd have his upholstery business up and running in three weeks.

Berwyn's called Berwyn because that was the name of the railroad agent who platted the place in 1886. He set the town there because every ten miles, the trains needed water—so every ten miles, there's a town that built up around the downspout. Or at least, the remains of a town . . .

Mary Tiff brought out their history book, MUDDY CREEK MEANDER-INGS—six hundred pages of local lore and family stories. Pretty much everywhere I went had one of these impressive tomes, diligently assembled to celebrate each little place's centenary—it took two and a half years to put Berwyn's book together.

It said that in 1916, Berwyn was "a prosperous village of modest proportion, with a population of around 300."

And it told the story of Ulrick Sorenson, born at Thisted in Denmark in March 1882. He came to the United States as a baby that summer with his parents, three brothers, and a sister; when he was nine, his first job was herding fifty-eight head of cattle for a dollar a week. But when Ulrick grew up, he became a balloon entertainer—or, as he titled himself, a "Professor of Aeronautics." He rented a room in Berwyn's hotel, and from there he scheduled flights all over Nebraska.

"The balloon was inflated by hot air generating in a trench about two feet wide by two feet deep, with one end open and a flue at the other end about the size of a thirty-gallon oil barrel. The trench was partly filled with wood and then kerosene; gasoline was then thrown on the fire to produce the gas. Mr. Sorenson worked inside the balloon anywhere from fifteen to thirty minutes to see that it filled properly. In this intense heat, he chewed on a lemon to insure himself from thirst."

He wore black tights, and sat on an iron bar; he went up in the air suspended on a trapezelike affair from the bottom of the balloon. Presumably growing bored with the limitations of this entertainment, he then built a glider in the Berwyn blacksmith's shop, and carried it aloft hitched to the balloon. When he attempted to fly off in it, however, it broke into pieces, "and he plummeted 3,500 feet in a minute . . . he had no unusual sensation while making the descent, with the exception that he knew he was going to land in a hurry."

Luckily, Sorenson had a parachute.

Later, when he married, his wife made him promise to stop this risky flying business—so he got a monkey from Chicago, and sent that up instead.

There's no hotel in Berwyn now. The abandoned buildings past the elevator include a defunct bank and restaurant too, and the disused premises of Elfco Inc.

Mary said, "We moved here in 1952, and the bank had gone under about three years before. They turned it into the post office, then that was moved too. The next building used to be a service station; the big white building was the Oddfellows Hall, they built it with their meeting room upstairs, and the downstairs was the telephone office. The operator lived right next to it in the same building, her name was Josephine Flint and she was blind; she died about four years ago, in her nineties as I remember. We still have the post office; that shares a building now with the fire trucks that our volunteer fire people use. And the Berwyn Village Board has its office there—well, its file cabinet. And that's it. There's only two businesses. The grain elevator by the tracks, and a bee company.

"There was a general store, of course—bread and milk and soda pop, and ice cream after school. That was in those buildings too. Then next to that is a building built by some people who came here in the late fifties, a guy named Ernest Elfgren—and get this, him and his people came from Connecticut in a covered wagon, would you believe, with four mules to draw them."

Cliff asked, "Were they Mormons?"

"No, they were just . . . unique people. They went into Broken Bow and Broken Bow just refused, wouldn't even let them camp. So they came back here. He was an amazing man, he was a brilliant machinist; he built his whole home out of oil cans and chicken wire with stucco all around it, and you know, it's still standing. It's probably one of the warmest houses here—he was a brilliant man. Eccentric, but brilliant. He was an inventor, he set up a co-op, a machine shop; he made cattle oilers, something they'd put in the pasture and the cows'd rub against them, and get fly ointment on them. And he made some kind of trash burner, and he bred chinchillas too—he had 250 of them things. I remember when they started they had a dance, it was wonderful, a real country hoedown—it was right across the street there—and I thought it was the most wonderful thing in the world."

Berwyn, the prosperous village of three hundred, has only seventy people today.

But Mary Tiff was resolute. "We have people coming in with kids now; we're a bedroom town for Broken Bow, the location's good, and the economics. People can live cheaply, and control at least somewhat what happens to them. It's basically," she said, "about having control of your own life."

So I told them of my meeting with Pastor Schwarz.

"Well, the preacher's a person who deals with people in emotional need all the time, he's in close personal touch all the time . . . I can see his position. And what he's saying is true. It's different for us here, Broken Bow's only eight miles off and it's doing okay—they've got a company making medical things, test tubes, there's several hundred to a shift in there; it's the only industry for thirty or forty miles around, and we're close enough. Whereas Arnold," she said, "is just a little far away."

Then she said something Cliff had said earlier, when I first arrived, that whatever happened, so long as you kept your school, then you'd keep your town.

Four years ago the Berwyn school had fifty kids, from the village and the farms round about. Now, it had half that . . .

"What did this was a few years ago, the Nebraska legislature passed the Choice Bill—if you could prove another district had better facilities, then your kids could go there. So of course, no small district can compete with Broken Bow, and the system's dwindling all around as a result. And it's pretty hard on a parent to sit down and say, Is it more important that the community stays together? Or should the kids have the education they can get in Broken Bow? Because it gets to the point where every kid you lose here, it's closer to closing."

So I asked which way the Critchfields had decided to go.

She said firmly, "They all go here to Berwyn. Much to Heather's displeasure—she'll be the only eighth-grader there next year. But I grew up in that school, and we have two excellent teachers here, and as far as the social life is concerned, we can replace that. There's plenty to do. Kristen and Heather and Rachel, they've just been on a pioneer class for a week at the Stuhr Museum in Grand Island, learning what history was like, I mean *living* the history—making rope and putting it in the bed frame, baking on an old stove, making corncob jelly, spinning and weaving, bringing water from the well—so they understand what kids their age back then would have had to do to get by."

Kristen chipped in, without prompting, that it was fun, too.

The way Mary Tiff put it, in this house of women, this was their side of the past being actively remembered—just as masculine history was held to by Wayne and his friends down at Caney.

Even so, making corncob jelly might keep the past alive, but it won't train a child how to do the same for the future.

And could they really hang on here? Was Pastor Schwarz just unlucky, that his town was twenty-six miles farther away than Berwyn from a test-tube factory? Realistically—in Berwyn and Arnold, in Oakley and Russell Springs—could they hope to survive against all the forces of erosion—against the blowing sand on the winds of the emptying land?

"Yes," said Mary. "Because I believe we have the best of whatever's available."

"Yes," said Cliff. "If anything survives—even if the big cities go under with all their turmoils—we'll still be here."

"Because people have to eat. And because of the values of working hard and being friendly and caring for each other."

"And in a big city they don't have that."

"But out here you *have* to have it. To live out here," said Mary Tiff, "you have to be persistent, you have to be really stubborn. And there's still a lot of people like that left out here."

Between the departing sadness of Pastor Schwarz, and the down-home hospitality and resilience of Cliff Critchfield and Mary Tiff, I had already come, back in Oakley, on what I think the future will in fact most likely be—and the storm country attitude that most likely will shape it.

It was Barb Glover at the *Graphic* who pointed me to it; it was two miles out of town, it was called the Pioneer Feedyard, and it was run by a lean, strong, blond-haired man of thirty-one named Jim Keller.

Keller's background was German-Russian; his grandfather got to

Oakley from the Volga in the early years of this century. The feedyard
was started in 1960; Keller's father came in on it two years later. Five or
six years ago, Keller and his brother bought his father out, and now he
was running an operation whose total sales he put at seventy-five million
dollars. He said about sixty million dollars of that came from the feedyard itself, the rest from related farming and ranching activities. He said,
in all, they employed about fifty people.

Keller was working on a Saturday morning in clean, spacious offices—not the kind of place you'd associate with any kind of traditional
farming at all but, more appropriately, with an industrial corporation.
There was an airy reception space, with magazines on a low table;
among the wall planners and the desktop micros, about the only thing
that directly suggested a connection to animal life was a large stuffed
turkey on a table in the waiting area.

Then you stepped outside—and the rich smell of thirty thousand
cattle fattening in huge pens of mud and shit let you know exactly where
you were.

In the blazing sun by the office, white barns and storage bins gleamed
with a parched and blinding radiance. A truck loaded with grain drove
into the glaring concrete yard; a front-end loader dumped corn in
another one. Keller pointed and asked, "How d'you like that? That girl
can drive a truck as good as any guy—but you see that a lot out here."

There was a mill, a steam flaker, to compress grain after it had been
heated, with a great pile of grain hissing onto the floor from a chute;
farther off, there were silos the size of aircraft hangars being dug into the
ground by earth-movers. "We put one million bushels in there, compressed high moisture corn. Then another trench is for whole corn
plants, chopped—the animals got to have roughage, too." Two trucks
sat in an excavated hole so big, they looked like toys.

But the heart of the business was a half-section of pens, 320 acres—a
great camp of cattle stretching away all about us as we drove down the
tracks between the pens. Grey metal feed troughs ran all around the
sides. As we passed one pen Keller said happily, "That's nice—in this
pen they've all got the same color, that creamy brown. That's got some
eye appeal."

We passed a man on a horse moving through the cows in the glossy
scuffed dirt. Keller said, "We ride the pens every day, looking at the
health of the cattle. Our death loss is about one half of one percent. We
keep full pretty much all the time; some people like to bet on the

market, but we just keep a-rolling. You can't outguess the market, so we look to hit an average."

The feedyard's the next stage in the chain from what Alan Shields does down in No Man's Land; Keller buys yearlings off ranchers at maybe 750 pounds, feeds them up to maybe 1,200, then sells them on to the packing plants.

But while you can grasp the scale of a man running 600 cattle on 12,000 acres of empty plain, seeing 30,000 in just 320 acres is a size of business more gawp-worthy altogether.

"Out here," said Keller, "we're mid-sized, maybe a bit on the larger side. Go back a few years, you'd be feeding 100 head, or 300 head, and there's still a few guys back east that run that size—but it's consolidating. The average now might be ten times that, though out here you've also got the super-size yards. At Ulysses down in Grant County there's a yard that's got 95,000 head, and they're expanding to 110,000, 115,000. That'd be the largest yard in the world right there."

We drove between the pens under the shining sky, and I tried to imagine that—115,000 cattle. It would be a city, a cow megalopolis. It would, certainly, be twenty-five times as many cattle in one yard as there are people in Ulysses.

He asked me, "How many places in the city could you just pull up and go in there and talk to someone? To the boss? You'd have to get an appointment, they wouldn't be there—or they'd be there but they'd just look at you and say, Who the hell are you? But this is the Great Plains here; you'll find the people here are friendly, and industrious."

On the other hand, he didn't want me making a big thing of it. He said, "We're a little itty-bitty speck of sand out here. I like what I'm doing, I've got enough pride to get out of bed and comb my hair—but I'm not into promoting my thing."

His thing, however, was at least making money, which was more than could be said for a lot of people on the Plains these days. In wheat, for example . . .

"It's not affecting them as bad as they're putting out. We've gone through a tremendous consolidation in the past ten years, but for every guy who's gone bankrupt, there's others who've done well. You're right, in that the cattle business adds value to the grain—just grain, that in effect is a third world commodity economy. So if we didn't have the cattle, we wouldn't have anywhere near the economic base we do—it's the most important thing here. Basically, irrigated farming equals feed grain production equals cattle."

But as the little guys drop out of that equation, and the corporate farmers move in . . .

"It will never be corporate farming out here. People have got their life's blood in the land out here, they're willing to work whatever it takes. I'm talking about the industrious ones—there's people who'll bitch and moan, and they'll go out of business—but the people that are willing to get up at three in the morning and see to a calf, those people will stay, and those people will succeed.

"Whereas what you call 'corporate' farming—I put that in quotations because we're a corporation, but *we're family*—but those corporate farms, they're not close to the ground. Anything down from the hugest level, the returns aren't there, so the commitment's not there. They won't work till three in the morning on a tractor in the shop because there's planting to do.

"But yes, okay—on the other hand the steamroller's running forward, and there are people going under. But the thing is, you won't stop that. Farming in general is a great way of life, but a lot of people can't afford that way of life anymore, not the way they perceive things. Because if you really want to be successful now, you've got to put farming as a business first, and a way of life second—whereas a number of years ago, it was a way of life first and last.

"So you can't do it the way your grandpa did it anymore. But you know how time works, the value of time—and time's going at an angle, it's accelerating up, and you think it'll reach an apex, but it never does . . .

"There's still good ethics and values," said Jim Keller, "in this part of the world. But even out here, you can see the erosion of those values."

I asked him if he'd ever seen a tornado.

"Sure. I've seen several. I've never seen one that devastated anything, but I've seen them blow things around. The house I live in currently, that got destroyed back in '71—but do I worry? Do I live in fear? No. It's like a rattlesnake—am I going to worry about it? It's not a big issue to people who live here. It is to people who *aren't* from here . . . Besides, thunderstorms are beautiful. We stand in awe of nature out here. You go to the Sand Hills, now that is a place of true natural beauty. That is God's country."

But the weather, I said, and the market—like tornadoes, there was nothing you could do about those things. And there were only those two things hanging over your life, defining your chances in any year of profit or loss.

"Is it scary to me? I've fought and I've struggled and I'm successful, but am I scared? No. Do I feel threatened? No. Am I concerned? Yes, I'm concerned about the water, and about extremish animal rights people, but as far as the market goes . . .

"We're not speculators. We're in it to add on pounds as efficiently as possible. And we've got the capital to withstand the bad times—at least we think we do, 'cause you never know how bad bad can be—but we've been in a good cycle these last few years, so we'll have a bad one, no doubt. But the thing is, every time we go through a tough spot, we come out better. Because it's not just the big getting bigger, whatever people say, it's the good getting better. And the harder you work, the luckier you get, so it's not really luck: It's just working your butt off."

What about the water then, and the pumping of the aquifer? What about the greenhouse effect, and the place just drying out?

"No, I discount that. There's something to it, but it's tremendously long-term; we know we can screw it up, but I don't think anything will ever be documented on it. And water out here—okay, we're pumping our underground table, and some spots we're pumping it faster than it's recharging. But there's a movement here to control that pumping, and people think some of that's radical, but they're helping us. That could be a crisis in twenty years' time, but I would say we'll adapt.

"As to the rivers being dry, they've always been dry. Yes, they're *more* dry . . . but that's because of the dams, and the terracing, and that's just better farming. I like to see dry rivers—that means the water's staying right here."

He said, "The land's not going to change, and the weather's not going to change—just the people. We don't need all these towns anymore.

"We picked thirty thousand bushels in a day with one combine last year; thirty years ago, we'd only have picked three thousand. That's why the towns go, because we just don't need so many people. And our infrastructure's good, so what's an extra half an hour in the car? It's no inconvenience. Yes, a lot of these little towns may die—but Colby will still be there, Garden City will still be there. There's a Wal-Mart at Colby now—and that wipes out whole downtown businesses in Oakley, in Colby too—but overall it means Colby draws more people, and Oakley less. Is that bad? Wal-Mart are keeping prices down, and that's the way it's going to work. The dollar's going to drive everything the way it always has done."

So the towns will die.

Jim Keller said that was history, that was progress, that was economics.

He said, "You don't want to stand in front of the freight train, do you?"

Back in Coffeyville someone had shown me a headline over a piece in the *Independence Reporter:* PORKERS INJURED.

A truckload of hogs had got stuck on a rail crossing, and a train plowed into them. When I think of it I can hear the crunching rip of metal, and an unimaginable squealing.

And several times through the trip I heard on the radio of people dying on the rail tracks. One time, I think it was in Omaha, drunk kids were playing chicken with their cars on a crossing, and one of them never made it off. No one knew whether he'd got stuck, or couldn't get his engine started, or if he'd just passed out.

When I think of it I can see him turning the key, and nothing happening, and the great engine bearing down in the urban dark . . .

In Coffeyville I sat on a bridge over the Verdigris, the oily brown surge of the river shoving past between high banks of dirt and stone, the water strong and lazy under dense stands of bright trees. The woman I sat with had been hit by one kind of freight train or another pretty much from the time she came out of the womb; she began to tell me her story . . . and on the way back into town, we had to stop at a crossing.

I counted the freight cars going by, 115 of them. The air trembled and the ground shook under our car, as the coal went south for the power plant at Oologah. The clanking, shrieking mass of metal thundered slow and remorseless along the rails, the iron bending in its bed of wood and stone beneath the weight as the engines moaned and roared . . .

Jim Keller was right. You don't want to stand in front of the freight train.

And, hurling dirt and debris and shattered houses around and around in its black belly on its howling march towards your little town, we all know what sounds like a freight train.

## The Vanishing Point

I left Roosevelt at dawn, heading east on 40 through more red rock and rubble; after sixty miles I got to Dinosaur on the Colorado line.

Northwest Colorado wasn't red like Utah, but yellow and grey, pocked with scabrous little tussocks of dry and scrawny vegetation. It was a scarred place, a rolling heave of worn rock and chipped stone. At some point I stopped to make notes and, instantly and mysteriously, the cab filled with clouds of tiny silent insects, bobbing on micro-thermals in the broiling air.

Things got greener beyond Craig, along the valley of the Yampa; there were trees and fields, and there was water—but I didn't feel refreshed. I had a slumberous dullness in my head, numbed and throbbing to the slow beat of the V8. Asphalt, hills, green, blue, trees, clouds . . . it was a world put in the blender and poured my way down a tube of road, a thick tide of rock and color pushing against me. Butterflies committed suicide in orange splashes on the windshield.

The climb into the mountains after Steamboat Springs woke me up. I got over Rabbit Ears Pass, cut off 40 northeast on 14, then took a short cut on dirt towards Rand. The dirt led onto a bleak, unpeopled, scrubby green plateau, rimmed around with white-topped ranks of grey mountain. A duck or two sprang in panic from ponds in the verges; prairie dogs made their madcap scuttling sprints between the wheels. The clouds were an entire streaked, spiraled, turreted airborne city, a sci-fi skyworld in lilac and cream—and rolling along the rutted dirt in the monumental silence I realized: You can't buy this. There's no money that can buy the way it feels to be here.

Rand was the Rand store, a post office, a fire station, the Liar's Lair, and a couple of houses, one of them covered from ground to eaves with antlers. The police department was a dented old Jeep on the roadside with a white star and the words Rand Police stenciled on the door; in the driver's seat sat a grey-wigged dummy in a straw hat, shades, and a Freddy mask. A sign said, WELCOME TO RAND. ELEVATION 6,280. POPULATION 14.

I crossed Cameron Pass, 10,276 feet, then dropped off the mountains past roaring waters down the Poudre Canyon—over fifty miles of turn and turn round clefts and crags and chasms until I felt dizzy, and the truck under the endless splintered rockface felt matchbox-sized.

Then, suddenly, I emerged from between red walls into a void of sky and space. At Laporte I spun back out onto flat land as if spat there, as if landing from outer space into this huge flowering of earth and air, this great spirit-rich emptiness under the singing blue sky . . . I crashed out of the mountains east through Fort Collins on whatever road I could find just so long as it was east, just so long as it got me back and far away onto the Plains . . . My road petered out into dirt, I was surrounded with radiant corn—and ecstasy rising in my soul would not be too strong a way to put it.

Sometime here I turned the radio back on, and the first thing I got tuned to was a public service announcement of the precautions you should take in the event of a tornado.

Welcome back, said the Plains.

It was five-thirty. The front range looked fine behind me, a cobalt haze topped with thunderous clouds dropping scattered curtains of rain here and there; the sun threw eruptive shafts of dense, mote-rich light through the gleaming murk of the peaks.

But the Plains ahead looked better. Here there was nothing, only vast fields and pasture spreading away forever under cloudless blue. I saw my first grain elevator, white and shining, a motionless tanker in the sea of the land. I crossed some railroad tracks, then passed a pig farm, packs of porkers all muzzles to the trough, did that smell good—and the distant dots of farms and ranches with their little clusters of trees specked the windswept horizon way out there in the parched bare grass. I found 14 again, and rolled on deliriously east in my whale-truck through the glowing ivory of early evening.

The radio offered temperatures tomorrow from 92 on the southern Colorado plains, to 105 in the north. . . . It was six o'clock, and behind me the mountains were gone already; the west was cloud, and every-thing else a soft and edgeless blaze of light. Up to the north—into Wyoming, probably—I saw a massive tower of radiant white rapidly rising, the best I'd seen yet. Every stage of its motion was clearly visible, the thunderhead boiling, pulsing, curling over on itself, folding out great new florets of seething vapor . . . The jet stream caught the head of the tower, and hauled it out east into a perfect plume.

Behind to the west the sun fell lower; slowly the prairie took on its evening robe of numinous golden orange. The short grass bent away in the wind; I felt desperate to stop and get a picture. I saw a low curt rise to the north, misty-based and silver-edged in the horizontal light; it was one little slice of relief wedged between the gold-green flats and the great blue sky that might make a good image. I pulled over, and crossed the road onto the verge by a tatty barbed-wire fence. A meadowlark watched me come, then pounced away off a fence post.

I peered through the lens, and was about to take the picture when something odd in the foreground caught my eye. I set the camera aside, and looked into the pasture. What I'd seen was the severed base of a pipe of some sort, set into worn pieces of brick, just poking from the ground. I looked around, closer—and there, past cow chips and a single thin bundle of briar, was the foundation of a house.

It was barely visible; there was grass all over it, and it was swept as clean as if an F5 had been through. But once I'd seen it, it was plain as day—a slightly raised flat rectangle of ground, with a thin stone rim. Someone, once, had lived here, in a Little House on the Prairie more reduced now even than El Cuartelejo—and now the prairie had near swallowed it up again already, and this last bare patch of foundation was all they'd left behind them.

Things come and things go, in the heart of America.

I hopped over the fence. A rusting strip of metal, a bar out of some antique farm implement, lay to one side. Then, beyond the disappeared house, there was a hole in the ground, stone-lined, and the worn remnants of steps leading down to it—a storm cellar. It was maybe eight feet by fourteen; it was filled now with a thick tangle of twigs and branches, old wire and dry bramble, with beams laid over to press it down and pack it out, and stop cattle falling in.

The same guy that built the house would have dug this little bunker, and it probably wasn't Highway 14 that went by his door when he did it. But it is now, and his door's long gone—and all that's left is this choked-full hole, and a flat foundation blown clean by the winds of history . . . I had found the vanishing point.

The last light grew to an ever deeper gold. Far in the distance, a single tree stood out against the storm on the northern horizon, among rustling waves of wheat lit ruddy vermilion by the dying sun.

That was twenty-five miles west of Stoneham, Colorado.

I carried on that evening to Sterling—a 422-mile day—and when I got there, I found the Fountain Lodge Motel. I pulled up into a court-yard painted a mildly orgiastic sort of pink—and they absolutely refused to tell me their rates until I'd seen the room. Because I might not like the room, in which case they'd show me another, because all the rooms were different.

It was the first motel I'd been to—the first and only motel in the universe, surely—where they'd got someone ready specifically to give you a tour until you found the room you wanted . . . but the first room was just fine. The walls were a hallucinogenic sky blue, with pictures from the Woolworth's scenic school; the bathroom was tangerine, with bile-green trim. It was lovely. Perfect. So I went back to the desk expecting some heinous and impossible rate, after these labors of individual and creative design—and it was twenty-two dollars.

Then the old lady launched with fanatical pride into how they never, never said what it cost beforehand in case people said, Yeeeuucchh, that's way too cheap, it must be dirty or something—and they were having the main fountain sandblasted just now, she was real sorry I couldn't see it, but here was a picture . . . It looked fabulously, dementedly garish.

But then, the one that was on was bad enough, a double circle with a kind of pulsing disco affair going on beneath the water, green, white, red, blue—it wouldn't have been out of place on a *Star Trek* set. And the third one to the side, well—a spectacularly tasteless grotto scene with water running down through turquoise pools guarded by frogs, owls, lizards, a plastic stagecoach, and a fishing gnome.

So now I said I was hungry, and the old lady directed me two blocks down the street to the J & L Cafe. The J & L was a kind of quasi-pyramid with spacious booths along each side wall, with seats of finest black Leatherette; along a central aisle, two counters with stools lined either side of the pie-dispensing zone. He who was boss patrolled between the counters there, looking fiercely amiable, while his girls pelted about in a kind of hyper-talkative tranquility.

My waitress was so unbearably pretty that I feigned absolute ignorance of all my options—what dressing to have, what kind of potato, what drink, what a sherbet was—just so I could have her stand there and run it all by me. She brought me a sample of sherbet to make me happy. She succeeded. And the salad had carrot in it, and radish, and purple cabbage, and the lettuce was crisp and fresh. And I knew the steak was going to be just awesome way before it ever arrived—and it was, it really was.

So what can I say? Only that the Best Motel in the Heart of America, and the Best Diner in the Heart of America, are both to be found within the space of three blocks in Sterling, Colorado.

It was good, good, good, to be back on the Great Plains.

# 6.

# Minatare

In the middle of Nebraska I left the Tiff house, grateful for a fine lunch and good company; at Broken Bow I turned north on a county road into the Sand Hills. At Milburn I crossed the Middle Loup: it was full, a regular river rolling through glossy green dunes. After that the road was dirt, or, sometimes, just sand—like driving on a beach.

The air was dense with a floating fluff of seeds, and bright with the darting of dragonflies; prairie dogs skittered through the dust under blazing blue skies. In the north a wall of crisp, gleaming white cumulus rose to line that whole quadrant of the horizon. I turned on the Weatheradio.

"Be cautious, but don't be afraid. Stay indoors, and keep informed."

There was a Severe Thunderstorm Warning—not a Watch, a Warning—for all of Rock County until 7:15. Just then I was in Blaine, immediately southwest of Rock.

"Routine programming is suspended."

They were tracking a storm moving southeast into Rock from Keya Paha; in Keya Paha it had produced up to golfball-sized hail. Other storms were reported in Brown and Holt, either side of Rock. I was headed into Brown, and I could see them all up there, a massive pile of thunderheads filling the wide rim of the sky.

"Know what the storm is doing. These storms can and occasionally do produce tornadoes, so be prepared to move to appropriate shelter should it become necessary."

I drove on in there. The closer I got, the more the wall lost its original pure whiteness, beginning instead to take on an angry, deepening grey-blue. This wasn't like that itty-bitty item that ended with my landing in a ditch back in No Man's Land; this was a whole horizon's worth of action. Towers punched into the jet stream.

I crossed 91 through Brewster and got on 7, due north over the North Loup. The river was a swollen sheet of blue, pushing full and sluggish through the sand; and there were forty-four miles of nothing now, until you got to Ainsworth up in Brown. It was 7:10 in the evening.

The Warning was extended to 8:15, covering all of northern Brown, Rock, and Holt. A new storm was reported five miles north of Ainsworth.

"If you live in the warned area you should take shelter."

As I drove into the thickening blue, the treeless dunes all about took on a subaqueous glow. I was in a vast, matte green moonscape, scooped and hollowed, camouflaged under deep patches of shadow; it was like driving along the floor of some dimly luminescent ocean. At 7:30, the upper western edge of the clouds swallowed away the sun; the wall ahead was now livid, an intense, shining slate-blue.

The radio warned the town of Stuart in Holt, "You can expect some possibly large hail in, uh . . . the next few minutes."

7:37. The first lightning crackled down straight ahead. I crested a rise above the Calamus River; and across miles and miles now the blue was darkening to a marbled black, a veined and implacable density in the clogged and fearsome sky. At 7:42 I went in under the edge of it; horizontal lightning flew beneath the low ceiling from cloud to cloud.

At 7:47 I stopped to take a picture, and an old couple came driving the other way, out from under the weather. When they slowed up to check I was okay—the way they always do—I asked them what it was like up there.

The old boy grinned and said, "Wet."

So here I am thinking I'm being terrifically bold—and there's these oldsters just a-cruisin' along . . .

"Drops are big," he said, "you might have to slow down a bit." Smiling, they went on their way.

At 7:58 the rain came abruptly smashing down. I drove the last twenty miles in a grey blanket of torrenting downpour, going slow like the man said, while the lightning popped and flashed all about.

In Ainsworth I got a room at the Remington Arms Motel. The guy on the desk told me he was from Ainsworth originally—but he'd worked thirty-five years in construction in L.A., until a few years back when he picked up an injury. Then he took his retirement, came home and bought this place.

I asked if he missed L.A.

He said, "I don't miss it one bit. Ever. The influx of Orientals these last years," he said, "it's been just . . ."

He searched for the right word.

"It's been just . . . *magnanimous.*"

I walked down the street to the Texaco truck stop. Outside on the lot a truckload of porkers oinked and squealed, imprisoned in panic under the dark and thundering sky; clouds still flared in the east with explosions of sinister light.

I got a Reuben sandwich, took it back to my room, and watched the Weather Channel. Locally, the Elkhorn River was reported dangerously high. "Persons downstream from Stuart should take immediate action to protect life and property if the river starts to approach bank full."

And nationally, from the Texas–New Mexico line, through Eastern Colorado and the Nebraska Panhandle, on in a curve through South Dakota to Minnesota, there was a string of storms firing up a thousand miles long.

In Denver there'd been mighty confusion; police officers saw seven funnel clouds in twenty-four minutes, and the sirens were set off. There wasn't any warning officially issued, but the City Council went ahead with the sirens anyhow. . . . A Denver station said tomorrow looked set to be the same.

And there was news of two tornadoes hitting a town called Minatare, two hundred miles west, at five-thirty that afternoon.

In the morning I headed that way.

West off 7 on a backroad past Willow Lake and Elsmere, I passed sunstruck ponds basking in the hollows of the Sand Hills. By one of these I came on a large and crotchety snapper turtle, catching rays on the blacktop; when I went to inspect him he hissed and—being a snapper turtle—he snapped.

Up the road, another turtle was roadkill. The shell lay overturned, cleaned out by scavengers, nothing left inside it but a bleached red smear.

From Elsmere to Purdum, the dirt after the rain was gullied tan gumbo. I slithered and skidded through a shining, duochrome world— green dunes, blue sky—until I hit blacktop again, and then Highway 2 at Halsey. From there, it was 140 miles to Alliance.

One hundred and forty miles of nothing but Sand Hills . . . Here and there, ever so rarely, I passed a windmill, or a shining pond, or the dots in mid-distance of a few cattle, or a speckled, loose-spaced little copse of trees, or a freight train hooting through the void—otherwise, nothing. Just the rise and fall of the great dunes, the wind-plucked swoop and ridge of green wave upon wave of gleaming emptiness. For long stretches in the middle, even the radio fell near-silent—just farm prices, or snatches of static-warped Christian babel . . . it was like having a lobotomy.

A long, slow, sensuous lobotomy.

If the Lord in his harshness stalks any place, then he surely stalks out here—and turns your mind to blank craziness.

From Alliance it was forty-two miles down to Minatare.

Coming towards the town it was as if the fields had not been rained on, but somehow rained *through*. . . . It wasn't just ponds filled up in the hollows here, but a whole fierce hurling of water all about, a water cannon job. Bits of fence and tree poked from sodden ditches, ragged and torn.

The turn into town was sealed off; a guy in a reflective jacket asked, "Do you live here? If not, there's no entry."

I said (feeling, I'll admit right here, shamed and vulturish) that I'd come to see the police chief.

He waved me through.

I came in on the east side, which hadn't taken the direct hit. It looked just all messed up, dirty, unkempt, strewn with branches and leaves, litter and wood and earth. The carpeting of muck was crunched into tire tracks by a quiet coming and going of pickups.

At the end of Main Street by the elevator, I found a police command post. I said what I was doing, and one guy asked another a most American question.

"Who's doing the PR on this?"

They said they had their power back, but the well was still out—no water. They were waiting for the railroad company to bring in some tankers. Then they pointed me to the American Legion building, where the local volunteers and the Red Cross had set up.

A woman there had a Polaroid of the first tornado in her pocket. It had set down in the fields north of town; it looked tall, thin, deadly. People milled about greeting each other, giving each other news to confirm they were all okay; I gathered in the hubbub how that first tornado had got them alerted, so they were mostly sheltered already when the second one tore through.

The second one had shredded an area four blocks square on the northwest corner of the town; I went out to have a look. Trucks hauled big chunks of broken tree away from that quarter, to a soundtrack of buzzing chainsaws. Ahead of me one guy said to another, "Boy, you really find out who your friends are at a time like this."

In Alliance a fund had been started already, collecting cash and nonperishable foods. In Minatare they'd had a call from Grand Island, that got hit itself ten years back, offering help—from three hundred miles away . . .

The town had a stunned, paused, openmouthed look about it. People gathered, talked, organized; houses were flattened, roofs ripped, but more than that what you felt was how lives were abruptly, arbitrarily arrested . . . but under the blue afternoon sky they were picking up, and they were going to work.

They were going to work in a place where all the trees were stripped bare, big branches hanging down all tattered and torn. A caravan lay on its side, the roof peeled back, the front end crushed to half the height of the back. A playing card—the five of diamonds—lay among a litter of twigs and bark in the middle of Avenue A. House after house was posted WARNING! KEEP OUT. Dented cars were plastered with mud and leaves, the leaves looking like they'd been blown onto the metal so hard they'd been flattened, glued on. Clothes and cardboard boxes hung high in the debarked remnants of the trees.

Avenue B was worse. The walls of wrecked houses were smeared with heavy sprays of thrown mud. Broken windows darkly gaped; drapes hung out over jagged sills. A three-wheel lawnmower lay in the gutter, front wheel sheared clean off; a camper on a debris-strewn lawn looked like it had been driven head on into a wall at a hundred. The houses had been thrown inside out, their contents turned into a pulped and soggy chaos of garbage on the grass. Kids' toys lay broken on the sidewalk, dolls, bears, cars, bits of puzzles and books.

There were trees, not uprooted, but twisted and snapped away, clean through the trunk. . . . I talked briefly to a farmer from outside town, and tried to pin down when all this had happened exactly.

He said, "Shit, I don't know. We got a basement full of water up there, thought we was hit bad, but I don't know . . . Hell, Lucille didn't have her Cadillac very long, did she?"

I walked on, and Avenue C was worse yet. The gutters were filled with mud and splintered wood, unidentifiable pieces of house. People salvaged bedding and food and pushchairs from homes that had barely a wall left standing. An exercise machine lay amid torn planks and beams on somebody's lawn; downed trees were crashed into one another like drunks, or fallen in on the shells of houses. Overturned cars were buckled heaps of junk; whole roofs lay flat on the ground. Everywhere was just fragments, disintegrated piles of wood and fabric thrown down in a muck-splattered mayhem.

It was entropy made instant flesh, matter turned to anarchy, ordinary life gone upside down into raging unreason. It was a chair on top of a wardrobe on top of a mattress on top of a shattered heap of two-by-fours festooned with scraps of yellow insulation that, twenty-four hours ago, was the place you lived in. . . .

Talking about it in the next few days, the inevitable analogy people reached for, over and over, was war: "It looks like we was bombed."

But it was more malevolent than that, more deranged, more deliberate. It was like a giant went through Minatare with a baseball bat, picking each swipe at each house with conscious intent—then kicking the wreckage about afterwards, just to make good and sure.

So here on Avenue C we had the TV vans humming with all their gear and their dishes, 7 Uplink, Skylink 9 . . .

One of the reporters—seeing me taking notes, and assuming I was press—came out from his van with a stills camera. He asked me to take a picture of him and his crew in front of the wreckage of the house they were parked by.

One of the crew wasn't too keen on that; there were people in that wreckage, still salvaging bits of their lives from the rubble. He said, "C'mon, we don't want to bother these people."

The reporter shrugged. He said, "That's the way it is."

"One of the things that bothers me, every time I look out the door at that ballpark . . . my dad helped put up those lights. When I was little."

Now they were down flat on the ground.

Bonnie Kaufman was on the school board. She said, "There was a warning, and the school is the shelter—and I have a key. So I knew to go over when the siren sounded, and a lot of people were there—maybe fifty, seventy-five—and they were watching the first one in the north, until it dissipated. So then everybody went, except me and the superintendent and his wife—and then we heard this horrendous roar. The west was all ugly-looking and it just roared, real loud. We said, Let's get back inside, and as we got on the step real forceful hail was falling, the type that could knock you out; and people came running back, I don't know how many 'cause the lights went out, but possibly more this time. There was one couple that was ready to get in their house, then they saw the roof just *breathe* . . . [she mimed with her fingers a great swollen pulse] so they came. And we were down there, it seemed forever—probably an hour, or more.

"But that first one," she said, "that was such a freaky-looking thing. It wasn't so much frightening . . . It started like just a little white tail, and then almost instantly it was a straight black streak, with a transparent covering like there were two tubes there—real strange. You were tempted to watch."

She said, "I'd just come back from Gering, and when I was driving home there were thunderclouds, and my house was real stuffy. But the siren couldn't have been more than half an hour after I got back and I thought, Wait a minute, it doesn't look that bad . . .

"And then it was there. It was just *there.*"

As far as her own place went, she figured the roof was probably okay; she'd had it redone only a couple of years back. But she'd opened all the windows because the air was so close, so muggy; then she'd had no time to worry over shutting them when she ran to the school, so now every room was soaked. Her bed was "like a swimming pool." And the house had hail damage on one side—but then, she said, what did she have to worry about? She was worried about other people a great deal more.

"How do you go to work, when your house is matchsticks? How do you get a bath, so you can go to work?"

Still, she said, they were lucky—nobody died.

While we were talking, a farmer came in. The tornado had ripped up his irrigation channels, sending water spilling everywhere; his ground was all gullied and wrecked, the crops all flooded. He had a neighbor, he said, who'd had seven calves drown.

Someone asked him how things were up there now. He just smiled, and shook his head.

"Well," he said, "I'm alive."

I stayed at Harry's Motel, a short way east down 26.

On CNN in my room, a weatherman named Flip Spiceland said there was flooding in New Orleans.

I went outside, and found flooding here too. Next door to the motel was Harry's Drive-Up & Restaurant, with a garage and truck stop along after that—and the forecourt was a lake. Vehicles trawled in through the water to the gas pumps, Harry's red neons reflecting in dreamy ripples in their wake. People stepped gingerly from their cars, and tiptoed through the water to the store.

The woman at the counter said it'd take a few days to dry out. When it had all happened, she said, "We couldn't see the road from here, there was so much rain and hail—and we didn't even know that thing had hit, till people came and told us. So we was lucky."

She said, "God rattled our cages, and let us know what He could do."

A kind of necessary myth-making began. In the next few days I heard stories told and retold, as people struggled to define the event—and kept the knowledge of how much worse it might have been tucked quietly away inside.

Because for many of them, outside the one flattened corner of town, it was as if they'd stood in front of the freight train—and it had turned out, this time at least, to be a ghost train, passing with a sinister but intangible roar that left their houses still standing.

So they looked at the houses that were gone, and they couldn't believe that theirs weren't gone too. It was as if they *ought* to be gone—as if to be spared was a piece of luck you'd done nothing to deserve. The woman at Harry's garage said she felt almost guilty that nothing much had happened out there, and I heard that feeling expressed several times—because what had happened to those who had been hit, to their neighbors and friends, was so comprehensively awful.

Dick Nerud's business was Poor Dick's Used Car & Parts, three quarters of a mile northeast of town. The operative word there is *was*—the tornado went right through it. Now, the man himself was numb with shock, and just kind of quietly, intently hanging in there.

"It tore up the buildings, and my house—it's gone. I had nice evergreens—we're in a semi-desert and I watered them all these years . . . they're gone."

In the middle of his devastation Dick Nerud summed up the impact—his carefully nurtured trees in dry western Nebraska, all just gone.

Then he said, "There's not much I can do. You don't like it, but there's no need to complain. Only thing is, I'm sixty-six, and it makes it harder for us to retire. Where it's dropped that roof in on those cars; I was going to sell those, use part of that money . . ."

They'd been fine old cars, forties and fifties models lovingly polished and restored, and kept carefully inside. Now half of a building was caved in on top of them.

He said, "It's kind of wiped us out. But I'm not going to feel abused or anything. It may create a problem down the road a ways, but my dad was quite a guide, not to get too excited. Things'll work out. He went through the thirties, out north in Sioux County, he was a rancher and he got in debt too deep—and he came out of it."

His wife Maxine pulled up with a load of clothes she'd washed at her daughter's place. With the roof of their trailer gone, everything inside had got soaked through and muddied; now she'd brought the clothes back clean, and there was nowhere to put them.

Dick Nerud walked through the blasted remains of his buildings; here and there he picked up a broken plank, then set it down someplace else. Where do you begin?

The acting chief of police, Roger Sterkel, sat in his cubbyhole of an office and said bluntly, "It's a real disaster out there. It's a wonder we didn't have any deaths."

He'd gotten trapped right in it; they'd just put a new windshield in his patrol car. "I was out warning people, and I was going down Avenue B when it hit. It snapped branches off the trees and threw them through the windshield; I tried to back away, but it took the power lines and whipped them round the back axle, wrapped them clear round like a lasso. So I was trapped; I wasn't about to get out of that car, not with the power lines there. So I'm just sitting there, with trees picked up like toys all about me; it uprooted two, threw them against a house right by me. And there was shingles, lumber, metal, tin, all just flying by—a roof, a wall—just in a matter of minutes, I'd say three or four minutes at most. For a little bit it rocked that car, too, I thought it was going to pick it up, throw it; I didn't feel very secure. I don't mind telling you, I was scared for a little bit."

It wasn't his first. "Down at Bridgeport I was sheriff for fourteen years, you do a lot of weather watches in this job—and one time I got too close. It took the top of the back window, pulled it out, filled the backseat with rain and hail, then put that window right back in again, sealed it up perfect—strangest thing I ever saw. That put the hairs up on my head—it was an eerie feeling."

I asked how he thought it would affect people.

"A lot of them are still in shock; they can't believe it happened to Minatare, Nebraska. It's going to be a couple of weeks before it really soaks in ... but it makes the community pull together, it makes it more tight-knit. And everybody helps—we've got volunteers of all kinds. But the thing is, a lot of times ... the people on B and C, they have so many people helping them, the adrenaline probably won't die down for a while. But then they'll realize—they've lost their homes, they've lost everything. When the activity dies down, when the supporters and the helpers go about their own ways again, then they'll realize."

He said, "This is the most homes I've ever seen wrecked in one bunch. See, living here, there's probably about three months of the year it gets real scary; how the people in Kansas and Oklahoma live, I don't know, it's on a daily basis down there. But here we get warnings, we see tails hanging down—it's threatening, but it's not as bad as down there— and then it just happens. Four minutes, thunderous wind—and suddenly, it's like the houses are made of paper. Next thing, you look around—and it's *total destruction.*"

In the Legion Hall I met Dennis Kumm, a bulky man who worked for Nebraska Civil Defense out of Lincoln—and he'd been having a busy time of it. There'd been the flood in Crawford a month ago, the flood in Howells last week, and now this.

When someone asked him if he was married he smiled wearily and said, "I was when I left home."

He'd driven 450 miles through the night—and through the storms— to get to Minatare at 5:30 on Monday morning. Now, he sat amid the dim and bustling to-and-fro of the volunteer center and, interrupted occasionally by his portable phone, attempted to do his part in putting things back together.

In between times, he told me about the weather in Nebraska.

He said, "The state's 470 miles wide, so it's possible to have things going off all over. But April through June, that's when it gets crazy. Last year it started mid-March, and we had forty-five counties affected out of ninety-three. So this year people were saying, Would we have it as rough as last year? And it didn't start till late. But May 10, it started raining in the northwest, and at Crawford there, it's rained every day since. They got hail the size of grapefruit ... and the White River never had a flooding problem, *never.* But it sure has now.

"Still," he shrugged, "it's the spring, I guess we expect the weather to do things. It's just rare that it goes on like this, I mean, *continuously.* For four or five years we didn't have any major damage that involved us getting out the disaster recovery deals—but now, this is the second year it's gone federal."

And did he have any explanation for that?

He shrugged. "It's just an act of God. It's something that happens, nobody can explain it. The last few years, we've had an officially declared drought. Now look at it."

Looking at it here in Minatare, he was preparing with Sherry Blaha, the local Civil Defense person out of Scottsbluff, and with various other agencies, a damage assessment. They were holding it off from the press until they were sure they'd got it right, so state and federal assistance would be set at appropriate levels—but at that stage they figured ninety-four private residences were affected, two businesses, and two public buildings. Of that total:

Thirteen family homes were destroyed.
Seven had major damage.
Forty-eight had minor damage.

Six apartments were destroyed.
Ten had minor damage.

Two mobile homes were destroyed.
Two had major damage.
Six had minor damage.

Crop damage was set at $6,200,000. Or, putting it another way: 90,000 acres.

About here it's worth pointing out—this was not a major tornado.

And, mercifully, most people were insured. Not that that's much consolation.

"All the things that come in," said Sherry Blaha, "so many things. Someone brought in a bunch of tiny kittens they'd found someplace this morning—looked like they'd only just been weaned, and they were hungry as sin. What do you do?

"Yesterday I felt like we were organized; today I feel like we're losing it . . . but we're not really." With determination she stressed, "We're not."

We talked at a paper-strewn table in a tight booth in the Legion Hall, with volunteers hustling round us to get coffee at the bar, and a steady noise in the background of children at the makeshift day-care area—and all the while as we talked, an old man stood there beside us.

It looked like he was crying, but he wasn't; he had cerebral palsy, so his face didn't work right—and he was saying over and over, he felt guilty guilty guilty.

He said, "Why didn't it hit *me?*"

On Wednesday morning, a computer-printed letter arrived at the mayor's office.

It was addressed to:   Minetara [sic],
                              c/o Mayor Minetara
                              Scotts Bluff NE

It was from:              F N Bosco Weather Engineers
                              1411 8th Street
                              Golden CO 80401

The envelope also noted, "Offer 20% Commission. It works!"
The letter said:

Sorry about the tornados [*sic*] just past! Tornados are repetitive. This is to help you avoid future damages!

To Citizens of Tornado Alley, as: KS, NE, OK, CO, Kentucky, Tennessee, Ohio, you can free yourself, and your family, from tornadic destruction, in minutes, if you have a package of:

Bosco's Handy Dandy Tornado Condenser. $25 each.

in your car or your kitchen. These ignited into your local air, will condense, at once, the heavy, overhead "Tornado Forming" cloud, and the there [sic] will occur, immediate condensing, and disappearance of the dark, capping cloud, and you will forget even the thought of a tornado! This has occurred! As we have found in Abilene, Texas, Blair, Nebraska, etc. Inquiry invited, or order, with $25 each, advance, and this can make you safe!, as others have found. Consult reference, newspaper files: Abilene, Texas, or Blair, NE.

There was no signature.

"I wished I had twenty-five dollars, just so I could see what it looks like. But I'm surprised we haven't had people selling 'I SURVIVED A TORNADO' T-shirts already."

Kevin Misner was thirty-two; he was Minatare's utilities superintendent. Before that, he'd been mayor, a post he was first elected to when
he was twenty-four.

He was a chirpy, busy little guy; when I told him about the TV
reporter getting snapshots of himself in front of those people in the
wreckage of their lives, he smiled the irritation away.

He said, "What really amazed me was, we were a big story in Denver
at noon. Then Denver gets a baseball franchise, and at five o'clock we
don't exist anymore."

And he said, "We've had the governor's office call and all that, with
condolences, which is nice. But on the other hand they remind you of
all the other disasters, which worries you. It's maybe a way of saying
there isn't any money, and you're on your own.

"Still, the local help's been amazing. Next morning—that night,
even—we had every fire department within fifty miles of here coming
in with crews and rescue units. The City of Scottsbluff brought in
barricades, so we could block off roads—see, we're just a little dinky
town, all we've got is a '52 Chevy farm truck—and that's our *new* truck,
we just got it two years ago. The other one was forty-something."

The local motels had all offered beds; the water companies were all
bringing in water. People were sending in everything from payloaders
to toothpaste. "And I tell you, there's been food everywhere. It's a city
worker's dream—coffee and doughnuts all the time."

We got in the city pickup, and went round to Mike Nuss's place.
Around us, the streets were a slow crawl of trucks like refugee carts,
loaded up with every imaginable thing as they made their slow way
through the sightseers. As he drove Kevin said, "I can't imagine the
whole country hasn't been in by now. Still, I guess I've never seen
anything like it either. I hope I never do again, that's for sure."

Mike Nuss's dad, Bill, was working with a friend in Mike's backyard,
trying to save a cherry tree that had been split through at the fork of the
branches; they were winching it tight back together with a wire brace.

Right now, Bill had one particular regret. "We were supposed to be
at Oklahoma City this morning. Mike was in a World Championship
Livestock Auctioneer contest, and he's a good one, he had a chance—
and now we ain't gone. And I feel sorry for him, 'cause every year you
get older, and the new ones come up . . . He was in the top ten this year,
no doubt."

Another of Mike's talents was music; he had a country & western band. Bill pointed at a garage by the yard; it had one wall down, two teetering, and the roof clean gone. "There was a van in there with seven thousand dollars of musical equipment in it—and all it did was blow out a taillight. Yet it blew a twenty-foot boat off its trailer, carried it a block, and set it down right behind that van in the yard here. This whole yard," he said, "was just all full of people's houses."

On the other side of the house, the life jacket from the boat hung forty feet up in the debarked skeleton of a Chinese elm.

"You can't imagine," said Bill, "how things can fly so fast, and land up where they do."

System Tree Care arrived from Gering to take down the shattered elm out front. A guy got in the bucket, the crane arm raised him up there, and with a chainsaw he started bringing down the bare branches from the top, chunk by chunk. When one piece fell to the lawn, someone pointed at it and said, "Will you look at that?"

It was bedded with nails, driven deep into it like darts in a board.

And everywhere around now, on the third day after the tornado hit Minatare, there was a feeling of intense industry rising from the debris. People were cleaning yards, men were out on roofs sealing them back up; tree firms and carpenters and glaziers and plumbers came and went, with insurance men among them working fast to get the checks out to pay for it. Bill Nuss and his friend worked to save his son's cherry tree.

There was a guy who'd just driven to California for his vacation, taken three days doing it; then he'd turned right around, and driven straight back in two.

Because this is *our town*.

Jacki Johns stood on crutches on Mike Muss's front lawn. The lawn was grey, covered in a dried-out coat of loft insulation. Jacki was thirty-three, a strong, good-looking woman with long black hair—though her color was a tad more pale than it might normally be. She'd been in the hospital thirty-six hours; she'd gotten out the morning before.

On Sunday afternoon she'd been at a picnic; they'd first heard a tornado warning at, she thought, about four-thirty. Then about five, the first one came. She said, "We watched it bounce back and forth on the hill . . ."

I asked what it looked like.

"I don't know how to explain it—just a column of wind, with a bunch of dirt swirling in it. It was black, scary—but kind of . . . I'd never seen a tornado before, and I always wanted to see one. Not *be* in one—but it was kind of neat. Scary, 'cause it was kind of close too. Then it whipped back up. Two of our kids were with some friends, so we went looking for them, then it started hailing really bad. We took the pickup to put it in the garage, right over there . . ."

Mike Nuss's house was on the north side of Minatare; Highway 26 ran east to west across the top of the town. Jacki's house—what was left of it—was in the field on the other side of the highway.

"Right over there," she said. "It's not there anymore, but it was, one time . . . Anyhow, we had one of our kids with us, our eldest son, and I was getting out of the truck with him. Greg, my husband, he went out of the garage, and the next thing he says is just, Get the hell out of here. And when I came out of the garage, the tornado was right there—right in the field by the house."

I asked what this second one looked like.

"Actually, it kind of looked like a bubble. There was so much rain and hail, and it was like a bubble in the middle of all that, kind of greyish-brown. And it was very dark all about, with big hail, golfball-sized hail . . ."

Didn't that hurt?

She laughed. "At the time I didn't even feel it. I was just worried about that tornado."

How big was it?

"Huge. It was huge. I couldn't even tell you . . . That was all I saw, that tornado, and it was huge, coming right at us. It was maybe two hundred yards from us—and we just ran, I mean *ran*—mostly focusing on a place to hide, only there wasn't any place. So we just hit the ground, laid on the ground—face in the weeds, pretty much. My husband laid over my son, he had a hand over his head and a hand over mine, and we just hung on. All you could hear was cracking wood and wind, very loud wind, and things just crashing into things. Greg stuck his hands up trying to protect his head from all the sand and dirt and hail—there wasn't a moment when something wasn't hitting you—and this sleeping bag flew into his hands. So he pulled that down to cover us, so we wouldn't get sandblasted so bad. . . . I got hit by a couple of things, once in the leg, once in the shoulder. I don't know what hit me."

I asked how long it lasted.

"It was no more than thirty seconds, a minute; it seemed like forever, but I don't think it was that long. All I could hear was just terrible wind—and the thing I remember was wood popping and snapping, the house just breaking apart . . ."

They were twenty yards from the house. The roof of the garage landed ten feet away from them.

Afterwards, they ran for shelter in what was left of the house. But with the roof gone, and the rain pouring down, the ceilings started caving in on the dining room and living room; Greg poked holes with a chair in the hall ceiling so that wouldn't come down on them too, then went to find help.

Jacki said, "It was about then I realized I had a chunk of my leg missing. It's pretty much a gash, down to the bone, cut the muscle in two, and there's a big chunk just gone; I was in surgery two hours, maybe, I don't know. And I got a hairline fracture in the shoulder blade—with a nice bruise, I mean purple. My son says it looks like I got hit by a baseball bat. Which is pretty much what happened, I guess."

I asked how she felt now.

She said, "I'm glad I'm alive. I'm very glad I'm alive. I'm stiff and I'm sore, and I'm taking one day at a time."

Then she said, "I don't think it's sunk in. I don't think it dawns on me that I'll never live in my house again—that when I heal up, I can't just go home.

"But we're gonna make it. I don't think I'll be running any races for a while . . . but we got family to stay with, and we've got lots of people have volunteered us places to live, and brought in food and stuff—people we don't even know. It's great."

She said, "I wouldn't live any place but a small town."

I asked if they'd figured what they'd do; would they rebuild?

"I don't know. We haven't decided. Probably not. I think we'll maybe buy another house here—'cause that's an old, old house, it's thirties, it's been there a long, long time. So it stood up pretty good."

It was down to little more than a couple of walls, the roof clean gone, the interior gutted.

She said, "We lived there four years, and we'd pretty much got it fixed up how we wanted it." Then she laughed, with a determined good humor. "Now it looks like it did when we bought it."

So I asked how she felt about the weather now, and this storm country she lived in.

She said, "The weather here this spring has been really strange . . . I know last night when the wind came up, I got very nervous. I'll be more conscious of it, I guess—but I don't think I'd ever leave here."

. . .

Going into his house, I found Mike Nuss in his living room with Jane Kelly from the state governor's western office. The room looked superficially okay, albeit strewn with broken glass from the windows, and matted and smeared with a fungal mess of insulation.

And the mayor was in Alaska; so auctioneer and country singer Mike Nuss, since forty-eight hours before the tornado hit town, was the acting mayor. Or, as he put it, "The very inexperienced acting mayor."

He was a courteous and good-looking man, fair-haired, tall, and in good trim—and he was, plainly, a good deal more acute than he made out. With Kelly there, his answers to my questions were sheathed in unforced but politic tact.

He said, "Normally all the acting mayor has to do is show up twice a month and pay the bills, deal with somebody's dog complaints . . . but I want to stress the help I'm getting, I'm getting an awful lot of good help. The Red Cross, the government agencies, it's all very friendly; they don't tell us what to do, they just show us ways to do things.

"Then there's the law enforcement—those boys had a big job to do, controlling the spectators, screening people, keeping it cordoned off at night to prevent looting. 'Cause there was no street lighting . . . and not everybody here is old honest country Joe, I can tell you that. You think that, you'll have your pocket picked in no time."

His house was bang in the strike zone, a spacious bungalow just down from the highway. I asked him what it had been like to go back to it through the wreckage, after the tornado had gone through.

He said, "All I had on was a pair of shorts and tennis shoes, I'd been mowing the lawn, so I was freezing to death. I climbed through the mess to get in here, over all the debris, to get some clothes; then the fire department came and told me to get out, and we had . . . well, we had a little altercation then. I said it was my house and if it was going to collapse on me, that was my problem . . . I guess I wasn't thinking too straight just then. And they stayed, and they made me get out."

But what did he think, when he first saw his house? Compared to the pulped wrecks round about, it looked relatively unscathed . . .

"The first thing I thought was, What do we do first? It looked better than I thought it would, given what all else I could see. And right now, at first glance you think, We got carpeting, we got paneling, we got a roof, hey—let's go.

"But then you look closer and all the walls are shifted off true by an inch, or more. It's like the whole house had a hernia, it's like everything got sucked in, then blown back out again. You can see how it's blown all the glass from the windows in—but all the drapes are hanging out. And it blew the loft hatch up—but then it sucked all the insulation down out of there, blew it all over the house, and outside. There's not enough left up in there to wad a shotgun; I think most of it ended up in my van out front. And the steering wheel's egg-shaped. How did it do that?"

The horn had been sucked out of the center of the steering wheel; there was just a hole there, with the wires trailing out. No one had found the horn either, it was just gone. The interior of the van was caked with the fibrous grey fuzz of the insulation; the vehicle was dented all over, with a window or two blown out. "But," he said, "you can still drive it."

At another house, there was a wooden post fired into a concrete wall like a bullet. The impact had been so unimaginably abrupt that there were virtually no cracks in the wall; the post was simply planted there.

Mike said he'd found a plastic Pennzoil bottle with a stick blown through it so tight, it hadn't leaked a drop.

There was a garage where three walls and the roof were gone—yet on the remaining wall, sets of circular saws and wrenches still hung in the sun on their little nails, in descending order of size, as if nothing had happened at all.

In Mike's living room all the furniture was shifted about, and all the glass blown in—he said, "If you'd have been in here, you'd have been chewed right up"—yet the pictures on the wall were all still hanging exactly straight. Books in the bookcase were untouched.

"I had a garbage bag with baseballs and softballs and gloves in it, right here on the step. And it was still all there, bar just one glove—and that had gone fifteen yards into the back garage. It's as if in the low pressure, some things just . . . they just *floated away.*"

Then he explained how Minatare's trash was collected by a private firm, and how the firm had fifty or sixty dumpsters round the town— double bins that would weigh maybe 250 pounds empty, and 1,000 full. So the guy from the firm came to check them Monday morning, and three were missing; missing from different places all over a five-block area, one here, one three blocks off, the other five blocks off from that. Yet they found them three quarters of a mile off, on the other side of Dick Nerud's place—*within fifteen feet of each other.*

Mike said, "I always wondered what it'd be like. You see it on TV. . . . I guess now you get a pretty good understanding of what other people go through. Still, we're talking disaster here, I know—but you just talked to Jacki, and she's the worst-injured person here. And frankly, that's a miracle."

He'd had the city building inspector over, and his own contractor, and they both agreed. His house was totalled.

And these weren't the best of times for Minatare and its nine hundred or so people to begin with. One of the reasons Kevin Misner ran for mayor at twenty-four was that "our business survival rate isn't real good"; he'd thought the place needed a change. And Bonnie Kaufman worried about hanging on to their school; she worried whether people would rebuild now—or just pack in and move out to the bigger towns of Scottsbluff and Gering ten miles west, where they'd have doctors and drug stores, and better facilities all round.

Mike said in the early eighties in particular, "We saw a lot of bankruptcies, a lot of hard-pressed people . . . a lot of people going, I don't know—close to off the deep end."

So I said how it seemed to me that in the heart of America, people in small towns were up against the weather, and the market—up against inexorable, uncontrollable forces in a battle many of those small towns were now losing.

And I mentioned how people say tornadoes sound like freight trains; how Jim Keller said those small towns probably would die, because that was history, that was economics—and you don't want to stand in front of the freight train . . .

Mike Nuss said, "Well, he might say that, because he's driving the freight train. He might have a different idea if he was standing on the tracks, he might have a different idea then . . . but this is America. This is a free enterprise system. And the guys who are most intelligent, the guys who are most constructive, the guys who are most *aggressive*—those are the guys who get to drive the train."

While the rest of the people just persist, I suggested, as best they can, stubborn and proud, raised in an attitude that says, when calamity strikes, Don't Give Up.

I asked, was that America?

"I don't know whether it's America, or if it's just human beings. Sometimes we get skeptical, with all the negative things, all the bad things in the news . . . but this has made me a believer. It's not just Americans, it's people—people like to help people. All the kindness there is here . . . I'm sure in your country it'd be the same."

. . .

"That first one was so long and skinny, I never seen one like it. It was gorgeous, actually, if you can think of something that destructive as gorgeous."

Annette Heussmann was a big, smiley blonde who came to interview me at Harry's for the *Scottsbluff Star-Herald* ("English author including last week's devastating storm in book about heartland"). Naturally, I interviewed her right back.

She said, "The thing that kept us from picking up bodies after this was that first one being on the ground so long, so people were alerted. One of the Red Cross guys timed it at 22½ minutes, and it stayed in one place 90 percent of that time. Then it bounced west, east, then shot off back west; it covered a lot of ground, when it finally decided to move. Then it hit the bank of a canal; we never saw the tail go up, it just . . . it just broke up, somehow.

"We were on the county road two miles north of town, and about then we got hailed on, horribly heavy hail, couldn't see anything—so we came back to 26, to go to the Stonegate Road to Lake Minatare. We'd met a patrolman who said it started up that way, so we were looking for damage photos up there. But then we were two miles north again, and again we were getting hailed on; and my friend Cindy that was with me said, 'You don't get paid enough to do this to your pickup.' So we turned back around.

"We came back to 26, and turned west to go home to Melbeta. We'd probably been on 26 ten, fifteen seconds—and Cindy was watching the cloud 'cause we were afraid of another one coming, particularly with the hail we were still in—and it started to form and she said, 'Oh my . . .'

"Before she got 'God' out it was already down, and we were right in the edge of it. In the truck. I thought, we can either bail out here and hit the ditch, turn and try to outrun it east, or try and cut on past the edge of it going west. So that last is what I did. I was going seventy-five trying to get through it, and it was a matter of seconds before we couldn't see anything other than water just swirling round the hood of the truck, everything was grey, all you could see was water; it was kind of like being in a blender. I was afraid if we stopped and opened the doors, we'd just be sucked straight out, so I risked keeping going.

"Right before we came out I remember seeing one of those black diamond signs about twelve, eighteen inches from the side view mirror—I was on the median of the highway. I thought, God, I don't even know what I'm driving on here. Then the first thing we saw when we came out from the greyness was the deputy's car and the sheriff's Suburban, both headed for Minatare with the lights flashing. At that point we slowed down."

She said, "I had to decide then whether to go back and get pictures, but we were so scared, we just wanted to go home. I'm an emergency medical technician so I should have gone in anyhow, I figured there was bound to be injuries . . . but I was afraid, I just wanted to lie down.

"So, well, I took the chicken's way out and went home—then I got clothes and ID, and went back. I'd have got there by six, or soon after. And I thought, by then, I wasn't shaken up by it. But there was a firefighter directing traffic at the Legion Hall where I parked, and I walked within two feet of him—and he said, 'Hey, what're you doing?' It was a guy I'd been dating for four years, and I didn't even acknowledge him . . . I realized I was shook up then. And he was real concerned; when he heard what we'd done, he gave me a major lecture about that. Then . . . well, I guess I just went to work. On autopilot, really. Talking, taking pictures."

But she shouldn't have done it, should she? In a car in a tornado . . .

"It all happened so fast. At the time all I could think was, I hope I made the right choice. It only sank in when I lay down to sleep that night. In Melbeta we had no power or water, and feeling how grubby I was . . . I just lay there in bed and thought, My God, I could have been killed."

Then she said if it had happened in her little town, Melbeta, population 116 . . .

"There's more homes been damaged here than there are homes in Melbeta altogether. If that had hit Melbeta, that would have been the end of that town. Forever. 'Cause it's got no school, just a post office, a church, a welding shop, a gas station, an agrichemicals dealer—that's it. We'd have had no reason to rebuild there. Melbeta would be gone."

History.

At 8:30 on Wednesday evening, seventy-five hours after the tornado hit town, they had a meeting in the Minatare school gym. It was closed to the press; it was for victims only, to let them know who was who, and which agency was doing what, and to ask if there was anything that anyone could do better. If necessary, said one of the rescue workers, it could be an out-and-out bitch session—just so long as people knew that things were in motion, and they weren't on their own, and they could get things off their chest.

So in a spartan, echoing, chair-clacking room, maybe sixty or seventy people gathered together, young and old, and sat waiting.

The rescue workers sat at a line of desks along a dais at one end of the gym; Mike Nuss opened the proceedings with a well-pitched little speech that put the long rank of strangers beside him in the best possible light. "I couldn't have done anything without these people. As a matter of fact, I haven't done very much at all."

I don't believe that for a minute, but there you go.

A large and earnest Red Cross lady got up and described all the services they could offer: food, clothing, housing help, medical help, occupational supplies and equipment. "Our assistance is an outright gift, because the people of this fine country contribute to enable us to do this."

Jane Kelly from the governor's office said, "Our role is to keep informed. We can't do very much at the moment, but somewhere down the line we will." Carefully, she mentioned other disasters.

Sherry Blaha talked about volunteer coordination, and explained the security concerns that made their ID tags necessary; she said by tomorrow they'd get permanent tags, and then they'd not have to register every day any more.

Dennis Kumm explained how the damage assessments got passed up to state level, and apologized if it seemed to be taking a while, but they had to get it right.

One by one, they were all lightly, politely applauded.

Kevin Misner got up to talk about when they'd have their water back and potable, but Mike Nuss held him up. "Let me interrupt you a minute there, Kevin. Folks of Minatare, you got a good man here."

Then a mental health official gave a little speech about stress, and stress management. He said, "All the emotions associated with tornadoes are normal."

He also said, somewhat obscurely, that he wore a lot of different hats, prompting the balding patrolman Dennis Richard to say, "Folks, I *have* to wear a hat—otherwise I get sunburn." Then he explained how they were running the security side of things.

When they were all done Mike said, "Well, folks, we didn't gather here for everybody to give us a hand." He told them the floor was theirs.

So people started asking when they were going to get their cable TV back. . . . You got hit by a tornado, and you're worried about TV?

Only in America.

It got more serious after that. Someone complained that the radar hadn't picked up the second tornado; that sparked a low little murmur of grumbling round the room.

Sherry tried to explain that tornadoes are unpredictable.

Yes, but was it two? Or was it the same one going round and coming back at us?

This was an issue that had been tossed back and forth all round the town for three days. Was the second one just the first, looping back for a second go—or had there really been two different ones?

One of the law enforcement people told how in Grand Island in 1980, there'd been five. "They went every way possible, sometimes three of them in the same area at the same time. They're totally unpredictable; you can't say *what* they'll do."

But here in Minatare, there'd been two tornadoes. And they needed to be told that; they needed to know what had *happened* to them.

And what they did next—when they got round to thinking about it—was their business. So they asked practical questions about utilities, and trees, but I got the feeling you'd have trouble finding anyone willing publicly to ask for *help*.

Mike told them the streets were going to be swept off at six the next morning. "So please, move your cars if you can. Also, demolition—we're going to request, no, we're going to *insist* that you come to the city, and sign a demolition form first. It limits liability on your part, and on ours, and it informs us that you're going to do it. Because it's going to create a bunch of confusion, if you have your cousin's loader just start knocking your house down. Someone went at it last night, and they tore up a water main."

Help? Hell, no—these people were getting their insurance checks and getting on with it already.

The meeting settled down to a bit of quiet back-and-forth about lost property—or, to be more precise, vanished property. People were missing precious things, sentimental things, practical things—from jewelry, to saucepans.

Mike asked, "Is Munro still here? I was going to tell him, he got his boat out of my yard yesterday—he can come and get his life jacket now too."

He was calm and unassuming, wearing boots and jeans, T-shirt and baseball cap. For a man whose house had been parted wall from wall, and who said he didn't know what he was doing, he was doing it extraordinarily well.

He knew exactly when to end it. He said, "If you want to stick around and visit, or ask any questions, just go on ahead."

The gym quickly emptied, and the people of Minatare went away about their business.

It was about ten; the air was bug-ridden, close and muggy. Slapping at mosquitoes we stood about outside, and Kevin talked happily about the doughnut bonanza. "We've had cops coming from miles around to do their carbo-loading."

Chris Overman told how he'd heard in Scottsbluff, they'd all been out on their roofs watching, and videotaping. "Gee! There's a tornado tearing up Minatare!"

"They weren't just watching," said Kevin, "they were calling us up. You know, 'Hey, how's it going? There's a tornado!' You say, 'No kidding.' So they say, 'What are you doing?' And you say, 'Well, right now I'm just crawling down this little hole in the closet here, and could you hang up please?' My brother even called me from the golf course."

Mike introduced me to his cousin Walter, and to Walter's wife, whose name I'm afraid I forget. She said an odd thing; she said, "The first one looked so mild when it came down, it was *hypnotizing* . . . then it hit the dirt and, you know, just vicious, then."

They'd been taking their son to a church program; they were parking the truck under some pine trees to protect it from the hail, and they had no idea at that point another tornado was coming in. They were on the east side of the park . . .

"Then the wind really got up, and the trees in the park were laying over at ninety degrees. I happened to glance in my rearview mirror, and this fifteen-foot camper was just kind of sliding down the street behind us. About that point the pickup started to feel buoyant, like a boat in water—you could feel that in your stomach, I tell you. So we decided to get out, I thought it was going to go. And we were almost driven into the pine trees, we just grabbed one tree and hung on; we must have been a few minutes just hanging on there, in a wind like you wouldn't believe. We were soaked, just drenched—and somewhat rattled too."

Mike said happily, "How d'you like that? People who went through a tornado hanging on to a tree. That should about wrap up your story."

I asked them what that wind had sounded like.

Walter said, "People say it sounds like a freight train, whatever. I couldn't hear nothing but hail, really."

His wife grinned and said, "I couldn't hear nothing but me yelling."

We stood talking there, with the bugs busy about us in the hot, thick night air. And I thought, well, wouldn't you know it . . .

Far off in the southeast lightning popped and flared yet again in the storm country sky.

It doesn't ever let up.


### Trans-Nebraska

I left Sterling at noon, running east on 6 out of Colorado into southern Nebraska. The radio said corn prices were tumbling on forecasts of cooler temperatures next week—but it wasn't cool today. In McCook the signs outside the banks read 100. I thanked God and Red Nose Sam for the air in my truck, and drove on through the wide and glaring land.

The Plains marry subtlety with mass; there's so much space that every little feature is simultaneously prominent, and yet barely visible. I passed a dry creek, a gully, a grain bin, a solitary tree, a piece of discarded machinery, pigs in a mud yard, cattle at a trough, a windmill, a barn, some unincorporated little outpost with a gas pump and a welding shop and an elevator by the railtrack, a guy moseying down the shoulder towing some great flopping, elaborate hunk of farm machinery—and each thing, as I passed, was just a speck of definition on the unending earth.

The road shimmered, heat rising like silver steam off the blacktop; the green land hummed, lying baked and still. For a while I felt tranquil, disconnected, a dot of perfect motion on the glazed ribbon of the road. A wonderful song told of a man meeting cowboys from outer space; they ride interstellar stallions, their bandanas caked with stardust. He asks where they hail from, so they get out a star chart: It's past this exit on the cosmic interstate, they tell him, the biggest place in outer space—a whole wild world whose name is Texas.

But mostly the songs were sadder than that. A woman sang how she had so many holes in her life, so many holes that if she piled them all together, she'd fall in there forever . . . and as the miles slipped by, that sadness began to mix with a rising fatigue. The heat blurred the edges of the world, and the wide land became oppressive.

East of Atlanta, Nebraska, for four or five miles, the verge between the road and the train track had ignited, burning away to black smears of ashy dirt. Low flames licked and rippled in the yellow grass; smoke drifted across the highway. Here and there, fire crews played hoses over the smouldering earth.

Precious water: I passed blue rainbows flashing in veils of fine spray from the slow-turning irrigation arcs . . .

Center-pivot irrigation was born in Nebraska. In the ten years from 1972, with a capital investment of over a billion dollars, corn production in the state rose by 44 percent.

But the flow of the Platte River—once a thing of dazzling strangeness to the hundreds of thousands trekking west on the Oregon Trail along its shores, an inland sea in the springtime inches deep and miles wide—has been reduced in this century by 70 percent.

In the first thirty-four days I'd driven 3,082 miles. In the past five I'd driven 1,562 more; I was adding another 409 to that tally today. So maybe I was tired, I don't know, or maybe the smoke got in my eyes—but around about here's where I cried to the country music on the radio, when the DJ said it was going-home time on a Friday afternoon, and started playing songs in praise of America.

I sang along as the road rolled by with a tribute to the working man, the auto worker in Detroit and the steel worker in Pittsburgh, the wheat farmer in Kansas and the coal miner in Virginia. I sang along with Randy Travis, with a song of desperately apt naïveté straight from the Reagan-Bush speechwriter's canon, a song proclaiming that if you could see what was wrong and you could do what was right, then you would be *a point of light.*

I sang along and I cried as I drove, because I had a moment here where I felt sorrow more strongly than ever at the big hope of America's ideal, its ambition to be a field of dreams for all; a moment where I felt bitter sorrow at the gulf between that and the way it really is—the people struggling to stay afloat in their struggling little towns as the sky turns black and the wind gets up, as the small farms go under and the water table falls, as the cities catch fire on the horizon in their violence and division, and the deficits and the murder rates and the paranoia all rise . . .

America—a country good enough and bad enough to make any man weep to the soundtrack of its deluded heart, on a green and burning highway in Nebraska.

.  .  .

In the evening I picked up a warning from a singularly affable state patrolman named R. Hanneman. Luckily, at the time, I'd slowed to sixty to light a cigarette; I told him, of course, that while lighting it, I must inadvertently have accelerated to that speed.

"So strictly speaking, you weren't in control of your vehicle," he said, and smiled.

I didn't tell him I was barely in control of myself anymore.

He said it'd take me two, two and a half hours to get to Nebraska City, "If you drive like you're supposed to. Take care now."

The town he stopped me outside of was called Friend.

And it was the only time I got stopped. That Ford must have been a Stealth pickup.

East of Lincoln, a trend that had been gathering in the landscape for some time became definite, a new reality in the day's last gold of swelling, dipping little hills—and there were trees, so many trees . . . It was gorgeous, it was sylvan, it was positively bosky. I was in the Midwest.

And darkness was falling—but I was, by now, gone dark in the head myself, cackling hysterically at the radio as the road bucked and rolled. Every time the "Hooked On Phonics" ad came on I bawled it out, matching the manic emphasis of the voice-over word for word:

> DID you KNOW there are only FORTY-FOUR SOUNDS in the EN-GLISH LANGUAGE! FORTY-FOUR! And WHEN you KNOW these FORTY-FOUR SOUNDS, called PHONICS, you can learn to READ and SPELL almost ANYTHING! We've TAKEN these FORTY-FOUR SOUNDS and SET them to MUSIC!

At the end, you're told to CALL 1-800-A-B-C-D-E-F-G!

But how can you, I screamed, if you're illiterate?

I drove into the darkening evening. The last light in the sky behind me over Lincoln was another crazed opera of rose and tangerine, a kind of atmospheric version of the Fountain Lodge Motel . . . then it was gone, and it was night.

My eyes were throbbing; my back was one long stiff ache. I stopped in Palmyra, an up-and-down little town tucked in a tree-smothered dale, all steep-sloping streets and basketball hoops—but no motel. I went on, to the Mustang Motel in Syracuse—and it was full.

So I ended up in Nebraska City after all. Exhausted and thirsty in the hot and sticky night, I found Ron & Nean's on Main Street. On the TV behind the bar, Johnny Carson was holding a large frog. He said, "Oh boy, doesn't he look like Jim Bakker?"

I got a Miller Genuine Draft (Best Beer in the Heart of America), then checked out where I'd landed, after those 409 increasingly mind-gone miles.

There was the barmaid, and the local drunk at the bar; there were two guys in seed caps at one table, and three girls and one guy at another. There were five booths, a Budweiser clock, five stools at a meal counter by the door, and a long thin mural of a mountain scene on the wall opposite the bar. . . .

I left after midnight, and got a sandwich in the Kwik Stop across the street from the Apple Inn. A fat girl buying gas offered me a beer; I followed her outside to a vanload of Nebraska City Jaycees on a late-night joy ride. And they were all delighted to give me a beer, except for the drunk one in the passenger seat.

He said, "Why don't you go back where you came from?"

# 7.

# The White Tide

In northwest Nebraska, on the night of May 10, Moni Hourt came home to Crawford from Chadron. A bright and lively woman in her early forties, she'd been studying for several years to become an English teacher at the college there; that Friday night, she'd just finished up some classes she'd been taking.

Her home's a few miles out of Crawford, on a dirt road past a little farm with an old red barn, then up a short rise. The house sits on a low knoll above the Chicago & North Western train track; the White River's beyond that. When I got there, Moni poured me iced tea; then she told me what happened that Friday night, when she tried to get home.

"I couldn't get here. Down where the barn is, it had flooded across the road, and there was a car stuck there already. I was coming to get my horses, 'cause they were in the river bottom; it was hailing really bad, and they'd said there was flooding, and I could hear the river, but to be honest, at that point I wasn't too concerned, I just wanted the horses out. So I went back to town to get my husband Joe and the four-wheel drive, and we got here and he said, I know the horses will be up out of this. There was nothing we could do.

"So we walked down to the track and looked at the river—and it was fifty times as big as it had ever been, I'm not joking. Trees, trees as big as this table, were floating . . . no, not floating, there was no floating involved—they were snarling and snapping, they were just *shoving* down that river. It was this dirty brown river that I'd never seen before, it was so much wider, so much larger . . .

"At that point a railroad car came up the tracks and went past us, he said it was flooding down below; then suddenly he came back the other way just as fast as that little yellow pickup could go. He never said nothing, he never even honked, he just whooshed right by down the rails. And my nineteen-year-old son said, 'Dad, what is that noise?'

"You could hear it like . . . like when the cattle move through the underbrush, snapping, echoing. We looked up the track and there was this great, muddy, chocolate milk–colored wall of water coming straight down it right at us, about four feet tall. Joe said we'd better run.

"There were ditches five feet deep either side of the tracks, we went down, and up; and the water followed us, it *followed* us—it was like it was trying to catch us, like it was *a thing*—it was coming up the hill behind us, just licking up that hill, surging, *licking* . . . I was fascinated, I kept stopping. What a klutz. Joe was getting real unhappy with me, real excited. But I just could not believe this was happening, in a country that gets fifteen inches of rain. Water is precious here, you pray for it . . .

"We got up to the yard and it hit the barns and the chicken houses, then it split around us. It filled the corrals, it got within five feet of the house, it went into Kenny's alfalfa field to the west of us, it filled the gully on the east side; we were surrounded. Joe said we had to get out of there. We drove to the bottom of the drive, but it was four feet deep on the road there, we couldn't get out. So we cut the fence and went across the alfalfa field, we just gunned it across there. The truck tried to die on us halfway, the water was getting up the doors by then, but we got across, higher up the hill to our neighbor's place.

"Even then, I still couldn't understand that it was dangerous. And you got to understand that in this country, you do not drive across your neighbor's alfalfa field, especially at this time of year—*you do not do that,* it's not *courteous,* to beat up on someone's life like that. So I was standing there apologizing. I mean, the pickup's dying, the hail's hailing, the river's flooding, your house is surrounded by water—and I'm saying, Kenny, I'm sorry, we drove across your alfalfa field. Crazy.

"But I wasn't the only one that was incredulous. The sale barn people were warned that the water was coming, so they moved the cattle out of the barns into the pens—but that didn't make no difference. And people living on the river at the city park didn't move. We got into town and told people about the flooding, and they just smiled at us. There's an old lady down at Whitney, she said she had 150 years of history in her head, and the White River wasn't ever going to flood. So people really didn't perceive this."

Then she told me what happened to her horses.

She said, "Our little mare swam and fought its way three and a half miles to Fort Rob—but it broke her hind leg. My daughter had to sit and hold her head while they put her down. She learnt to ride on that horse. And she had a colt six months old; he was on a hillock, and he was so scared. And we had another old horse, we found him submerged in the mud. He was dead.

"I want to show you the emotions of this thing. These horses are minor, compared to the whole sum of what happened here, but this is the *emotion* . . . My daughter asked some construction workers if they'd seen an old sorrel with a blaze on his forehead. Now these guys weren't from here. And one of them said, 'Well, he *used* to have a blaze on his head. There's a dead old horse in the mud over there.' And we *love* our horses in this country. So Buffy cried. It took four hours to cover him up. And it seems minor, but it isn't—I mean, people lost things. They lost *parts of their lives*.

"But this community fought back from the fire two years ago, and they're ready to fight again. Take the rodeo. That's the most important thing in this community, it brings thousands and thousands of dollars in here—and the rodeo ground was destroyed. So, fine—we're going to move it to Fort Rob. We're going to call for volunteers, and two days from now we'll have a rodeo ground out there. It won't be so good, but it'll be there.

"And that rodeo will happen."

The fire that started in Fort Robinson State Park on July 8, 1989, was the biggest in recorded Nebraska history. For weeks beforehand, temperatures had been 100, or higher; in the previous six months, there'd been only five inches of rain. On July 8, the temperature hit 110; then the lightning came, and forty-eight thousand acres in and out of the park went up in smoke.

To get it under control took three days round the clock. In a whirl of volunteered labor and donations at the food hall one fireman joked, Could they get him some marshmallows and some wieners—and a very, very long stick.

Moni's husband Joe was one of the firemen who fought the fire, so she rode his truck with him, then wrote an account of the event for the local paper, the *Crawford Clipper*. Among the groups whose contributions she acknowledged were the local bikers, who rode all around and even into the flames where the fire trucks couldn't get to, herding cattle out of the way, picking locations for fire breaks and back fires, and generally acting as the eyes and ears of the operation.

And in the same way that she'd worried about Kenny's alfalfa, she reported one of these bikers saying, "I kept worrying about cutting fence lines. Finally a rancher came by, and I told him I needed to get through the fence. He gave me a pair of wirecutters . . ."

Two years later, the tree loss from that fire contributed to the speed of the water's gathering in the White River. One guy joked to me that they were going to have a Crawford T-shirt saying I'VE SEEN FIRE, AND I'VE SEEN RAIN.

Moni said she'd been saying of her teaching course for years, "I'm going to graduate come hell or high water."

Crawford got both—and on the morning of May 11, in borrowed clothes, Moni Hourt graduated.

Crawford's seventy-five miles north of Scottsbluff; the drive up there on Highway 71 was wild and empty, uninterrupted by communal settlement of any kind. Every five or ten miles, I crested a wave in the road and a sudden great new sweep of grassland spread open before me, spring's rain-spurred green blanket veined with the brown fractures of gullies stretching off to the next ridge.

Under a shining dome of cirrus-streaked blue the land was luminous, potent and sad, rich with the ghosts of Sioux and Cheyenne, and the countless thousands upon thousands of buffalo . . .

The land changed about twenty miles south of Crawford. Rocky clefts and outcrops began fairly suddenly to get sharper, to become genuine hills; a coating of dark pines began to layer the land, breaking up the outlines into something almost cosy, after the implacable openness of the Plains. Then, past pale crags and dusty, steep little slopes, I came down between the wide arms of two ridges. To the east, there was the jagged stack of Pine Ridge itself—while to the west stood a butte whose ocher rock rose in the sunlight so smoothly, so abruptly, whose face was so trimly edged and joined, it looked more like some massive Inca fortress than any natural formation.

Crawford lay just beyond, between the ends of these two arms. It seemed a battered little place, lying defeated and breathless in a burning midday sun; bar signs hung tattered, peeling and weary over the bleached and glaring sidewalk. The Elite Cinema, opened in 1931, was closed, the awning rotting slowly away. Houses were for sale; here and there, closed businesses collected dust between whatever was left.

Before flood and fire ever came, the economics of the Plains in the eighties were already working their more steady curses out on Crawford. Like Boise City, it had lost one in seven of its people in the past decade.

The *Crawford Clipper* was closed—it opens only two and a half days a week—but the editor's number was posted in the doorway, so I called her, and asked who it might be good to talk to. Before she came up with Moni's name she said, "I'm trying to think of someone, but . . . they've all passed away."

I bought some postcards. The lady in the store picked one to show me and said, "That's what our fish hatchery looked like. Before the flood."

It was just a mud dump now.

I arrived in Crawford on the day lightning killed a spectator at the U.S. Open in Minnesota, and there were storms here too. I booked myself into the Fort Robinson campsite, then drove past the buffalo on the pine-dotted slopes up Smiley Canyon Road. Two heavy grey cloud caps were coming in from the west, spitting lightning, massive flattened toadstools on electric beds of rain, lids of fire and water over the raggedy jostle of the pine green hills. I felt like I could reach up and touch them. The leading edge came over me; the wind got up, whipping dried flood-silt in the valley below into whirling dust devils. The grass hissed and whistled, and the trees bent away.

I went back into town in the driving rain, and got a beer at O'Doherty's. When I remarked on the weather the barman said, "We've had more rain in a month than we'd normally get in a year. But then, normal—we haven't had a normal year for five or six years now."

Outside, the thunder rolled. A bunch of women came in, talking about "hellacious hail up by the Watson ranch." One of them, Rosemary Petersen, said the flood had totally rearranged the country out there. Her son, a patrolman, had shot video the next morning from the air—"and I couldn't believe it. It looked like the Missouri River, it was hundreds of yards across."

Normally, where it runs behind Moni Hourt's place, the White River is just a few feet wide.

Rosemary said, "The night it hit I was standing on the porch, and it sounded like the wind was coming up, but the trees weren't moving. It was the water. You could hear it hitting, wood smashing . . . It sounded like three freight trains."

All bearing down roaring together.

She said, "It's greatly affected our tourism traffic. Everybody thinks we're all washed away, but we're not. The thing is, the media . . . We're going to have to get to the press, and tell them we're still here."

I went in the morning to Dale McCroden's house. He was a highway patrolman, and had a copy of the tape Rosemary's son had shot; he and his wife Kim had their own morning-after footage too.

Dale ran the video. It showed trailers tipped on their sides in a debris-strewn park; the ground was a sheet of oozing mud, water still spilling across it. Cars lay overturned, brim-full of dully glistening muck. The carcasses of cows poked part-buried from the wet wreckage of the earth, belly-up among the shattered remnants of trees.

"At the sale barn," said Dale, "maybe 190 cows survived from 600. One stood stock-still for twenty-four hours after, then keeled over and died. They spent four days with rendering trucks, just picking up dead animals."

Kim's voice on the soundtrack sounded tearful. "This is what our city park looks like. What's left of it." Water poured over sodden tracts of mud.

"From a river," said Dale, "not as wide as this living room. I don't know what . . . Every time I look at this I shake my head. How wide that river went was unbelievable."

At the sale barn the high water line could be seen way above the tops of ground floor windows. The phrase, "What's left of it," recurred over and over on Kim's soundtrack, as she filmed one slime-coated scene of devastation after another.

"This is everybody trying to help Carl and Jane. This is the barn. What's left of it."

The tape shot from the air showed huge plains of silt thrown out over the land. Dale said, "Out east after Crawford the water was massive, stretching a quarter mile wide, or worse. We had friends downstream put their stuff up on cement blocks, then the water came through three feet high, at two in the morning. And cement blocks ain't high enough for that."

There was tape shot two weeks later, where Kim had stood in the same places all over again, and it didn't look a whole lot better. Water went on streaming over the rearranged land.

Damage estimates in the aftermath had risen from three, to six, to thirteen million . . . Kim said, "We've never had it happen here. Never.

But I tell you, if people say there's a storm coming—boy, you should see them move now."

When I said I'd been in Minatare she said, "We very rarely get tornadoes up here, 'cause of the buttes and everything. But I'm not going to say it's an impossibility. Not now."

And she had a theory for it. "Every time the space shuttle goes up, within five or six days we get one whale of a rainstorm. Now I don't know, but you watch. They send the shuttle up, something happens. And Kuwait . . ."

She said, "Something's affecting our air."

The Recovery Center by the town hall was a single room, dingy and file-packed, dotted with the obligatory takeout coffee cups. I found Jane Kelly from the Governor's Office there, with three or four other people; it was like we were on a disaster circus, a calamity tour . . .

She said Crawford and Minatare were totally different. Minatare was 95 percent insured, except for the crop damage; people with totalled homes were getting insurance checks right now. But here, no one had flood insurance, it was unforeseeable. So now, she said, "They're caught up in federal and state funding, and it's a maze."

The legislature had appropriated $1,800,000 for Crawford's recovery. But the damage assessment they had in the office stood at $12,262,855, and nearly half of that was to public facilities . . .

Crawford, in the meantime, couldn't be waiting on legislators. A guy from Civil Defense said, "People here had a damage assessment together in three days, in conditions you wouldn't believe, but they weren't sitting with their hands out waiting for the federal dollar. These are impressive people. We had to go and search people out that had damage, 'cause some of them here, they're too proud to ask for help."

Moni took me for a walk up the railroad behind her house.

The five-foot ditches on either side of the track that she'd scrambled away through that night were gone, filled near to level with the bed. As for the track, it was shifted clean off the bed, shoved away to one side; it was a tangled strip of junk, the rails buckled out, and all covered as far as you could see with the bleached remnants of trees tossed together in jumbled piles of dead wood.

Below, said Moni, the river had a whole new course. It now bypassed the rail bridges it had smashed, leaving them irrelevant and marooned;

whole tree trunks dangled off them, or lay washed on drifts of mud to the side, their roots damp thickets of shredded vegetation. The flood's wake was scattered all over with trunks and branches like bones.

The rail company said it had lost twenty miles of track, and forty-two bridges. It didn't look like they'd bother opening the line again . . . bang went more business for Crawford.

The city dam was smashed too, a ruin of ooze-smeared concrete that the water had pushed past like it was no more than a stone on the stream bottom. A big buttress leaned broken on its side behind it; one side wall lay sheared off and spun out of the water's path, left flat under a sheet of muck and flotsam.

To one side of the dam the flood had torn a huge, crescent-shaped chunk of earth out of a high, sandy bank; a fence fell like a piece of string into the void the sudden landslip had made, the posts hanging from the wire until they lay down in a tip of brown slop at the base.

It was estimated that getting the city's water supply properly restored would cost $2,600,000.

Crawford was, in short, a riverbed equivalent of what had happened to the northwest corner of Minatare. But tornadoes at least happen every year, you know they're out there—whereas this was an event you'd not expect more than once in every several hundred years. At one place upriver, half a normal year's rainfall had fallen *in two hours.* . . .

"In this country," said Moni, "you see a wheat field, and it's beautiful—and then the hail comes. So what do you do? You plant again. Because you can't live in this country unless you're prepared to fight, you can't live here unless you're prepared to be a total optimist, and always believe that tomorrow will be better than today.

"It's true that in the early eighties we had a lot of crashes here, ranchers, farmers; and it would kill you, to see these people who'd been the epitome of the success of this area declaring bankruptcy, and selling their herds. So it's not been good, but I wouldn't use *bad* to describe it, 'cause bad is terrible. And people have pulled themselves up by the bootstraps somewhat since then, so they'll do that again.

"Take the sale barn, that's real important to the town's economy. Now they need $175,000, but people have already pledged a good portion of that. Not officially, not on pieces of paper—you don't *need* pieces of paper in this country, it's done by handshake. So they'll be back.

"I'll give you another example. There was a rancher in Sioux County had cancer, and the insurance wouldn't cover him going to Omaha to try to get that treated. So he was going to die. And this is back when the farms were bust, there wasn't much money in the country out there—there's not many people out there either—but they raised ten thousand dollars in a day. And that man's still alive.

"Now they couldn't believe in Omaha that a community could do that, and it may be difficult to understand, with all the problems this country has economically. But there is such an *incredible* bond to these hills, to these people, to these *ideas*. I walk down the street and I talk to this guy and that, and I know their history; I know about their children who failed, and their children who succeeded, and *we're all here together*. We're here because we want to be, and because *we love where we're at*.

"Over the years I've talked to so many older people that have stayed here and succeeded; or maybe they've not succeeded—but they've stayed here, because they've got something they couldn't get someplace else. See, very few people *have* to be here, you can always move on—but we stay because we believe in it, we believe in optimism, that you *can* succeed, and that you *will* see tomorrow.

"So this whole thing now, it's no different to when somebody's grandmother came out here, and can you imagine? They came out here from back east where they had trees and nice houses with sedate parlors, they got off a train at the end of the line, which was generally Valentine—and all they could see was nothing. I've had women tell me their eyes ached, just looking for *something*.

"And I'd say, What d'you mean, something? And they'd say, Anything. Anything that wasn't nothing . . .

"But those women got in wagons, and they jolted and jammed out here, and they cooked food they weren't familiar with, and they dug houses into the ground out of dirt banks, and they stomped the floor down, and they put down doilies, and they *survived*.

"And that's what this country's about."

That evening I drove up Smiley Canyon Road again; buffalo cantered cumbrously away from the truck under skies of vermilion and cobalt, turquoise and tangerine. The stark buttes shone pink and gold among the pines.

The next day I talked to Kathy Reeves, the press information officer at the Recovery Center. She was a slim, strikingly attractive blonde of thirty-nine; she came originally from Iowa, but went to college at Chadron State—and, because of a man, she'd stayed here ever since.

"My poor mother," she smiled, "every time she comes across the Sand

Hills, it's, Why? Why? I grew up with rain and green grass and lots of trees, and rich black earth and cornfields, and a road every mile, and a town every eight . . . so it's different. But here I am."

It was the end of the afternoon, and she was the last person left in the office; outside, the sky was darkening, and threatening more rain. On a black-and-white TV on her desk a videotape played silently, showing water spilling over plains of greasy mud. It was, she said, to show to state senators—to show what had *happened* here.

The flood had destroyed the heart of the town—the park. Everything went on there, all year round, school functions, family reunions, dances, Fourth of July celebrations; it served as the rodeo ground, the ballpark, the golf course. . . . They were planning a clean-up there the next day, if it didn't keep raining and they had to put it off again.

Thunder rolled, deep in the dense indigo of the sky outside. . . . Moni, I said, had told me it could easily not rain for a year, once this was over.

Kathy said, "Oh yes, by the end of summer I expect we'll want rain. It'll be hot and dry, and the hot wind'll blow . . . who knows? But all this rain just now, it's depressing; we can't clean up, and we can't do our normal summertime stuff. See, I know people moan when it's dry, but we're sun addicts here really. I love the sun; when you've had a long cold winter, you need the sun."

All the same, the sun hadn't been enough to keep one in seven of Crawford's people . . .

"Well, it's hard to find stuff for young people to do. We don't have the money, and the older people don't want to bring in any manufacturing, any industry, any jobs . . . even the golf course, there was a lot of people against that. There's a lot of little old ladies that don't like golf, they'd rather have flower gardens in the park, I guess . . . but the school, even that has trouble getting money. I can't understand that. And all it leaves us is tourism, tourism's all we've got—and the flood's destroyed it."

In 1990, Fort Robinson pulled in nearly 300,000 visitors. In the Fort's campgrounds there were 170 electrical hookups; after the flood, about 40 were left. Tourist revenues were projected to fall that summer by at least a million dollars. . . .

"Outside this area they think, Flood, that's it. They think everything's gone—and it's my job to tell people it hasn't. I've been at it . . . well, one week. In fact, I didn't know it'd be my job to get the tourists back until last night."

She said, "It's funny. I planned on having this nice relaxing summer. I'd always worked, and I was going to spend time with the kids, but not now. I suppose I could have said no—but someone has to do it, and I'll give it a try. I've never had to do anything like this before—I just work at the school, with the pre-school special eds—but here I am. And I'm learning about journalists, I can tell you. And the government . . . but it's not all bad. It really isn't all bad."

Outside, the rain was falling heavier from grey banks of cloud tumbling in over town. I asked, did she look at the weather differently now?

"Every time you get a rain like this, you wonder . . . you don't know what's going to happen anymore. Well, I do know it's the end of tomorrow's clean-up; I know that much."

Heavy drops shattered on the concrete in the alley out back; thunder cracked and roared, as water ran thick yet again down the gutters of Crawford. How long, I asked, was it going to take them to get over all this?

"It's going to take a long time. And it'll never be the way it used to be—but I'm enough of an optimist to believe that when we're through, it'll be better. I know a lot of people don't agree with me, but with federal money, I think we'll get a lot of improvements we couldn't have had.

"As for the golf course, well, it was beautiful before, but so much has happened to it, it's going to be a real challenge now. I mean, we're talking some major sandtraps, right? It's cleared all the brush out from under the trees too, so it'll be easier to find your ball . . .

"I think," said Kathy Reeves, "a lot of good'll come out of this."

Which is the way these stayers think.

"We don't know any other way. You live here, that's how it is. And why should you question it? It's life."

Spray danced a yard high off the ground outside. On her desk the video silently, ominously played on, the water rushing in a white foaming tide over the dirty wreckage of the earth.

"White men think they're so smart. And then they carry their own snot about with them."

That was an old Cheyenne woman Moni'd talked with one time. She'd been talking with many old people, hoping one day to make a book of their stories—it'll be a book worth reading—and she'd come on an old Indian story that goes like this:

A deer is on a hillside. She sends her eyes ahead of her up the hill, and when her eyes get to the top of the hill, they look back. And then the deer wishes, looking down on herself with her blind sockets below, that she really was blind.

Because behind her on the Plains, her eyes can see a great white tide pouring in across the land. . . .

Red Cloud, chief of the Oglala Sioux, was a smart operator. In 1868, while the Brule leader Spotted Tail signed the Fort Laramie treaty pretty quickly, Red Cloud waited nearly six months before coming in, then haggled another month after that before he signed. What he got was, in effect, a political victory for the Indians: The whites had to close the Bozeman trail, and abandon their three forts along the length of it.

More importantly for today, the treaty also acknowledged that the Black Hills in South Dakota were Indian land.

For a while after this the Indians, albeit bored and sometimes hungry, were mostly peaceful. The Red Cloud Agency was moved from the North Platte to the White River in 1873, and in 1874 there were, according to the records, 9,339 Sioux, 1,202 Cheyenne, and 1,092 Arapaho camped by Fort Robinson.

In the same year, Custer confirmed that there was gold in the Black Hills.

Troops were ordered at first to evict any trespassing miners. But in November 1875 President Grant instructed the army to ignore them, and the last great Indian uprising began. Or at least, the last great Indian uprising *of that period* . . .

Custer was killed with his men at the Little Big Horn; troops massed for the army's response. Meanwhile, the government fraudulently "bought" the Black Hills, when all those who'd have voted against such a deal were away fighting.

It was a fight, of course, they were doomed to lose. In the spring of 1877, Crazy Horse came in—of his own volition—and was subsequently killed at Fort Robinson, in a devious complex of circumstances no one's figured out for dead certain to this day. The Oglala Sioux, that branch of the Lakota nation to which Crazy Horse belonged, were taken off to the Missouri River; but they hated it, and were settled eventually on the Pine Ridge Reservation instead, northeast from Fort Robinson in South Dakota.

·   ·   ·

The following year, 1878, Fort Robinson featured in another of the last flarings of Indian resistance, the Cheyenne Outbreak.

The small band led back by Dull Knife and Little Wolf from Indian Territory got to the Sand Hills in September that year; they split up, and Little Wolf survived the winter undetected in the Little Chokecherry Valley. Dull Knife, however, with about 150 others, mostly women and children, was captured, and taken to Fort Robinson.

Once there, they refused to return south; death, they said, would be better than that. It got to a point where they were denied food and water for five days, so they broke out, as death or escape seemed indeed the only options they had.

For the next twelve days, they fought a running battle in the bluffs and buttes around the fort, scrambling and stumbling through the bitter snows in the depth of winter. When it was over, sixty-four Indians and eleven soldiers were dead.

An attempt was made to try some of the seventy-eight Cheyenne who survived for the deaths of the settlers back by Oberlin in Kansas, but no evidence stuck. They were sent, finally, to the Tongue River Reservation in Montana.

Fort Robinson played a part, tangentially, in one last key episode in the suppression of the Indian nations by the flooding white tide. In November 1890, one thousand four hundred troops were sent from there to the Pine Ridge Agency and Wounded Knee—but the display in the museum at Fort Robinson says little of what happened next, come December 29 of that year. It's now reckoned around three hundred Lakota people died in that massacre.

At Fort Robinson the event is referred to only elliptically, "a disaster"—and the display moves hurriedly on.

Tourism has made Fort Robinson a place of evasion and omission, a place of historical slippage in other ways, too. When you go into the museum there, the first thing you get is a video program. Over scenic shots of fine local vistas, backed with appropriately mystic-epic music, a voice heroically, atmospherically intones, "Your footsteps are not the first to walk this land. Your voice is not the first to echo through these canyons."

So you think, Great—they're going to tell me about the people who were here first.

"The U.S. Army was here for seventy-four years . . ."

.   .   .

Moni Hourt said people generally had one of three attitudes toward the Indians.

First, there were people who didn't think about them at all. Second, there were people who still thought they were animals and savages—dirty, drunken, flea-ridden layabouts who got everything they had coming to them. And twenty or thirty years ago, pretty much everybody thought one of those two ways.

But today there was a third attitude too, an attitude that she hoped was slowly but steadily gaining more ground. There were people, she said, who now acknowledged that what was done to the Indians was a tragedy and a disgrace—that they'd been robbed and cheated and lied to and murdered and starved, and white America didn't come out of it looking pretty.

But what could you do about it now? In 1991?

She answered her own question like this. She said people who lived in that country out there suffered floods and tornadoes, and personal tragedies, but they got up, they went to work, and they carried on. When you buried a loved one, say, should you give up because of that? Of course not. What sort of testament would that be to them then?

And, she said, there was an analogy here with the Indians. For sure, it wasn't that they'd been loved, because very plainly they hadn't been. On the contrary, the likes of Custer had been praised as a hero when, clearly, the guy was an egomaniac gloryhound who'd shoot down Indian women and children without compunction, quite the opposite—who'd shoot them down with thrill and lust as if it were sport.

But it was an analogy in the sense that, because now the white man knew what he'd done, should he lie down and give up for guilt over that?

Should they give the land back, she asked, because of what their forefathers had done? Those weren't the same Indians now that the land had been stolen from; and this wasn't the same land anymore that had been stolen, either. You couldn't go back: everything was changed, changed utterly.

That particular freight train, she said, had gone through a long, long time ago, and all you could do in its wake was make the best of what is, for today, and for tomorrow.

Besides, she then said, if you gave the land back now, they'd trash it. It'd make no more sense than giving it back to the buffalo. Because the Indian had a whole different way of seeing things than the white man did . . .

Look, she told me, she grew up with Indians working for her dad, and she loved them. But every Saturday they'd get their pay, and they'd go to town—and every Monday her dad would go and bail them out. It'd take six generations just to work the booze out of them, let alone everything else.

And yes, she knew who sold them that booze—but like she said, should she give up because of that?

We were standing above the broken dam just then. The river was a sullen, foaming streak, slipping indolently past the damage it had done. And it was a glorious afternoon, burning blue over the sandy green hills along the river's shattered path—and I liked Moni Hourt very much. So perhaps what I said next was a cruel thing to say.

But I said it seemed to me that she spoke of the Indians—of growing up with them when they worked for her dad, and loving them, but you couldn't give the land back because they'd trash it, because they were, by implication, irresponsible children—she spoke of the Indians, I said, in exactly, in *precisely* the way you'll hear the third or fourth generation of white settler in Africa speaking of the black man.

I might as well have slapped her in the face.

She turned away for a bit. Then she said, "I know. I know."

Then she rallied. She said if the sins of the fathers came down then, yes, she was guilty. But she couldn't sit and grieve over that, because if she sat and anguished at the guilt of the past, over and over, she'd be sitting there forever. She'd give up. And Plains people don't do that—they *don't give up*.

Because, she said, if you do—if you give up and sit down—you'll get hit by the freight train every time.

She said she could no more sit down and worry over the past, than she could sit down and worry about nuclear war.

Which would, of course, be the ultimate white tide.

## God's Finger

In Nebraska City I asked how I could get to the Missouri River, and the woman at the desk of the Apple Inn said, "You want to get *close* to it?"

It was odd. The town wouldn't have been there without the river—thousands got off the steamboats there after 1849, using the Nebraska City Cut-Off to join the Oregon Trail by Grand Island—yet now the river was like a secret, almost hard to find, as if the town had turned its back on it.

At the foot of a dirt road by the train tracks, I came on three guys unloading grain off trucks into storage bins; the grain hissed like rushing water through the grates, under a scorching sun. At nine in the morning it was high 80s, and humid; I'd walked only a few blocks, but sweat was cascading through my eyebrows already.

The men directed me a block along, between tin hangars and past a weighbridge, and there it suddenly was—a silent surging of water, not as wide as I'd imagined, but strong, with a pulsing, whorled surface like it had muscles. It pushed along, ferociously intent on getting down to join the Mississippi.

A faint mercy of cool breeze sighed softly off the water in my face. An old boy fished off the bank, under two idle cranes on the barge wharf; a cardboard box blew in slow, ragged bursts over a white glare of concrete. Up the hill, the town slumbered on a Saturday morning.

So what was here in 1805 when Lewis and Clark came by? Animals and Indians . . . I walked back past the brick two-storys of Central Avenue lying flattened, gasping and shadeless in the terrible humid sun; the cab of the truck when I climbed in was a sauna.

I crossed into Iowa; the radio said in the United States of America there was now a murder every twenty-four minutes.

In Iowa I drove through Massena, HOME OF FRIENDLY PEOPLE, and Fontanelle, A GOOD PLACE TO CALL HOME.

Then I came to Des Moines, and spent the weekend there with friends. One of them said, "I can't think of a better place to do plant molecular biology—except it's Des Moines."

He said, "Farming here is an industry, a professional corporate trade. The families go by the way; the successful farmer here is the mega-farmer, planting huge acreages with computer support programs mapping input and output, this variety or that, soil conditions, weather—making corporate decisions, basically. That's what farming is now. Totally a business. The family farm, all those values, that's gone. And if you want to blame anything, blame the market. Because there's money in it."

There's money in farming?

"Absolutely. Big money, big margins. Anything over 120-, 150-bushel corn, you sell for it $2.25, $2.50—it doesn't take much math to see what you're talking when you take that to the elevator. See, corn is such an extraordinary crop, and the soil here is this incredible black loam; in the heart of the corn belt, say Champaign, Illinois, you're talking 200-bushel corn."

He said, "It's a very efficient way of producing large amounts of protein, oil, and carbohydrate."

It's a business . . . the plant research outfit this guy worked at before up in Madison, Wisconsin, got taken over three years back. At quarter to five in the afternoon the buyer sent in a lawyer to read a statement; they had an hour the next morning to clear out their stuff. There were people crying, throwing their things in cardboard boxes; vans were parked across the gateway so you couldn't get a car in, it was barricaded, and armed security followed them out. That night the place was floodlit, and the locks all changed.

He said, "It was weird, treating a bunch of Ph.D. scientists like they were militant unionists; God, it was awful. It was drought year, '88, the heat was unbearable, we were stressed out all summer . . . and then on top of all that we had to come to Des Moines. You know what Iowa stands for?"

Idiots Out Wandering Around.

"When we came here they sold us this bill of goods, that it was a clean, community kind of place, a good Christian place to raise a family. It's a crock of shit. We've had the car stereo ripped off in the driveway twice in two months. It's just the same as everywhere else. No, it's worse—there aren't any decent restaurants."

Des Moines had just had its first drive-by shooting. The local paper was full of hysterical and largely fact-free gibberish about how seven hundred fifty or eight hundred kids in the city were either in a gang, or *wanted to be* . . . What did they do, a phone survey? Like, Hey—you want to be in a gang? Well, sure . . .

It's a business . . . at work, this friend of mine coats microscopic particles of tungsten—particles one micron across, one thousandth of a millimeter—with pieces of DNA. The DNA in question is YFG, Your Favorite Gene. The coated particles are dropped in solution onto the front of a plastic bullet, the "macro-projectile." The bullet then gets fired at a corn plant from a .22 gun with a 10-cm barrel, a piece of rifle stock. The bullet hits a screen with a hole in it, the tungsten particles fly through the hole—and $x$ thousand of them, out of your ten million on the bullet, get punched into the cells. They go in with a marker gene, to show where they've hit; it turns the cells red. Red corn . . .

You thought genetic engineering was guys with a tiny techno-needle and thread, minutely sewing away at the molecule chain? Forget it, this guy's an artillery expert. He comes home from the lab with gunpowder on his hands.

And he works, he said, for the only major seed company left that's not owned by a chemicals company. At his place, they were trying to develop hybrids that wouldn't need the chemicals so much, but what the other guys were up to ... A colleague said he figured the chemical outfits were just hedging their bets, storing research against the day when controls on the use of chemicals in farming got stricter.

But in the meantime, nitrate contamination in Iowa was now such a big deal, you'd get ticker tape warnings about your water across the bottom of the TV screen, just the same way you did with tornadoes.

My friend's colleague was from back East. He said, "The heartland's a pissy place to live in terms of weather. It dominates your life.

"We had one ice storm two years ago, it was the worst to hit this city in a hundred years. The rain falls, and it freezes the minute it hits, so a mild one's really pretty, the trees get coated like crystal. But a heavy one, they get coated an inch thick or more, and if they're not used to getting regularly pruned by that like they are further north in Minnesota or Wisconsin, that's devastating. Everything comes down. It was like a war zone here, there was no power, there were people in the ditch everywhere, and hot wires, live wires—you could hear the transformers popping, and the branches crashing. It took the city a week to get back up again."

My friend had pictures. You couldn't see his lawn for the wrecked trees all over it. He said, "Can you imagine lying in bed and hearing that come down all night?"

On Monday morning I drove northeast towards Wisconsin. I took country roads through the endless corn, roads that sounded like food additives, roads called E27, E29, V18. The rivers were all high, with black, muddy evidence of the spring rain's overspill all about them.

I curved on C7X through rolling hills towards the Mississippi. The sky was darkening, grey with more rain. It was muggy; showers roamed round the hills like curtains, shutting out patches of horizon.

I took X56 to Marquette, and crossed the river into Wisconsin. As I rode the bridge into the wall of green trees on the far shore I thought, Boy, some river—then I got through the trees, and there was another

bridge still to cross, and a second vast amount of that river all over again
... this is, remember, still a thousand miles upstream from New Orleans.

There was news on the radio of a tornado in Germantown, just north
of Milwaukee; a Severe Thunderstorm Watch was issued for eastern
Iowa, south and central Wisconsin. Running east on 18 for Madison, I
could see a mass of big weather to the northeast, towers stacking way up,
with blocks of rain falling a murky indigo beneath them.

The Weatheradio described two lines of storms, one from Racine to
Green Bay, the other from McFarland to Wisconsin Dells, with the
heaviest action coming in over Madison.

I could see that moving across the horizon ahead, so before I arrived
too near beneath the edge of it, I pulled over to take a look. There was
that old familiar sheet of angry grey-blue, deepening to black along the
rim of the ground, and in back of it, no question—there was a wall cloud.

A Madison weatherman said, "It's very, very strange—it's touch and
go."

The west and north were glorious blue, but all the east before me was
dense with dark, submarine colors. Directly ahead was an eerie sheet of
falling white, a curtain of hail; to the north, a rainbow marched along
under the front edge of the storm. Then, maybe ten miles ahead, maybe
less, a thin blue tail slithered from the back end of the weather, God's
crooked finger of trailing cloud ...

Driving on, serious rain came tumbling down, a blinding wash of thick
water racing over the windshield.

"Frequent bursts of static on your radio may indicate lightning."

And there I was thinking Phil Collins had catarrh ...

The skimpy funnel dissipated. It was, I think, the nearest and clearest
I got to seeing a tornado, and it wasn't really much—just a skeletal,
momentary, idle little flickering of the big possibility ...

I crept through Madison. The rain was torrential; my eyes were glued
on the taillights in front through a silver mayhem of splashback and
spray. Then, turning north on 51 on the far side of town, suddenly it was
past; the sky was cloudless and gleaming blue again over the drenched
and glistening highway.

Twenty miles north of Madison, I turned east off 22 onto County B.
Skidding through pools in the hollows of the road, I came to the little
town of Rio.

# 8.

# Welcome *Thunderheart* Crew

> What treaty that the white man ever made with us has he
> kept? Not one. When I was a boy the Sioux owned the world;
> the sun rose and set on their land; they sent ten thousand men
> to battle. Where are the warriors today? Who slew them?
> Where are our lands? Who owns them? What white man can
> say I ever stole his land? Yet they say I am a bad Indian
> . . . is it wrong for me to love my own?
>
> —*Chief Sitting Bull,*
> *Hunkpapa Sioux*

Sitting Bull never signed the Fort Laramie treaty. The leader of the
10,000 Sioux, Cheyenne, and Arapaho warriors who, in 1876, defeated
General Crook on Rosebud Creek, and eliminated Custer shortly afterwards, finally came in from Canada in 1881, with 186 remaining followers.
He said, "Let it be recorded that I am the last of my people to lay down
my gun."

The government had already forced the sale of nine million acres of
Sioux land, including the Black Hills, after Custer's death. In 1889 they
took more, breaking what was left into six smaller reservations. The next
year there was drought; rations, meager enough already, were cut
again—and the government told the Sioux they couldn't hunt game
anymore. Dispirited and hungry, they were ripe for the Ghost Dance.

In the late 1880s, with the aid of some rather dubious miracles, a
Nevada Paiute called Wovoka had proclaimed himself the risen Christ;
he preached a messianic-apocalyptic vision in which the world was
destroyed and reborn, the Indian dead returned, and the land became

theirs and abundant once more. At the heart of this desperate religion was the Ghost Dance, hours and days of dancing in which Wovoka's devotees, exhausted and ecstatic, attained visionary trances; it spread through the Indian nations of the West like fire through dry forest.

By the autumn of 1890, there were many converts among the Sioux. A missionary called Kicking Bear visited Sitting Bull in October; with at least his tacit encouragement, the Ghost Dance spread until, by November, it was pretty much the only thing happening across the reservations of South Dakota. Local whites grew alarmed; at the Pine Ridge Agency, the agent sent a message to Washington, "The Indians are dancing in the snow and are wild and crazy . . . we need protection and we need it now . . . an outbreak may occur at any time."

Troops arrived at Pine Ridge from Fort Robinson towards the end of November. The former Indian agent Dr. Valentine McGillycuddy asked, "If the Seventh Day Adventists prepare their ascension robes for the Second Coming of the Savior, the United States army is not put in motion to prevent them. Why should the Indians not have the same privilege?" But there were now several thousand Ghost Dancers camped with Kicking Bear in the Badlands, refusing army orders to come in, and in a generally hysterical atmosphere, wise counsel like McGillycuddy's went unheeded.

On December 15, at the Standing Rock Reservation to the north, an attempt was made to arrest Sitting Bull—considered, erroneously, to be behind these disturbances. In the resulting melee he was shot, along with thirteen others, including six Indian policemen. Around two hundred of his followers fled south; some of these joined with the Minneconjou Chief Big Foot, another Ghost Dance convert.

Escaping from the army (who had orders to arrest him too), Big Foot led his band on a trek through the fierce winter cold of the Badlands, hoping to find protection with the Oglala Chief Red Cloud at Pine Ridge. Along the way, he fell seriously ill with pneumonia—so when news came on Christmas Day that Kicking Bear and his band were giving up, Big Foot sent word that he too would come in peacefully. On December 28, he surrendered unconditionally to a battalion of cavalry; he was escorted with his starved and freezing people to the soldiers' camp on Wounded Knee Creek.

There were 370 Indians, the majority of them women and children; there were 470 soldiers, with a four-gun battery of light artillery. On the morning of the twenty-ninth, an attempt was made to take from the

Indians what few weapons they had; the Indians became scared, restive, and resentful. In the scuffling confusion of the mishandled disarmament, a shot rang out—and the Seventh Cavalry let rip.

Thirty-one soldiers died, some of them caught in their own cross fire. And maybe 300 Indians . . .

A physician who saw around 150 of the bodies being buried in a mass grave a few days later, after a blizzard had passed through that prevented it being done earlier, said:

"Fully three miles from the scene of the massacre we found the body of a woman completely covered with a blanket of snow, and from this point (traveling towards Wounded Knee) we found them scattered along as they had been relentlessly hunted down and slaughtered while fleeing for their lives. Some of our people discovered relatives or friends among the dead, and there was much wailing and mourning. When we reached the spot where the Indian camp had stood, among the fragments of burned tents and other belongings we saw the frozen bodies lying close together, or piled one upon another."

Today—in the wake of the Columbian Quincentennial—it's worth noting that the United States Government has never properly apologized to the Lakota nation for what was done at Wounded Knee.

The Pine Ridge Reservation in South Dakota is home to the Oglala Sioux, the largest of the seven bands of the Lakota nation. From Crawford and Fort Robinson, it's seventy-five miles to the town of Pine Ridge itself, just across the state line; it's a short drive farther to Wounded Knee. My South Dakota Centennial Fun Map marked the site as a "battle."

Where you turn north off 18 to get there, a historical marker on the side of the road records the deeds and character of Crazy Horse:

> This sign is dedicated to the greatest of Sioux warriors Chief Crazy Horse. Light-haired, fair-skinned, grey-eyed, he was modest, courteous, generous, of great physique, and known for his self-denial . . . he was never involved in any of the numerous massacres on the trail, but was a fine leader in practically every open fight. "Listen now," Crazy Horse said, "you cannot sell the ground you walk on." He never signed a peace treaty . . . he never was photographed.

Unlike the more substantial historical markers of white America— slabs of finely engraved marble or stone, or plaques of thick carved wood hung neatly from rough-hewn posts—the Crazy Horse marker is a hand-painted sheet of tin. Similarly, compared to the pristine gloss of Fort Robinson, with its white history so manicured and polished, there's nothing neat or fine up at Wounded Knee.

There's a bare cement visitor center, unfinished; on a low hill above the road, there's a tattered little chapel by the graveyard there—and another tin marker. It says the death toll was 146. Where it records how the Indians were ordered to surrender their weapons prior to the massacre, someone's etched into the tin, "They had no arms." The soldiers did, in fact, collect about forty old rifles, before the shooting broke out—but it's still a potent, angry little graffito, and it's near enough right.

While I was looking a young guy came along and said, if I wanted, he'd go over the hill to get the keys for the center; they had blown-up pictures there, taken three days after the massacre: the frozen bodies on the ground, tossed in the wagons . . .

His name was Manuel Hatchett, and he was twenty-two; he was a full-blood Oglala. He said, "We're trying to build that visitor center, and create jobs, because we need jobs, we need a lot of jobs bad. So we've got the structure up, and we've laid a concrete floor inside—but we still need maybe five thousand for the roof, and a couple of thousand each for the plumbing and the wiring."

It seemed a bitter contrast to the investment at Fort Robinson—this weed-strewn place with its rutted track up to the cemetery, and the roofless grey stump of the unfinished building. When I told him how the display at the Fort slipped in hasty embarrassment past the Wounded Knee "disaster," he kind of snorted, mildly—like it might be funny, if you didn't know that kind of news from way back anyhow.

Then he told me a story. The year before he'd been here by the marker, and he heard an awesome low roar, a growing rumble like a jet plane; next thing he knew, 130 bikers were coming over the hill, a seriously mean-looking outfit all on Harleys. These guys pulled up all around him, engines growling, which reduced him—just being a kid on his own here—to a state of some anxiety. The leader came over and asked a question or two; so, controlling his nerves, he explained a little bit how they were trying to put up that visitor center there.

The bikers' leader had one of those German helmets with the spike on top; so then he passed it around all these hairy-assed guys on their bikes. When it came back, it was overflowing. Manuel shook his head and said, "Boy, I collected one thousand dollars that day. And that's how we poured our floor in there."

I asked him if many people came by.

He said, "There's a lot do stop, especially after *Dances with Wolves*. There's going to be a whole lot this summer."

I went up to the cemetery. It was a worn little place with a weathered chain-link fence, and two shabby brick gateposts; the wind whistled and moaned over the hill. Some of the graves were marked by bare sticks, with ribbons of cloth floating off them in the wind; others had plain wooden crosses. Among them, in the center of this sad patch of dirt, stood the memorial to those who died in 1890: Spotted Thunder, Shoots The Bear, Chase In Winter, He Eagle, No Ears, Wolf Skin Necklace, Pretty Hawk, Yellow Robe ... there was one sadly apposite name: Blue American.

There was another, more recent headstone. Among Lakota inscriptions it recorded: "2,000 and 500 came to Wounded Knee in '73, One Still Remains. Lawrence 'Buddy' La Monte.'

The stone said: "By This Sign: Victory."

The marker below said Wounded Knee in 1890 was the last armed confrontation between the Sioux and the American government—but just as the marker's casualty figure probably isn't the whole truth, that statement's not true either.

In 1973, AIM—the American Indian Movement—occupied the site at Wounded Knee in an armed standoff with federal forces that lasted seventy-two days. Nor is La Monte the only one who died in those days; many more followed him in the next few years, as the Pine Ridge Reservation went through a convulsion little short of civil war. It had, at that time, the highest per capita murder rate in the United States, worse than New York, worse than Detroit ...

Now a bunch of people had come to make a movie against the background of those events. They were based in Kadoka, seventy-five miles northeast at the far corner of the reservation; so that was where I headed from Wounded Knee, through expansive green hills past pines and rocky crests, steering by hand-painted signs through Kyle and Wanblee past the bruised and fading pickups and trailer homes of the Lakota people—through something, in short, uniquely American ...

Welfare apartheid.

Kadoka's fourteen miles beyond the White River, the northern boundary of the reservation—and eighteen miles along I90 from the eastern entrance into Badlands National Park. It has motels for the tourist traffic along the interstate; that's why the film crew was billeted there. Their headquarters were at the Best Western; the sign outside said, WELCOME THUNDERHEART CREW.

Kadoka was founded in 1906, when the Milwaukee Railroad came through; now, it lives off the traffic on the interstate. There was a mileage chart on a drum in the lobby that you spun around to find out how far you were from everywhere: Missoula 754, Chicago 807, San Francisco 1,514 . . .

With *Thunderheart* in town for four months, Cindy Wilmarth at the Best Western reckoned a million dollars would be sticking to Kadoka, easy. "The phone company's done overwhelming business—they do a lot of phoning, these people could not survive without phones. Plus gas, groceries, lumber, clothing stores, the second-hand store, motel rooms—there's about a hundred of them, we've got eighteen, nineteen rooms of them just here."

She said, "They're mostly from L.A., or New York—and a lot of them, it's really surprising, they're vegetarians. They really like fruit. And they like Swiss cheese a lot, not your good old American Kraft. And they like nuts."

Definitely not your South Dakota diet there. I asked what these strange-eating people from far away were like.

"Very nice. Supernice people. Our daughter got married last week, and Graham Green that was the medicine man in *Dances with Wolves,* he came to the reception at the City Auditorium, and he gave them a big hug and a kiss, and he gave them five hundred dollars. Superneat guy—I mean, he blew her mind, he's common as an old shoe. And the production crew that stay here, they went together and bought them this humongous piece of Samsonite luggage, and I know that sells for over two hundred dollars. It's crazy. But you couldn't ask for better. Everybody's on first-name terms, Sam Shepard, whoever . . . it just blows everybody's mind."

In the City Bar (also called the Video Bar, 'cause you could play video poker in there) it looked like I'd lucked out again. I'd got into town for the busiest night of the year—there was the Firemen's Ball across the street, it was the Reunion Weekend with the Alumni Picnic, and a great deal of beer was going down all round.

At the bar I talked to Tom Brown, twenty-four years old, a boxy-shaped little ox of a guy in a leather jacket, one of your friendly bear types. He worked in the hardware store, so I asked what it was like having a movie in town.

He said, "Man, they just spend money like, *boom*. They buy every-thing, tools and building supplies, nuts and bolts, nails and eyescrews, pots and pans and lamps ... We're not really set up for something like this. Some days they'll come in and buy most of our stock. I had a guy come in the other day and buy thirty-six light fixtures."

He shook his head. I asked how long it'd normally take to sell thirty-six light fixtures.

He laughed. "I can't even *imagine* how long it'd take to sell thirty-six of them things in this town. We had to special-order them in; we're special-ordering a whole lot of stuff all the time, it's complicated—but it's good. I'm going to hate to see these people leave; I've made good friends out of this, the construction guys ... See, as far as the business is concerned, I'm just a clerk, I don't really care about the business end—but it makes you feel good, when you can help somebody out like this. 'Cause this is a small town, you know?"

So what was this small town like, when it didn't have a movie in it?

He said, "I lived here all my life; I think it's doing okay. If you run a bad business it'll go under, but there aren't many going under here; there's no one living outrageous life-styles, but you don't have a lot of poverty either. Get down on the reservation you do, but *that's brought on by themselves* . . ."

My italics.

The City Bar was packed, and cheerfully rowdy. The barman was lining up five glasses, putting a shot of Bacardi in each, then Bailey's, then Amaretto.

What was *that*?

"Don't ask me. I'm just making them."

Everyone wore cowboy hats.

I was stood next to Mark Zelfer from Scenic. "There's nothing there, but you should go. It's only about sixty miles. Then you go up Sheep Mountain . . ."

I asked why he'd come sixty miles from home.

He said, "I got a family reunion. It's not my family, but what the hell ... Hey, Tammy. This guy's from British Columbia."

Tammy said I should go to Scenic too, and get a drink in the Long-horn Saloon. "They got skulls and stuff, and sawdust; in August when the bikers come, they just ride right in there."

She said, "A couple of years back there's this guy there, he owns most of Scenic, and some Indians got mad with him, 'cause on the bar it said

NO INDIANS ALLOWED, when he's part Indian—and they shot him in the leg. See, the Indians come in, when they want booze and stuff—they'll pull the radio right out of the car and swap it for booze—and he sells booze to them for gads of money, I mean *gads* . . . so I don't know how he's still walking around, I don't know how someone hasn't busted his head. But I guess he's friends with them 'cause he gives them what they want."

Next to where it says NO INDIANS ALLOWED (the NO has been painted out, but remains visible—to give tourists, one suspects, some sleazy kind of shudder), the Longhorn Saloon has a different sign, written in the Lakota language. It says LAKOTA WELCOME.

Tammy said, "It's sad. . . . Did you go through there? They don't take care of nothing. The houses are all beat up, and trash, they just dump it any place—and people feel sorry for them. But last winter it was real cold, so people sent them coal down there—and that coal just about beat the trucks back to Rapid City, them selling it for beer. Now this isn't all of them, there's nice Indians—but we grew up around them, and it's sad. They get free housing, and all the windows are out . . . They don't look after stuff. And you got to be careful too. My husband was in here one time, he just went up to one guy meaning to be friendly, but he'd had a few beers and he said, Hey Chief—and the guy just about floored him."

You don't say.


Happily sodden people whooped and toppled about the pool tables, or jammed into booths, or wrestled their way to the three-deep bar through dense drifts of cigarette smoke.

I talked to the *Thunderheart* car coordinator. "We have twenty-five principal cars. At one point we have eighty-five vehicles—sixty Indian ones at a powwow, and twenty-five FBI. We modify the suspensions—when you're chasing through the Badlands you don't want the tires coming off . . . and the principal cars have duplicates, triplicates. You'll see us going down the road with two cars exactly alike."

I tried to imagine identical battered pickups in procession through the moonscape of the Badlands. It was getting weird. You could do acid and not get into conversations like this.

Lisa Horacek said, "You're going to North Dakota? Whooo no, yuk! *No one* goes to North Dakota."

Lisa's boyfriend was named Zane Pettyjohn.

Carol from Rapid swayed in the doorway and said, "When John

Lennon died I cried for two fucking years. And I still cry. I cried longer for John Lennon than I did for my own mother."

She said, "I graduated here in '69, and now I don't know anybody here. The Kadoka people I grew up with, and the movie people, they're real tight—it's like the movie people know them better than I do, it's like I'm in a different town. It's like I'm a stranger. It's like I'm you."

Fearful that she might cry again, for her lost past and John Lennon, and somewhat mystified as to how an unhappy drunk dancer from Rapid City in South Dakota could identify with me in any way at all, I walked back to the Best Western and went to bed.

*Thunderheart*'s director was Michael Apted, a tall, composed Englishman just turned fifty. He'd grown up in Ilford in Essex, and learnt his trade at Granada TV in the sixties, making programs like *Coronation Street*; he went to the United States in 1980 to make *Coalminer's Daughter*, and stayed.

We had breakfast in the Best Western. Apted said he'd been in and out of Pine Ridge for a year; before *Thunderheart*, he'd made a documentary about Leonard Peltier of the American Indian Movement. Peltier was serving two consecutive life sentences at Leavenworth in Kansas, for the killings of two FBI agents in 1975 . . .

So when he got the *Thunderheart* script, Apted was deep in the subject already. The film's about the murder of an Indian, and the two FBI agents who come to investigate that—Sam Shepard playing the senior partner, Val Kilmer the junior. And Kilmer's character has Indian roots, so it's about him discovering those roots, and discovering the government's true agenda on the reservation—which is land, minerals, and the dismantling of AIM.

Apted outlined the background. On the reservation there are two racial groups, mixed bloods and full bloods. In the seventies the mixed bloods were running the tribal council, supported by federal money; in power was Richard Wilson, a brutal character who organized a vigilante police force, and made all employment subject to him. So, said Apted, "You had the makings of a civil war against the full bloods, the traditionals, because . . . well, remember Vietnam—the government ran this the same way. They used Wilson and his goons just like they tried to use their puppets in Saigon."

A number of AIM's leaders were from Pine Ridge. There was a coalescing of AIM with the Pine Ridge traditionals; people came in to take sides in this civil war.

"It was completely scandalous, people were being murdered, and it was never getting investigated—so AIM came to try and investigate properly, because the traditionals had no power of law behind them. They came in a big caravan, and the feds were waiting for them at the Bureau of Indian Affairs building in Pine Ridge—it was sandbagged, they had heavy arms in there—so AIM took over the hill at Wounded Knee.

"There was massive escalation then. The government sent in federal marshals, state troopers, the 82nd Airborne, and the goons as well, and they surrounded them. Our feeling is it went all the way to the White House . . . Anyway, they negotiated, there was media attention, and considerable sympathy, so the government sat it out. It lasted seventy-two days, and in the end it petered out, and only two were killed. Though the Indians do claim it was more—that they killed more people than that, and buried them secretly.

"But either way, it heralded a period of major violence, and that's what my documentary deals with."

The government brought charges against AIM's leaders; they charged Russell Means and Dennis Banks with kidnapping, the works, and the judge threw it out: he said the waters of justice were polluted.

"But the government couldn't take the loss—the idea was to run them through the courts like they did with the Black Panthers, to keep them raising bail money, to keep warrants on them, to keep them moving from state to state. And they succeeded in that; they pretty much destroyed AIM, as it then was."

In the meantime, the government went on supporting Richard Wilson and his goons, and the violence escalated on Pine Ridge. In 1975, AIM was keeping arms and ammunition and explosives at the Jumping Bull compound; two agents who went to investigate were executed at point-blank range. Three hundred FBI poured in to clean the place out.

Peltier ran to Canada; two other guys were charged with murder, and acquitted—by an all-white jury—on grounds of self-defense, in that the government had created such an atmosphere of fear and violence in the first place. Then Peltier was extradited; the government constructed a rickety case, and Peltier got convicted. He gets out in 2035.

Apted described the conviction as "deeply unsound."

"What you've got with Peltier," he said, "is like America's Guildford Four—where the law enforcement bodies have to admit they fouled up. Which isn't easy to get them to do—but it's either that, or the president exercising clemency."

In a kinder, gentler America . . .

"So *Thunderheart*'s set in the whole atmosphere of that. Well, it's set in 1980, in the wake of it, because it's still going on. They want toxic waste dumps on the reservation, they want to mine uranium there—and if there's stuff the government wants like that, they just move in and do it, and fuck 'em. I bet you every reservation in this country is a projected site for waste dumps, because that's what they are, dumps. America's dumps. Ninety percent unemployment, 70 percent alcoholism . . ."

I asked then what he reckoned Kadoka thought, having this sensitive movie so close to home in their town.

"What are their attitudes to the actual film? I think a lot of people are very nervous about it, very ambivalent. It's not a shrill film, at least I hope it's not, but this is a place where . . . Sam's telling me he went in some bar down the road with Graham Green the other day—and some 250-pound lunatic comes up to Graham and he says, 'Who invited you in here?' "

Even something as basic as names get misshapen, crossing the gulf between cultures. Wanblee, the Oglala town used in *Thunderheart,* should correctly be spelt Wambli. The word means eagle; the town sits beneath the striking mass of Eagle's Nest Butte.

And Kadoka, meaning hole-in-the-wall—the town's sited by a gap in the fractured, castellated Badlands wall along the south of I90—might more accurately be spelt Hodoka. But if you can call Wounded Knee a battle, what's in a name . . .

The buffalo-based economy of the Lakota nation reached its high point in the first half of the nineteenth century; there was an active and profitable trade in furs and hides for guns, ammunition, beads, knives, pots and pans, tobacco, sugar and flour.

The Dakota Territory was organized in 1861; there were, at that time, only about five hundred white settlers in the southeast corner of the embryo state. Between Indians and grasshoppers, low rainfall, and less credit, it didn't look promising either—but that never stopped the white tide any place else, and it didn't stop it here. Swedes, Finns, Danes, Dutch, Poles, Bohemians, and, above all, Norwegians and Germans came pouring in. Drought in the 1880s held the flow back awhile, but— especially after the further diminution of the Indians' land in 1889—the tide kept coming. In the early years of this century South Dakota—for whites—was booming.

Indian children, meanwhile, were taken from their parents, and sent away to religious boarding schools; they had their hair cut, and their language kicked out of them. . . .

In autumn 1906 Kadoka had two stores, two restaurants and boarding houses, a saloon, and a livery. The first train arrived on Christmas Day; the first cattle were shipped out in August 1907, and the first passenger service ran four months after that. The town's first lots had been sold on April 5 that year; Jack Jones's establishment moved to its new lot and served supper that same night, with the building still up on its moving timbers.

The first white child born in Kadoka was Ida Ellen Quinn, in August 1907; the town got an ice cream parlor, a milliner, a newspaper, a baker, a jeweler, a druggist, a hardware store, and a real estate agent. By 1909 there were three churches; a school was built in 1910.

Before that, school was taught in a building that had formerly been a saloon. There were eight saloons to begin with—but once the railroad was completed and the heart of town built, the construction workers moved on, and the saloon trade withered; eventually there were only two, the way it is today. There's the City Bar, and the Discount Fuel Lounge—a bar in, of all places, a gas station.

One of the barmen from the City Bar, Terry Stout, was also the Jackson County library director. He said it was a weird job split: He saw half the population on Saturday night, and the other half, the little old ladies, on Monday morning . . .

We talked in the little library on Main Street. He was forty-five; he'd been born in Kadoka and lived there till he was five, but then they moved away—his father was in the air force. After a peripatetic service childhood, he lived in San Francisco, then moved back to Kadoka a few years ago, to take care of a family member who'd fallen ill. I asked what it was like, to make that move back here.

It was, he said, "Cultural trauma. Back in the city we called it nosiness, but here it's neighborliness. Hell, they know what brand of toilet paper you've bought before you've even got it home. . . . I won one thousand six hundred dollars on that machine in the bar, right? And there was people ringing me saying, Hey, did you really win all that money?—before I'd even cashed the ticket. But that's a small town."

And, he said, the impact of *Thunderheart* on that small town was "pretty impressive: ten thousand dollars a day for four months, that's a solid piece—that's a noticeable, substantial one-time shot. Plus the ego it adds, being the center of attention . . . it's an interesting diversion. It's new conversations."

I asked if he thought any of those conversations turned, among Kadokans, on the subject of the film.

He said, "I honestly don't think people have given it much thought. It's more being at the center of the process, the celebrity, whereas the conflict between the reservation people and the local people, that's been going on so long . . . it's not news, it's always there. To what degree, just depends on the individual."

I asked then to what extent there was interaction between the communities.

He said, "There's interaction economically—otherwise, no. Because whether people want to acknowledge it or not, it's still us versus them. I find it interesting, most of my life I met a lot of diverse people, I was used to tolerance, and difference—so when I came back here I was a little surprised at first at the animosity toward the Indians. But out here there's no blacks, no Chinese, no Hispanics, it's just red and white. The favorite phrase round here is, 'Hell, I got nothing against those Indians—I just don't want to sit and drink with them.'

"But then, here you see the ones that don't do much for themselves—you miss the ones that are trying. People work their butts off here, they get irritated to see government subsidy going into wine in the trunks of cars to Wambli, and that's built up over so many years—it goes all the way back. Hell, you killed Custer—that's engraved. And some people just aren't going to change."

Alfred High Horse came in for the *National Geographic* and the *Saturday Evening Post,* a huge, lumbering, shattered-toothed bulk of a man. Terry said, "He works, he drinks . . . nicest guy you'll meet. Then there's Wilbur and his wife, every bit of money they get goes on booze, on video gambling—but there's a lot of whites do the same. Probably more.

"And I've noticed in the five years I'm back, the number of people from the res coming to shop in town's the same—but the number going to the liquor store's been dropping a bit."

Should they sell the Indians that booze here in the first place?

"That's a good one. In some ways no, we shouldn't. But who are we to tell them what a man should or shouldn't buy? One part of me thinks they'd sure as hell be better off—but I can't rightfully tell anybody what's legal for me isn't legal for him, can I? And you might be your brother's keeper—but how far d'you want to keep him?"

It's estimated that one third of all preventable deaths in the United States at least are contributed to by alcohol abuse. . . . In the Oglala Lakota College's course schedule for fall 1991, two out of fourteen pages were given over to warnings and information about the dangers of drugs and alcohol.

The college has been going twenty years; the schedule quoted Chief Sitting Bull:

> In the future your business dealings with the whites are going to be very hard, and it behooves you to learn well what you are taught here. But that is not all. We older people need you. In our dealings with the white man we are just the same as blind men, because we do not understand them. We need you to understand what the white men are up to. My grandchildren, be good. Try and make a mark for yourselves. Learn all you can.

On a dirt lot behind the Best Western four trailers were set up for the *Thunderheart* production offices—offices for Michael Apted and the producers, for the production management and the set designers, for accounts and admin, for PR and casting. In one of these trailers I talked with the production manager Chris Cronyn, a cheerful, sandy-haired guy in his mid-forties, about a $15,000,000 film landing in this town of 750 people in South Dakota.

He said, "I sense the Kadokans . . . I can smell that they're being very careful. They have a sense of what the picture's about. I think individually we're probably reasonably well liked, we haven't torn up the town; as far as I know we haven't got anybody pregnant, we're not a bunch of drug addicts, we pay our bills . . . but I guess they probably think we're a bunch of liberal flakes. They probably laugh at some of us."

When I asked Ken Wilmarth at the Best Western what it was like having these people in town he laughed and said, "Well, I figured it out. The guys got the ponytails, the girls got the short hair."

Cronyn said, "We're coexisting. Both parties are happy." Then he got out the adding machine, and worked out how the money was spilling into Kadoka.

He figured $350,000 on motel bills, $50,000 at the gas station, the same on lumber and hardware, $150,000 out of people's pockets on bits and pieces of groceries, beer—and maybe $35,000 on Kadoka labor. Not including extras.

As for the reservation, he figured he'd spend $125,000 on extras there, $75,000 on location fees, and the same again on Indian labor. The production was being impeccably liberal too, giving trainee jobs on the crew to Indians, work as carpenters, set builders, drivers; one or two had gone off on benders, but it was mostly working very well . . .

Some people on the reservation weren't too happy all the same. The next day, the *Lakota Times* ran a long and rambling lead titled THUNDER-HEART LAWSUIT IN WORKS. It wasn't easy to gather exactly who was threatening what, but it was easy to see that Richard Wilson's daughter wasn't pleased.

Dan Bishop was the production designer; he and his wife Dianna Freas, the set decorator, were sharing a room for the summer with their cat, Sharkbait.

Dan said, "Eighty-five percent of the film's around here. The FBI town's nearer to Wall, and we don't have a uranium site yet . . . Is that sensitive information? Oh well, basically the crux of the script is that for a while there's been a lot of testing and exploration for uranium out here. It's private companies, they'll buy or lease land from corrupt reservation leaderships—but if you get uranium pollution in the water table . . ."

Dianna said, "It turns out to be a pertinent issue. They've found zeolite on Pine Ridge here, it's impermeable in some way, they use it as a kind of casing in waste dumps—and to get it out would mean strip mining."

We begin to get to the heart of the matter. Strip mining, always, is a horror show, enduringly, unforgivingly destructive—and, no doubt, an Indian reservation's as easy a place as any to get away with doing it. And people talk about *Indians* trashing the land . . .

An Indian named Jim Garrett said to me, "The multinationals, the government, they want to strip-mine for zeolite—but it's in the Bad-lands, a lot of it, and you can't strip-mine there. You can't reclaim the Badlands—there ain't nobody on earth who can recreate that. Anybody who says they can thinks they're God, and they're full of bullshit."

White-man techno-progress . . . Dan Bishop asked if I'd seen the missile silos. "They're everywhere. There's one west, one east, there's others on the way up to Philip. You know what they look like? They're sort of unassuming. Just a chain-link fence, and a concrete nipple where the missile lives."

Jim Garrett was a big, rangy guy from the Cheyenne River Reservation with a wide toothy smile, and his hair in a long grey tail; he'd been working six weeks now with Jody Hummer, the girl in charge of casting extras. Jody was a pretty, open-faced blonde from Ohio who'd moved to L.A. three years ago. She said, "I really miss Ohio."

So was she happy out here?

"Oh gosh yes. It's beautiful."

I found them in a cubbyhole office in the back of one of the trailers. Their role was to get word out round the reservation that there were jobs to be had as extras; to have meetings, to explain what was wanted, then build themselves a pool of different ages and types of people.

Jody said it was hard to do. "I don't think the Lakota people are traditionally people who'd want to do a thing like this."

Jim said the people coming forward were doing it because *Dances with Wolves* was such a good experience. And—he'd graduated in environmental studies in California—he had good words for these films beyond their content too.

He said, "What I like about it is it's a nonpolluting industry that's come to our land. Too many times before people just came, took everything, and left their trash behind when they were done. But all a movie leaves behind is memories—and that's what Lakota people believe in right there."

"But *Dances* was different," said Jody, "it was historical. This is *close*, this is painful. We're meeting people that were right in there on either side . . . we don't want to hurt anybody. But it's sensitive."

Jim said, "A lot who participated in those days are still alive. You can draw comparison to the Vietnam War—the healing's still going on, and a lot of people hang back, it still hurts."

But people who'd been on different sides back then were now working together on the film—and he had high hopes. He said, "For the first time people outside are going to see what our communities actually look like, the conditions we live in, the joblessness, the housing, all the things that have been dealt to us in the poker game. Because materially, it's a very poor hand—but then culturally, it's a rich one.

"And there's a lot of people realize how important it is to keep that culture going now. It was so fragmented—but these twenty years it's begun to repair itself, through the stand AIM took—and through thousands of Lakota peoples' efforts."

Jody chipped in to say of her own hopes for *Thunderheart*, "It'll show that effort, the way people help each other, the concern with education—the effort to bring the seventh generation through against the problems, the alcohol . . ."

The way people help each other, the concern with education—it sounded like another troubled tribe of Plains people I'd been meeting. And the stubbornness of the Sioux, the last tribe to come in—is that a familiar trait too?

Well, maybe—but there's also that gulf of difference. At the party Kadoka threw to welcome the *Thunderheart* crew, Jim Garrett was in line with the other guys for the food—and they refused him a steak, and offered him a hot dog instead.

Jody said, "They should have been embarrassed."

Welfare apartheid . . .

"What it comes down to," said Jim, "is the U.S. government has a handful of bones, and it tosses them down. And the breeds are generally wily enough to get most of those bones . . . except I want to stress, what we get in benefits *isn't* a giveaway—it's guaranteed to us by treaty. And secondly, if you're talking welfare recipients, the farmers get more assistance than they'd ever *imagine* giving to Indian people."

But by their policy of divide-and-rule, by placing the distribution of the benefits into the savvier hands of the more pliable breeds, while too many others fell to the deep bottom of the bottle, the government had come close to breaking the last shreds of the nation. And that was where AIM had stood up and fought . . .

"I'd like to put an unqualified yes on that. They weren't saints, but they turned the whole thing round. And I'm not apologizing for the violence that happened then, I refuse to, to anybody—because sometimes you have to hit someone between the eyes to get him to listen. And nobody was listening to those grievances—those same grievances going around and around again."

Still, there were some on the reservation that were leery, or downright unhappy . . .

Jody said, "There's a lot of misinformation."

Jim said, "It's *personal*—these people realize what they did in their lifetime, and they're guilty. And this is bringing that out."

So I asked, could he forgive Richard Wilson now for the things that had happened?

"I'm a stickler that says if you're born in a society, you be loyal . . ."

But can you forgive him?

"My religion says to be sorry for Dick Wilson, to see he was so damn pitiful . . . but I don't know."

Dan Bishop said, "You grow up back East, you hear about the heart of America—well, I'd say more than any other place I've been, that's where I'm at now. You go down to the City Bar, you meet the mayor, you talk . . . Did you know that bar's owned by the city? When the bartender buys you a drink he shouts, 'This one's on the city!' You kind of imagine the council sitting round saying, 'Well boys, how much shall we charge for a whiskey and soda this year?' "

I wandered around Kadoka from motel to motel. They were strung along the interstate, a scattered little blare of billboards and signs filtering dollars into the faded town tucked away behind them.

Bishop said I should find a set dresser called Dan Smiley, a guy who was half-Irish, half Rosebud Sioux, and who knew everyone in town twelve hours after he got there. "I tell you," said Bishop, "three movies in a row, in Montana, in Cincinnati, then here—Dan Smiley goes in the bar, the bartender's named Bob, and Dan goes fishing with Bob. Three times in a row."

I found Smiley with Paul Parry, a carpenter, in the City Bar, fresh back from fishing; they were in their mid-twenties, both from Sheridan, Wyoming. We had a beer. Outside in the early evening, Main Street glowed red under a heavy blue sky; the Kadoka Telephone Company stood out luminously pink and yellow in the dusk. Old guys sat on chairs on the wooden porches, shooting the breeze.

We went back to Paul's caravan in the campsite for a barbecue; we sat in the darkening evening, slapping bugs and talking as the steaks hissed on the grill. Two local girls rolled by, Jennifer and Amy. Amy said, "You guys'd be dead without a barbecue, right?"

"We'd be real skinny, that's for sure."

We were starting to get a spattering of rain; there was lightning popping on the horizon again, megabursts. Amy said, "Darn, we're not going to get any lightning over here, are we? I don't want no lightning where there's cattle, 'cause then I have to ride around on a horse and see how many are dead."

Paul said, "Put in there she's the first girl you ever met who chews tobacco."

Amy was nineteen. She said, "I chew Skol. It's a dietary measure."

I asked her what it was like having the movie in town.

She said, "It's action. It's something going on here. It's a lot of parties."

"It is," said Dan contentedly, "like having a couple of stud rams in town."

"Well where are they *at*, Dan Smiley?"

The horizon all across the north and east had gone to war; blue-black clouds flared and ignited in the distance.

Dan and Paul took out all the panels in one of the film's houses in the Badlands; the FX people wired in explosives on eight thousand feet of wire. They covered it over with balsa wood, then took out the windows and replaced them with candy glass, a sugar-based simulacrum that shatters harmlessly. I pestered the publicist; I wanted to get lucky again, and see a house get shot up.

But you can't get lucky every day of the week. The Kadokans were thrilled with all the unnatural rain; Cindy Wilmarth talked excitedly about how the country would look in the movie, rich and flower-specked and vivid, a great glossy ad for South Dakota . . .

But rain comes in cloud, and when cloud comes, light goes—and then you can't shoot outdoors. Chris Cronyn said, "This weather . . . You set up at seven outside. About ten, you call in the first team—then the cloud comes, and you're totally fucked. Write that down. Totally fucked."

They moved back to the auditorium in town. A dozen semis, trailers, and caravans stood stacked with equipment round the building in the sun. It was, of course, shining with a vindictive brilliance, now that they'd moved inside.

David Atherton, the makeup artist, slowly circled among the rigs on a bicycle he'd bought for fifteen dollars. "It's a three-speed with only one speed on it," he said, "but it's a pretty lime green. I suppose I'll give it to someone at the end of the picture—I'm not shipping it back to L.A., am I?"

Inside, the Kadoka High School Auditorium had a little stage, and a stand of bleachers for basketball games—but the court was buried under a second chipboard floor the crew had laid, and the whole considerable space was stuffed to the roof with the paraphernalia of the dream factory. The set—the FBI agents' border town motel room—sat at the heart of a beehive of lamps and reflectors and black curtains and milling people, grips and gaffers and hair stylists and best boys all scratching their heads and banging things in that peculiar kind of slow-motion, apparently aimless frenzy that characterizes a shoot.

Michael Apted moved through the throng and the clutter, giving off an air of calmness but plainly, deep down, not pleased. He said, "I had no idea the weather was going to be this unpredictable this late in the year. It's a bit of a curve ball, as they say. I thought the only problem would be heat exhaustion—just heat."

But, I said, at least he had the unexpected bonus of that lavish green out there.

"Well, I don't know if I wanted that. When I first saw it here it was all this incredible brown, this huge parched brown. And I wanted a heat film. . . . There's this spiritual side of the film, this guy having visions. It's not easy—but I thought that could come out of it being a hot film, out of heat haze. Whereas a lot of it right now looks like bloody England."

His assistant said, "If you read the later drafts of the script, all the description changed, when we realized the months we'd be filming. The heat just *radiates* from that script."

But it was only June. Terry Stout had talked of 96 at midnight, come high summer; they would, I said, get plenty of that parched brown heat eventually . . .

"Eventually could be a bloody long time."

Apted said being a director, when you were working, it was dawn to bedtime, you were rapt. He was beginning to do stuff like lose his room key . . .

But what, I asked him, do you actually do?

Someone pointed at the director's chair and said, "He sits there."

"I suppose I try and hold it all together. Do I?"

"If there was a general, he'd be it."

He said, "The director speaks in thundering clichés, and it's everybody else's job to turn that into resounding good taste . . . but in the end, you carry the can. It's like the baseball coach. If the team wins, he did it. If the team loses, he did it. So if the film fails, you watch the producers and the studio back away from it at the speed of light. And that's because it's my energy that's supposed to keep it all going. It's a collaborative venture, it's one hundred people's juices on the line—and I'm just, well . . . I'm the director."

Directing this film, he'd said they had to do it here. He said, "I had a big fight with the studio over that—they'd have loved it if we'd gone to Montana. Because it's very difficult, maybe dangerous, to come to the volatile environment of a reservation. Reservation politics are notoriously unstable, they could turn round and tell us to fuck off at any moment—but I insisted, for the freshness, the authenticity. And it really pissed them off. It makes their life more difficult, more worrying . . . but tough luck, I say. If it had to be shot in the San Fernando Valley, I wouldn't do it."

Atherton the makeup man appeared. He asked, "Is there air conditioning in this scene?"

"No. Hot. Flies. Sweaty armpits." Apted turned to Dan Bishop and asked, "You want Sharkbait to be in this one?"

"He's camera shy."

Sam Shepard roamed about worrying that falling asleep in midmorning was "deadly." Apted told him that was how Churchill won the war, on catnaps.

The crew lit the set, stumbling about in that odd frazzle of adjustments and rumination—clumsy molecules, jostling and colliding round the brilliant nucleus of a fabricated 1980 motel room. Then they shot the scene.

It involved Shepard and Kilmer running through files on ARM leaders—ARM being the picture's thinly veiled version of AIM. They were figuring who to go after for the murder of Leo Fast Elk, a character on the tribal council; they wore suit trousers with suspenders, and shirts artfully adorned with perspiration.

"Quiet, please."

Production assistants meandered around muttering on walkie-talkies to get the lobby quiet; someone took the payphone off the hook, and left it dangling. I wandered outside. There were more of those broiling, sculpted vortices of cloud moving in—they'd made the right decision after all.

"Here we go—stand by to lock it up."

Back inside, in Diana Freas's outlandish bazaar behind the heavy drapes round the set, I inspected old lampshades and pictures, gramophones and telephones, fans and furniture, rugs and suitcases . . .

"Rolling."

Basketball hoops hung woefully disregarded from the auditorium roof, in a deep still hush.

"Scene 57, take 3."

"Speed."

"And . . . action."

The scene was six lines—thirty-eight words.

"Cut."

You could feel the air move with the sigh of people breathing out.

"Resetting."

"Quiet please."

"Artists are set, everybody settle."

"Rolling."

Fingers to lips, that same still hush . . .

"Scene 57, take 4."

"And . . . action."

Again, the six little lines, the thirty-eight words.

Apted said afterwards, "Little snips like that—it's a jigsaw, it's a million bits and pieces. From *Coronation Street*, to *Thunderheart* . . . I prefer to do bigger chunks, but this is how it is, mostly. A million pieces."

Bruce Ellison was Leonard Peltier's lawyer; he was also an adviser for *Thunderheart*. Today, he'd brought his son to watch a movie being made.

There were attempts just then to bring Peltier to Fargo, for a hearing in pursuit of a retrial. Lynn Crooks, an assistant U.S. attorney who'd been a prosecutor in the original trial, was reported as saying, "I certainly don't want him here . . . I have no desire whatsoever to see Mr. Peltier again."

Ellison said, "Crooks can always be counted on for good quotes."

In his early forties, he wore a ponytail, and a T-shirt protesting plans for a nuclear waste dump in Minnesota. Originally from New York, he'd arrived in South Dakota four days after the shooting of the FBI men at the Jumping Bull compound. He was, he said, "weaned from bagels immediately."

When he arrived he was in his mid-twenties, just graduated from law school. He came to be a staff attorney for the Wounded Knee Legal Defense/Offense Committee, with a commitment when he came to do one year, tops—then he fell in love with the place, and he'd been here ever since. And, I asked, what had he got himself into back then?

He said, "A literal state of war. Mostly on the reservation, but sometimes spilling into Rapid City, and the highways in between. I was replacing an attorney called Roger Finzel who'd been attacked, and nearly killed. He was with a defendant, another attorney and two paralegals; they got stopped at gunpoint near the Pine Ridge airport, and they beat him, they tried to slit his throat; Dick Wilson's words were, 'Stomp him.' They opened his head, they broke his ribs . . . so there was a job opening."

In a different country from New York . . .

"Well, in New York you get the random violence, the irrational . . . At least here you knew who your enemies were. But it was different, having to go round where it's potentially life-threatening twenty-four hours a day. Having to be armed, traveling with people who were armed, staying in houses that were targets of attack—you had road blocks, you had to avoid certain parts of the reservation . . . The official BIA list was sixty-six deaths in three years, '73 to '76. We reckoned it was nearer two hundred."

In essence, he said, "What you had here was a right-wing paramilitary outfit created, funded, armed, and directed by the government."

When Ellison arrived after the shooting, no one had been charged yet. "My job initially was to try and help people being interrogated by the FBI—people were being arrested in paramilitary raids all over the country, so I flew or drove everywhere . . . and I had very little idea what I was doing, I was just out of law school. It was like being a doctor without having ever worked on a body—but you learn. You learn *quick*."

Then he said that around Peltier's trial, they created such an atmosphere of fear that some of the jurors were still terrified today. They sequestered them; once they were selected, they were kept under armed guard either in the courthouse or in a hotel room, they were transported in a bus with taped windows—constantly placed in circumstances where it appeared their lives were in immediate danger.

"No way," said Ellison, "no way could you have an open mind, no way could you not begin to fear that Peltier's friends and family might attack you. The judge too, he was told his life was in danger—he had armed guards round the clock."

And was that justifiable?

"No. It was absolute fabrication. It was fantasy."

Later that evening, I found the grip crew in the City Bar watching the Cubs play the Pirates; I talked with three of them, Tim, Jim, and Dan. Jim and Dan had gone cowboy already, in straw hats and Wranglers; Tim on the other hand was more Che Guevara, with burly stubble and a woolly beret on his head. But they were all baseball men—and in 1988 they'd worked together in Dyersville, Iowa, on *Field Of Dreams.*

"Great little town. Best people I ever met in my life."

"Go to the Office Tap, get the onion rings. Awesome."

"That's the great thing about this business—you end up in these places. We just been in Uganda, Mississippi . . ."

"And Mississippi's weirder than Uganda."

"But *Field Of Dreams* . . . that was a great film to do. I mean, a *mystical* film."

"When we got in this business, we always said we wanted to do one film that would be memorable—one film that twenty, thirty years from now, if it comes on cable, you'd watch it again. *Field Of Dreams* was that film."

"But this here, *Thunderheart*—this is the most interesting film I've worked on since that."

"I like it 'cause it's action-packed, gunshot and car chases—and people go, Oh, not another one—but they've surrounded it with this script that's really touching on stuff. I mean, it's *heavy*. Like, someone killed this woman out here, and—can you believe this—they cut off her hands and sent them to Washington for ID. Instead of taking fingerprints. Then they said she died of exposure, they found her in a ditch. So the family got a court order to exhume the body—and the exposure she died of was exposure to a .38 in the back of the head."

"Can you believe it? This is *America* . . . and what's scary is I didn't know *any* of this shit till I came here. In two weeks, I've learnt stuff . . . I tell you, this was locked up, man. Locked up."

At least now, said Ellison, Peltier's case was getting more attention, and not only in the media. The New Democratic Party in Canada had adopted a call for his return to Canadian soil, and that party had a good piece of the Canadian vote. In the United States, Senator Inouye of Hawaii had asked Bush to exercise clemency.

I asked if things were any better here, back where this story began.

Ellison said, "Well, the goon squad is gone, so there's no organized violence anymore. But the conditions that precipitated the resistance are still here; in some senses they're worse. Unemployment is higher now, for example, than it was back then.

"On the other hand, the locally guided effort—the KILI radio station, the college, the educational effort, the anti-alcohol effort . . . There are tremendous problems, but they are being tackled. Everything that AIM was trying to do is still in the works."

Then there was the environment, the waste dumps, the mining—issues, he said, on which local whites could join with Indians on the same side for once. For example: One of the defense contractors wanted to use a place in the Black Hills as a test range for their latest piece of techno-fantasia, a uranium-tipped tank-busting missile system—and they were stopped by the CIA.

They were stopped by the *who?*

By the Cowboy & Indian Alliance.

The day's shooting wrapped up about seven; I went with maybe thirty people from the crew to watch the dailies in a little projection room at the high school.

The film went to New York for processing every day, and then came back for review; today being a Tuesday, we were watching Friday and Saturday's work, a double dose. And to be honest—if you're not intimately involved in the construction job whose end result is these daily strips of celluloid—then watching the dailies is dull.

The dailies are the bits of the jigsaw thrown on the floor out of the box, the disconnected pieces from which the picture eventually gets shaped. You're watching scenes in the form of a dismembered stew, an orderless ragbag of takes on every component image in that scene. You're watching wide angles and close-ups, backs of heads and talking faces, fragmented conversations and reactions, shot through now and then with wild slews out of focus, or actors fouling up a line and smiling, or rolling their eyes to heaven with a snort of annoyance—but I'll sew together what I saw the best I can.

Against the backdrop of the White River flowing by the Badlands wall, Kilmer pulls up to the junk-strewn shanty of a young Indian woman. Dust swirls in the wake of a battered pickup; sweat runs down faces seen close through a tattered screen door. The woman derides Kilmer as "the government Indian." Children scamper about, nervous; he's rejected, but worms his way in on a second visit with a box of groceries for Grandma. Through the fractured mesh of the endless repeats and abrupt juxtapositions, it's possible to see how things might develop between these characters; while the woman hints at something wrong in the water, illness in the children . . .

But the abiding image in my mind is a different one, of an Indian running, and a goon coming after him in a car over the dazzling green ground. In the silence of the dailies the goon stands up from the door of the car, driving with one hand, firing an automatic rifle with the other. The rich long grass of the chalky riverside falls away beneath the dented fender of the bouncing, racing vehicle; the rifle spits soundless yellow flickers of fire against the pale pink and grey of the Badlands beyond . . .

Outside the school, the horizon was a brilliant pink, thickening along the rim of the huge land to deep ruby and crimson. David Atherton passed by on his lime green fifteen-dollar bike and said—thinking, perhaps, of his smog zone home, L.A.—"Isn't that something?"

Splashes of neon glared into the gathering dark along the Kadoka motel strip, a garish rash against the dying sky. I walked away down Main to the City Bar, and talked baseball with the grip crew.

## Field of Dreams

The first time I went to America I ended up pumping quarters in a pay phone in a doughnut store in Salt Lake City, screaming at TWA just to *get me the hell out of there* . . .

The second time I got drunk for a fortnight in New York, which has nothing really to do with America at all.

But the third time I went to Rio in Wisconsin, population 700—and among the rolling green sweep of the cornfields under the Valhalla-scale storms, with the Milwaukee Road freight trains hooting and clanking past through the day and the night, I was happy for the first time in America.

I drove into Rio again on County B, and rolled down Main Street. Nothing was changed. It still looked a little shabby around the station where the trains don't stop anymore. Our Place was still there, and the Village Pub, and the Friendly Inn—you'll never be short of a beer in Wisconsin. I bought a six-pack, then went out to Scott and Jane's place.

And like Ruth and OB have their lake, Scott and Jane have their wooded back forty—a magical place, a sudden Narnia out the back door, forty acres of trees and glades resonant with breeze and birdsong, rustling and humming with thick layers of nature busy about its myriad secret processes. We went walking in there in the golden evening; after the storm the ground and the grass were heavy with rain, gleaming and darting with prismic shards of crystal dusk light. We came on a clearing where the grass was waist-high, dotted with dark green thickets, and overlaid with a numinous wash of white mist; the low sun threw radiant beams of orange through the trees into a drifting haze of glowing vapor.

Towers rose on the pale electric horizon, lit lilac and gold—and it was like the world had light *inside* it, light singing in the heart of every cell, warm light softly pulsing in all the veins and arteries of the murmuring wood. I felt like I was floating, disconnected from care . . .

Heaven will be Scott and Jane's back forty, minus the unbelievable mosquitoes.

With the Fourth of July coming up, they had friends gathering for a holiday canoe trip north into the woods. They'd all been to college together; now, all but Scott and Jane were in the cities, mostly Minneapolis; one had driven up from Atlanta. So dinner was like *The Big Chill,* all these old friends visiting who'd passed into work, adulthood, kids, the city climate of fear . . .

Val was taking a self-defense course. If it had to be, she said, she'd go for your nuts and your eyes; she'd disable you, no question.

She said, "I'm ready to gouge someone's eyes out, because that's nothing to what those guys out there are prepared to do. There's people out there prepared to cut a woman's breasts off, or cut out her vagina—so frankly, what I'm doing is only reasonable. And a lot of woman I've met live in that mind-set in America now."

Someone else said, trying to define Americans for me, "We're a nation of movers. We're people who don't live in places; we only camp in them, until we go someplace else where things might be better. We go in and out of towns without leaving a trace."

While the truck got an oil change, I had lunch at Karen's Cafe on Main—Best Potato Salad in the Heart of America. The guy in the garage said the solenoid was going on the starter motor, but it'd get me home; otherwise, it was holding up fine.

In the forty-two days since I'd bought it, I'd driven 5,589 miles; and yet, of the forty-eight states, I'd been in only nine. Scott banged his big hand on the door of the truck, and laughed his rich laugh out loud at the preposterous Brit.

"*Damn* fine truck," he said. "That camper is . . . that camper is *unique.*"

Outside it was like Africa. Huge bugs roamed on clattering wings through an untrained expanse of tall flowers and grass under the implacable blue heat. Birds now and then chipped in a careful, reflective remark; wind slipped by occasionally, stirring the trees, a firm hot hand through the breathless air.

Scott had taken his son down to Milwaukee, and watched the Brewers lose 6–0. "Not a good experience. They have their moments—but they're few and far between."

But aside from baseball, he said Wisconsin was doing okay. "We've had an exceptionally good growing season, very timely rains. Last week, we had some real hot days, things were getting stressed out—so that rain last night, you couldn't have asked for a more perfect time. 'Cause it's ready to go, there's enough moisture in there to make corn right now."

In general, he said, "We don't seem to have the dips and bumps so severely. The dairy farmers have taken a beating, but everyone else is alright. And you can always find a job here. It might not be what you want to do, but you'll be bringing home a paycheck.

"See, the main thing is we have abundant fresh water—so I think the Plains'll go on hurting worse and worse, and we'll become the center more and more. And instead of just seeing cornfield after cornfield, you'll see more fruit, more vegetables—I mean, California, they have water police now. You wouldn't have that here. 'Cause those places, the biggest vegetable-producing areas in the United States—if they weren't irrigated, those places would be desert. Whereas here, we produce so much damn corn . . . we could lose the whole of Ohio and still have enough corn."

It was the same thinking that led Red Nose to hope Coffeyville, too, would survive in the end.

Then Scott said, "The only thing is, the government's got its hands so deep into agriculture, they manipulate the market so much—I'd just as soon see the government get right out of it and let agriculture go, so we'd have a *real* supply-demand thing here."

But that would devastate some regions.

"It would. But those who prosper will still supply the market."

Our Place, known also as Joe's Place, had a softball team, and Scott was on it. They played in Fireman's Park; they were, that night, playing the Quad Squad from Columbus. I went down to watch them, on a blue summer evening.

A father said brusquely to his young son, "You got a ball? Usually helps to have a ball if you want to play catch, buddy."

Parenting in America, one guy had said to me, was run on the good cop/bad cop principle—and Dad was the bad cop. I'd said over dinner the night before that I'd heard fathers speaking with extraordinary harshness to their sons throughout the trip, right to sticking a terrified three-year-old on a calf at the Boise City rodeo—and round the table people agreed: The greatest fear of the American man is the day his son's big enough to punch him out.

American men, they said, live vicariously through their sons, who *have to do better than them*. So as their bellies begin to hang over their waistbands, you'll see them bawling the kid out at Little League . . .

In the BJ's dugout in Liberal Mike Barlow had said, "Where I'm at school at Oklahoma State, I talk to the European students in tennis or track and field there, and they seem more content just to enjoy what they do; they're the guys all the trainers want to be around, those guys are courteous. They don't have this need-to-win-at-all-costs thing, this American win-win-win.

"And it can be a bad thing—a lot of kids by the time they're ten, they just don't want to play ball anymore. When you spend a lot of time around athletes, you'll know some that have a lot of talent but basically, they don't like what they're doing. Then it comes out they're just doing it for their Dad."

At Fireman's Park in Rio, the father playing catch with his son had another son, younger, maybe four or five. He was on a team already; a woman asked the kid how it was going.

"Good," he said, sternly, like a little micro-adult.

His dad said with fierce pride, "He plays soccer, too. He's a runner."

All the same, softball, at least as played by the six teams of the Rio Softball Association, seemed to me a civilized affair. Your team of ten had to be at least half women. The pitcher and the catcher had to be different sexes; the pitching was underarm, and there was no sliding home. "We don't like anybody to get hurt."

Joe's Place, someone joked, had twenty on the team, " 'Cause we're old."

Someone else asked, "He's writing a book? About *this?* Must be a comedy then."

"Or a tragedy."

We sat on benches under a tree in the warm late light, drinking beers from big coolers. Far off in the southeast, thunderheads roamed the green horizon.

The Quad Squad scored five in their first inning. The lady on first base for Joe's Place said, "How many errors can I make in one inning?" I mentioned to the guy next to me how it seemed a telling American kind of cruelty, the stark way the errors get marked against you in these sports of theirs.

He grinned and said, "You got to know who's slacking off. So you can let them know about it."

A freight train went clanking and rumbling by, letting go again and again with its melancholy hooting as it passed through the town. A thunderhead rose in the northwest.

"Let's go. Everybody have an up attitude now."

Joe's Place got even to 5–5 at the top of the fourth. Scott swung so hard he broke the bat; sweat-laced faces grinned, swigging ice-cool beer.

The Quad Squad got one in the fourth, and four more in the fifth: 10–5, and that was how it ended.

"Good ballgame."

The teams in two lines acted out an informal little ritual, walking past each other so everybody got to slap everybody else's upraised hands.

In the last pink and velvety light over Fireman's Park, Scott said happily that he had one out, one double, one RBI—and *no errors.*

The next morning I drove southwest back into Iowa, to the Field Of Dreams.

Either Tim, Jim, or Dan of the grip crew in Kadoka said, "This guy has a vision, he hears a voice. He's a farmer, but he plows under his corn, and builds a ballpark there instead. Then one by one, famous players from the past start showing up out of the corn; ghosts come to play on this guy's ball field. And he's lost half his corn, he can't pay for his house—but the voice told him people will come. And they do."

"His father comes, that's the point. It's about fathers and sons."

"And reconciliation."

"And love."

"And baseball."

"It was '88 when we did it—worst drought since the thirties. And our corn was insured—if it didn't get to be four feet tall by such and such a time, the film company got a payout. So we spent the whole time shooting every damn thing except for where the corn was—and it didn't grow, and it didn't grow, and eventually the insurance paid up. So then they irrigated the hell out of that field, pumped it full of nutrients—and a storm came through, that fired it up too. By the time we got to it half of Iowa was this knee-high brown wreck—and our corn was seven, eight feet, it was *too tall.* We had to build a foot-high platform right into the field, otherwise you couldn't see the actors. Hell, they couldn't see each other."

"But it was sad. You'd drive around, and everywhere all this corn was dying on the stalk. And everybody was panicking—how were they going to get through the winter? And there we were growing this great corn. To make a movie."

Then the grip crew said how the guy who plowed his corn over for the film, Don Lansing, had kept the ball field afterwards—and how now, in real life, the people came. They had fourteen thousand go there in 1990; one couple got married there, there were busloads of Japanese—and there were fathers and sons.

Fathers and sons going to Iowa, to play ball on the Field Of Dreams.

Three miles outside Dyersville, there it was—the white farmhouse with the grey-roofed awning over the deck, the red barn, and the little ball field with its lights set down into the green sea of corn. It was beautiful.

Lansing's sister said, "It was too pretty to plow under. When we were kids we always played ball in the yard here—and that was the cornfield we'd lose our balls in."

Now they had people from all over, Australia, Korea, Canada, Japan. She said, "It's kind of hard to believe, but families enjoy it. Fathers and sons, it's special to them. It doesn't matter if they're from California or Florida or wherever, they play ball together."

They didn't charge anything to let these people come; they just sold T-shirts and souvenirs from a little cabin by the drive. Lansing's brother-in-law said, "I guess it's about dreams. Dreams and fantasies."

There was a high school team there, in a yellow bus from Oelwein fifty miles away; a Little League team came too, a vanload of thrilled kids. And there were fathers and sons, throwing each other easy pitches, thwacking the ball over the bright little field.

"I guess as long as there's baseball and there's fathers and sons, there'll be that movie, and there'll be this."

In the film there's a line, 'Is this Heaven?'

And Kevin Costner replies, 'No, it's Iowa.'

"People like to come out of the corn, like in the movie. They like to pretend it's Heaven, which it *ain't* . . . but movies get people to believe things, I guess."

America now has 20 percent of its children living below the poverty line.

It borrows more than it earns, and it buys more than it sells.

The average American has a lower real personal income now than he or she did in 1980.

The deficit swells . . .

And in America in 1990, 23,220 people were murdered—well over a third of the nation's death toll in the entire fifteen-year period of its involvement in Vietnam, *in one year.*

These are not facts guaranteed to give you sweet dreams, and the average American knows it.

But all too often, it seemed to me, his or her response was not to quit dreaming and start facing up to those facts—but to blame them instead on welfare bums, spics, nips, niggers, sand niggers, drunken Indians, and in general the whole criminally vicious and scheming horde of the un-American other . . . then to go to self-defense classes, grumbling about liberals trying to take away their guns.

Like Moni Hourt said, "The land of milk and honey sprung a leak."

She also said, "Americans—we're like our weather. We're capricious, excitable, and given to explosive events."

And there was, at that time, another pack of dream images cropping up regularly on TV—not a movie, this one, just an ad, but a very filmic ad indeed.

In the wake of Desert Storm, it showed the Hum-Vees bucking over the dunes, and the sinister black designer-death profiles of the Apache gunships hovering in clouds of smoke and flying dust—all intercut with the flag going up the flagpole at the school in the little town, and the child putting its hand to its patriotic breast. The soundtrack was a thumpingly unsubtle chunk of rock music:

*My hometown is not like this*

as our brave boys ate grit, scrambling and diving through the Arabian sands,

> *But that's alright with me*
> *'Cause I'm out here for my hometown*
> *'Cause freedom isn't free*

And what use is that, if your hometown's dying?

But there you go. If you live on a field of dreams, the only outcome can be delusion, and then disillusion, as the spinning wind sweeps across the plain . . .

There is, I fear, a storm coming in.

# 9.

# Pine Ridge

I drove along I90 from Kadoka to get to the Badlands. The sky was a bruised, black and blue empire of unfallen rain; the clouds were ragged with that unearthly, spun-marble effect as if they were solid, and could fall down and strike you. . . . To the north, the prairie rolled away; along the south of the interstate, snatches of the wall were visible now and then, a pink dinosaur lip.

The Badlands were extraordinary, hallucinogenic—a crumbling shale moonscape mostly pale ocher and grey, sometimes yellow and maroon, honed by the forces of erosion into a jagged city of thrones and castles and spires, towers and turrets and serrated ridges. The rock was layered through with immaculately precise pink striations, capped with white crests of volcanic ash blown from the rising of the Rockies a hundred million years ago; it was like driving on time's shoreline.

Rain-green flats lapped from the south into a shattered jumble of rock, where water and wind unburied the bones of strange marine and swamp creatures, hippos the size of deer, horses the size of dogs . . . The late twentieth century drove through in campers, visitors from another planet.

I cut southwest on the dirt of the Sage Creek Rim Road, through wide seas of abrupt stone and yellow-flowering grass, plush with meadowlarks and prairie dog towns; the wind blew, under inverted cones and bundles of purple-tinged rain cloud. I passed through Scenic, heading south to Porcupine on the reservation, past the clumps and crags of white and grey dotting the green hills and grassland of Pine Ridge . . . and I tried to imagine men, women, children, pursued here through the bitter cold of a Dakota December.

For though it was green with rain just now, the harshness of the place, under that turbulent sky, was vivid and forbidding.

. . .

In 1986, five years before the centennial of Big Foot's trek through winter to Wounded Knee, a group of nineteen Lakota people reenacted that trip, going 180 miles through the Badlands. Jim Garrett from Cheyenne River was among them; another was Alex White Plume, now fifth member of the tribal council on Pine Ridge. But when I asked Alex in his office whether it wasn't a pretty arduous undertaking he said simply, "It was *beautiful*."

He said it was dangerous, maybe—but it was a spirit trail. It wasn't *meant* to be easy . . .

By 1990, the Big Foot Riders had grown to three hundred strong. This last time, after a ceremony to commemorate Sitting Bull at Fort Yates, they'd ridden 250 miles.

At Ellsworth Air Force Base, Lieutenant Robert Carver told me he'd seen them leaving from a school up on Cheyenne River. He said, "It was cold, just incredibly, dreadfully cold, I mean *cold*. And these folks were on horses, riding through the snow with the wind blowing . . ."

Lieutenant Carver was from North Carolina. He said, "You don't see that back East."

Nor, back East, if the dumpers and the diggers get their way, would you see the uranium testing, the zeolite mining, the toxic trash tips, the earth ripped out and the waste tossed back—the maw and rectum of our techno-progress, hidden away on the Indian land.

"From Porcupine to Wambli, there's sixty miles of zeolite in there. They've described the formation as, 'not finite, but infinite.' But some of those buttes are 100, 150 feet tall—and to go after that formation, they'll have to destroy them. Also, the zeolite holds the water here, so the environmental integrity of the whole reservation's at stake."

They could wreck the whole place.

"Yup. And I don't know how they can be stopped. We can organize, we can resist—but it'll take some sort of national consciousness to stop it."

It was late in the afternoon. In a neat little office at Our Lady of Lourdes Mission in Porcupine I talked with Bill Kunan, a moving force in the Native Resources Coalition. He was a Chippewa from Wisconsin married to a full-blood Oglala, and he'd been on Pine Ridge fifteen years; he was a big man with a strong, solid face, and an anger that lurked visibly beneath the quiet energy with which he put his case.

He said, "People have to understand what's going on here. The Indian

Wars aren't over; instead of wearing cavalry uniforms they're wearing three-piece suits, that's all. Because at the moment if it's Indian land, who gives a shit? Federal protection? We've got zero. So it's going to take a lot of prayer, a lot of strength on the part of the people to hang on to what we've got."

On Pine Ridge, the latest waste dump proposals had been blocked, so the dumping company just moved over to the Rosebud Reservation and was trying there instead. There was room on Rosebud, they said, *for all the nation's waste* . . . and the Indians didn't have a whole lot of resources to confront them. They put a few bucks on the table, said Kunan, and everybody jumped . . .

He said, "The only thing that unifies us is our prayers. We have nothing else but our spiritual strength. We all watch video, we all go to the dog track—you know what I'm saying. But we're trying to survive. We're trying to keep them from tearing everything up, and stealing everything, and destroying everything. And as we go on each day, we can see we've made mistakes—but we base what we do on research, and on vision too. We're still Indians, we can still see something—and we can see what's being done to us. Because we've been right on so many counts before."

Then he said, "What goes around comes around—and it's coming around right now. But we'll still be here."

He stressed, *"We'll still be here."*

Kunan wore a veteran's T-shirt. It wasn't his—he didn't seem a man likely to go fight for Uncle Sam—but it had been given to him by a friend. And he said simply, whatever the rights and wrongs of Indians getting employment in the white man's wars, "You have to honor them as warriors. You have to respect that."

Outside the tribal council buildings in the town of Pine Ridge, there was a large signboard dedicated to the Lakota men and women who'd gone to fight in Desert Storm. I counted 107 names painted on that board, in several cases two or three people from one family: Wanda Black Feather, Jody Birdhead, Louella Broken Nose, Ellen Fills The Pipe, Preston and Charles Good Voice Flute, Dino Iron Eyes, Dennis, Duane, and Randy Lays Bad, Jonathan, Darrel, and Lloyd Little White Man . . . like Kunan said, you have to respect that.

Then, inside the bare brick building on the bulletin boards, among flyers and posters announcing powwows and conferences, treaty days and rodeos and Desert Storm parades, I found a poster for the Ninth

Annual Sacred Hoop run: a five-day, 500-mile course round the Black Hills from Bear Butte to Angostura to Fort Robinson to Beaver Creek to Devil's Tower, and finally back to Bear Butte again.

The poster said cheerfully COMMITTEE NOT RESPONSIBLE FOR ACCI-DENTS, THEFT, OR BLISTERS.

People who can run like that, you'd surely *want* them on your side . . .

I drove twenty miles south on 87, through the grubby border stop and booze mart of Whiteclay to Rushville, Nebraska.

There's nowhere to stay on the reservation; there are few facilities of any kind at all. The next days became a strange shuttle between Pine Ridge by day, and the border town by night.

In Rushville I got a room in the Nebraskaland Motel, then found the Lazy River Saloon on North Main. It was an entirely Western establish-ment, at least judging by the nine wagon wheels on the ceiling, the sixteen saddles and the twenty-two branding irons on the wall, the forty-two rifles . . . There was an Indian couple in there, an old guy named Doc at the bar, and Brad the bartender. I went to talk with the Indians.

I'd have guessed them to be about forty. The man had muscled arms and a headband, and longish hair to his shoulders; the woman was stocky, heavy-faced behind big glasses. They wouldn't tell me their names. The man asked with some suspicion where I was from, and when I told him he said, "Great Britain? Where's that, Russia?"

It's in Western Europe.

"Where's West Europe? Shit, I'm ignorant."

I dove straight in. When you land on another planet, you might as well start at the beginning . . . I asked, was prejudice a problem?

The woman said, "It has to be. Any town round here, everywhere you go, people that have dark skin . . . It's no matter if you have education, it's skin color. There's Indians went to college, it makes no difference, it's real difficult to get a job—and they test you when you find one, like, Can you stay for a day? Indians *want* to work, they're *hard workers*—but somebody's always there to put them down. And Indians are short-tempered, you know."

They said Brad was okay, but that bar across the street, they didn't go in there. "Over there one time there was Indians playing pool, and this delivery guy comes in, he just sets all his stuff right down on the pool table there. But go to Gordon, now that is the most prejudiced town. Indians keep that town going, they get their checks every first of the month, and they spend 'em there—the first of the month, that's Gordon's economy, in the liquor stores, the department stores—but they don't appreciate it."

The woman said, "This is some years back . . . but these three white people undressed an Indian there, they was having a dance, and they made him dance naked into that Gordon Legion Club—he was just an old alcoholic in the street, they picked him up—and they killed him. They put him in the trunk of a car . . . You don't want to hear the rest of what they did to him. I'm ashamed to say. So AIM came down to Gordon, they had a march and a rally and stuff. It was good for a while . . . but it didn't make things any better.

"And they keep things under cover. Sometimes I hear that white kids take Indian women and leave them naked someplace . . . Indians tell each other what happens, they don't tell the cops. Cops aren't going to do anything to a white person. One time we went into the Legion Club in Gordon, and this one white guy was harassing his girlfriend . . ."

Her husband abruptly said to me, "Are you a fed?"

I said no, I wasn't.

He said, "This white comes and fights me, and it's 'Handcuff the Indian.' Then they just left us in the car, and went inside, when it wasn't us that started it. So don't go saying we're hostile individuals."

There were, he said, no swearwords in Lakota.

I tried to have them teach me some Lakota words—but between the Buds and our mutual ignorance, we didn't get very far. I sounded like a toad with a nose cold, attempting mangled, segmented translations in the back of my throat. Once or twice when I asked for a thing to be spelled the guy would say, "Hell, I don't know"—but that's not just down to him having trouble with pen and paper. As with Wambli/Wanblee, or Hodoka/Kadoka, it seemed more as if the Indian words simply couldn't, or wouldn't, be pinned down in the first place. And I felt, if you learnt this language, it wouldn't be like the finite transit to another specified country involved in learning French, or Italian. It would be like cutting loose from your moorings altogether, drifting away into spaces as wide as the Plains . . .

So we gave up and told each other jokes instead.

"One time," the guy said, "these two Oglalas gave two Rosebudders a ride to a Rosebud fair, they put them in the back of the pickup. And I guess those two Oglalas are drinking, you know, 'cause they lose control, they go into Ghost Hawk Dam, and the pickup goes down in the lake. And those Oglalas in the cab are the only ones who come out—the Rosebudders drown. So everybody says, How come?

"And this one Oglala says, I guess they couldn't open the tailgate."

Then suddenly he said, watching my notes go down, "You're not fucking with my mind, are you? You fuck with my mind . . . I could go get a pistol from my car right now."

I said no, I wasn't fucking with his mind. And no, I wasn't a fed.

He told me more jokes; when we quit talking, he taught me the Indian handshake. The woman said, "You're a brave person, just coming up and asking questions like that. I was about ready to slap you in the face."

I went back to the bar and sat quietly next to Doc, making notes, drinking beer, watching baseball. Brad said those two were okay, they came in once a week, shot pool, drank four or five beers and then left.

Two other guys had come in; they were talking together, laughing . . .

Next thing I know I'm being punched in the shoulder. The Indian guy's towering behind me and he says, "Are you laughing at me? Indians don't like to be laughed at. You remember, I got a fucking pistol in my car."

I told him I wasn't laughing at anybody. I wasn't laughing, full stop. And there was a staring out, a nervy moment . . . then the woman took him away.

Brad said, "Tough side to check on, man."

Next to me Doc said, "This town is entirely different than how it was thirty years ago. I was born here, but I been gone thirty years, and I don't even recognize it as the same place. There ain't nothing to write about here now. Except the prejudice, which is worse than it was."

Well, I was sorry to hear that.

"Oh definitely. All these minorities are prejudiced more against the white man than they ever was. Thirty years ago a nigger was a nigger and I let him alone—now he's forced me to dislike him. I understand England's got a little of a nigger problem coming that way too. Like that Injun, it wasn't the booze. It was the prejudice."

I told him he was an offensive old prick. It was the first time I'd expressed a personal opinion to a stranger in a month, but I was getting tired of this shit.

.   .   .

I talked to the other two guys.

"Look out there," they said, "there ain't a soul walking up and down out there. Thirty, forty years ago, those streets'd be full."

"Used to have bartering then. People'd take their cream, their eggs, their groceries to the store, and it was bartering, we had commerce here. That's all gone. It's all gone down the roads to the cities. Everybody just stops at home now."

"Saturday night used to be booming. When I was six years old I can remember my father would come to town, Junior Alayo used to have his grocery store right over there—oh God, he'd stay up till twelve o'clock at night. Guys'd get drunk, then go in there to get their cheese and lunchmeats to make sandwiches to go home with."

Brad said, "Just ten years ago this town was happy—but the farmer ain't making no more than he did ten years ago now. He just survives."

"These last years the bank's been on their backs . . . there's so many that's gone."

Brad said, "You've taken an awful proud nation, and you've locked them up same as you would in a penitentiary, and you've stripped them of all their rights. Then you turn around and give them everything, when they were used to earning everything, their name, their prestige. So consequently they turn to the booze."

And which proud nation was he describing?

Farmers losing everything, everything coming down to the government and the welfare and the wheat support price, leaving the likes of Doc marooned in the emptying towns muttering over whiskey on the rocks, head shaking, soul sodden. . . .

But Brad, of course, was talking about the Indians. Besides working the bar in the Lazy River, he taught seventh grade on the reservation. "So," he said, "I see it every day."

Four drunk Indian women had come in. One was slumped head down on the bar, weeping. With them, untended, was a boy of nine or ten, roaring around with all his energy undirected, or just watching, fidgeting, bored to death. The woman wept and moaned, a low dreary groaning.

Brad said, "There's only one way to change it—through the children. You've got to try and change it through the children."

These women were about the most depressing people you'd want to see in your life. It was fucking this, fucking that, swaying, shrieking, flaring into arguments and tears.

Brad said, "Teaching up there, I have no parental involvement at all. The kids respond; if you can get them locked in by fifth grade, if you can get them through eleven to fourteen, they'll hold, 80 percent could carry through. But I can't promise it—I've seen second graders come in looped, that's seven, eight years old. What can you do then?"

"Momma, I'm dying. Tonight I'm dying. I want to go home."

They could barely walk. The kid scuttled about, or came dejectedly to rest propped on the bar, staring dully at the lights.

Brad said, "Children need discipline, respect, care."

There was a wail then, "So who's gonna take care of *me?*"

One of the other guys said sadly, "To be honest with you, this town would not survive without all the booze that runs through here."

But Brad said, "Don't let what you're seeing here be the total. This is the down side. Up there, there's a top side too—a real top side. Don't go thinking this is it, not for one minute."

I tried Moni Hourt's three attitudes out on him then, that there were those who ignored, those who despised, and those who regretted.

He said, yes, and the third camp might be growing too. "But they're not going to do a fucking thing about it."

And the scale of the problem . . .

"Percentage-wise, you're seeing seventy percent of the res right there at this bar. It isn't a pretty picture—but that's down to two hundred years. And as a teacher, I believe the cycle can be broken. We have to get to the children; otherwise we pay for this forever.

"And there's another thing. I said there's no parental involvement— but at the same time, with the uncles, the aunts, the extended family, they still do take care of their own. So it may be bad, the cycle they've put themselves in—no, that *we've* put them in, you can't blame them . . . I mean, look where we put them. The Badlands, the worst fucking land in the country. I wouldn't bet a rattlesnake would want to live up there too long.

"But still, listen—I've lived all over the United States. I've lived with blacks, Cajuns, Mexicans—and the Indians are still the strongest. Inside, they're still the strongest. And if that could be let out . . . we wouldn't have any reservation then, we wouldn't *need* a reservation. They'd be your average Joe, your average tax-paying citizen."

Successful integration is, of course, the white man's fondest dream. To a lot of Indians, on the other hand, integration looks like burial: the final disappearance beneath the earth-trashing arrogance and craziness of the flooding white tide.

What a lot of Indians want might be summed up better, instead, by what Brad said next. He said, "They were here before we got here. They're still here now. And they'll be here when we're gone."

Brad said there were people in Rushville who'd drive an extra sixty miles around to Rapid City to avoid going on the reservation. It's another world . . .

I drove up there in the morning. I'd heard that Alex White Plume was a man I should go see, but when I got to the council building in Pine Ridge, he wasn't in. And I didn't know where to begin there, who to see, what to say . . . Alex's secretary said I should talk to William Horn Cloud.

I asked who he was; she smiled and said, "He's himself."

He was an old boy sat quietly in an armchair behind the reception counter, watching the comings and goings round the small, poorly equipped offices; there was no taxpayers' money gone into big government here, that was for sure.

And I felt uneasy already, landed in this other world now; so when it turned out William Horn Cloud was deaf, there was no way I was going to sit there shouting questions at him. In the hushed and unhurried to-and-fro, I felt self-conscious enough as it was; I didn't have any map there, I didn't know the rules—and I felt myself watched, not aggressively, but with a curious, cautious surveillance. After all, who was I? And no way could I sit yelling my clumsy questions at this deaf old boy in there . . .

I wrote on my pad that I was writing a journey to the heart of America.

William Horn Cloud said, "I can't read too good either, my eyes are weak."

And I was helpless.

He smiled, brown eyes twinkling deep in a handsome, leathery face softly grooved and furrowed with the best part of a hundred years. Stumped as to what to do or say next, I remember thinking it was an appropriate encounter—knowing nothing, I'd been confronted with a mirror to my own deafness, my own blindness . . .

William Horn Cloud leant slowly forward. He said without preamble, "The pipe was brought to the Sioux Indians seven years after Columbus landed. A beautiful girl brought the pipe to two Indians out scouting for buffalo. One had bad intentions towards her, the other told him not to, but he went to her—then a cloud came down and covered him up, and when it was gone there was nothing left but his bones.

"This other guy got excited. The woman told him to go back to camp, I'm bringing something to you, so erect a shelter. He went back to get everything ready, and she came and unloaded her bag. She said, This pipe I bring you so that you will use it in time of hardship, sickness, and need. And this pipe must be handled by a just man.

"She had showed what happens to the bad man, and the good. And now when a person gets a certain age, he takes the pipe and goes way off and prays for visions to help his people. He don't pray for personal gain, but for the welfare of his people.

"See, long time ago, before the white man came, the animal kind and the two-legged kind had a very close relationship, and they helped one another by the Great Spirit. He created the four-legged to instruct the two-legged in his creation—that means the grass, the roots, the herbs, the four-legged eat that, so they know which is which—and they turn that knowledge over to the guy who prays with the pipe. That's how the Indians learn to respect creation."

He said, "The Great Spirit created these things to be used by Indian people. We don't try to improve them, we don't try to be smarter than creation—which is how people got now. They try to use chemicals to improve the food we eat; Indians never tried to do that. Indians just give thanks to the Great Spirit for what He gives as it is."

He sat back, as if that was the end of the lesson. Then he said, "If I go among the white people and ask them to tell me their history, they're going to charge me. But we like people, and we like to tell our history. We get along better by knowing each other's backgrounds."

He sat back for good. I had been politely instructed. The office swirled slowly about him. He was motionless, and smiling.

A tall, striking man in cowboy hat, boots, and jeans had seen the old man talking to me. He wasn't happy.

He said, "You come in here to write a book—but what's in that for the Lakota people? You just write a book to make money—when we have a battle on our hands here, to keep what we got for the next generation, and to get back what is ours. Because the Black Hills are ours, that's what we want, we want the Black Hills back. But you people . . . you showed our young people money. And you're here for money right now."

I wondered how difficult I would find it on Pine Ridge. A wedding and a weatherman, a rodeo and a baseball game, even a tornado and a flood—these were all subjects where white people had told me their stories with the faintest of prompting. But on Pine Ridge, I supposed it would be harder.

I figured, after all, if I'd been hit by as many freight trains as the Indians have been, I might not be inclined to tell my story to any passing member of the driver's union either.

It turned out, in fact, that this guy staring me down was the only Indian who refused my questions all the time I was there.

Project Recovery stood to one side of the council buildings. It had bright painted signs in a little yard outside; one said simply IT'S OUR CHOICE. Another said NEED A DEATH RIDE? JUST DRINK AND DRIVE. A third showed FACES OF ALCOHOL, a livid string of Munchian screams in psychedelic primaries captioned PARTYTIME. ANGRY. FIGHT. SORROW. CRY.

When Red Cloud signed the Fort Laramie treaty in 1868, one of his stipulations was that there should be no alcohol in Indian country; alcohol had been illegal on the reservation from the start. Nonetheless...

I went through a tattered porch to a pleasant, airy reception room with light wooden walls and floor, and talked with Ed Starr in his office. He said the vast majority of deaths on the reservation were alcohol-related—but to his frustration, he didn't have stats on it. The government's Indian Health Service, he said, "only look at the physical aspects, they don't give us numbers, even though it's the Number 1 problem. Like, if a guy dies in a car wreck, they don't say it's alcohol—it's a broken head. So the only stats are for car accidents, stabbings, cirrhosis..."

With what stats he had, he suggested 88 percent of crime and illness on the res came down to drink—rape, theft, you name it.

As for Project Recovery, he said it had been going eleven years; last year, they'd sent seventy-five adults for treatment, and sixty-eight adolescents, out of a population on Pine Ridge of around fifteen thousand.

And I asked him why drink was such a problem . . .

He said, "I started drinking 'cause my dad drank. And just to be part of the crowd . . . I started when I graduated in '63, then stopped in '79 when I went to a treatment center. And it was hard: I had to change a lot of friends, I had to find different people that were sober. There's not too many . . . but people drink 'cause there's nothing else to do. You got your grants and your commodities, you don't have to work to stay alive—so the reason a lot drink is the way they feel about themselves. They feel frustrated with the way they're living."

Still, I said, I'd heard suggestions that things were getting better.

He said, "I think culturally we're relearning the old ways, how they lived without alcohol. We're learning through the Lakota College. We're learning that it's our choice."

Then he told me a Lakota creation story.

"God was called Inyan—that means rock, or stone—and he was lonely, so he created Maka, the earth. Maka complained it was too dark, so Inyan created the sun and moon to follow each other. Then Inyan created Ikce ('Ik-chay'), which means plain old common people, and these Ikces were all covered with hair, and he put them under the earth. But there was an Iktomi, a spider; and he went under the ground and told the Ikces there was a good place to come live up on top. So he tricked them to come up."

Ikce, Ed Starr interjected at this point, also means to make choices.

He went on, "Inyan got mad 'cause they'd disobeyed him. So he gave them a choice either to obey Woope, the daughter of Maka—Woope means law—or be turned into four-leggeds. Well, some refused. So the ones that refused were turned into four-leggeds, and they were the buffalo. But the rest that chose to obey, all the hair came off them, and they were the two-leggeds. And if they ever got hungry, they could kill the four-leggeds.

"So that's how Woope came about, law, and how to make choices. Well, that's a short form of it . . . but what it means is, we have to make a choice. We have to choose whether to destroy ourselves, or to walk the good red road to the Great Spirit."

Then he pointed to a poster on his office wall showing Wichoni Changleska, the Circle Of Life, and a mourning ceremony in which the body's not buried, but raised above the earth. He said, "It's like up there. We don't want to mar the earth, to break it up. . . . They used to take the bones after a year to a sacred place, an oak tree in the Black Hills, and burn the bones there, and scatter the ashes in the hills—'cause that's respect for the earth. And that's why there's so much opposition to the mining, the trash pits—'cause the earth is sacred."

It looked, I said then, if we went on as we were, like we'd be paying for the way we'd been messing with the earth.

Ed Starr said, "I hope not."

.   .   .

Each morning I drove back up 87 to Pine Ridge, through the long bend and curl of the hills, past the dusty beer barns at Whiteclay, past people walking the roads. And each day I liked it better, and Rushville less.

I talked with Alex White Plume, fifth member, in his bare little office in the council building; the conversation was punctuated by frequent phone calls, and a constant arrival of requests through the door. I drank coffee from a polystyrene cup I'd rooted out in someone else's office—like I say, no big government here. The place felt more like a volunteer organization, struggling along on goodwill, rummaging for coffee cups . . .

On Alex's door was a notice, handwritten. It said, THE OST (OGLALA SIOUX TRIBE) IS PRESENTLY OUT OF FUNDS. NO FINANCIAL ASSISTANCE UNTIL FURTHER NOTICE.

Someone had crossed out PRESENTLY, and added CONTINUOUSLY instead.

An imposing, elegantly dressed, and somewhat angered woman came into the office. She'd had her house broken into—then found a favorite belt buckle, which had been stolen, in a hock shop over in Martin, and the guy wanted $40 for it. And she'd had to pay.

Alex said he'd paid $130 himself to get a saddle back from a shop in Scenic, same deal. But, he shrugged, that was border towns . . .

Someone from *Thunderheart* called, worried about the stuff in the *Lakota Times* about lawsuits, and opposition to the movie. Alex told him not to worry, it was election time in ten months, "So everybody's trying to get in the paper. But the burden of proof's with them—you ain't got a problem."

Getting off the phone, he said he thought the movie was a good thing. For one thing, 250 of his people got employment for the summer—and then, there were very few movies about contemporary Indian life.

I asked him what it had been like on Pine Ridge, in that period against which the movie was set.

He said, "Oh God, it was like living in a war zone. It was like open season on Indians, people'd kill an Indian and just bond out like it was a traffic offense. So when AIM was invited in here, they were urban Indians not afraid to stand up and say, Hey, I'm an Indian—and that was a big thing. Since that time," he said, "Lakota people are Lakota again. We've gone from one Sun Dance a year, to twenty-four. And," he grinned, "they ain't making John Wayne movies anymore."

Later he said, "The reason this movie's making some people uncomfortable, in my personal opinion, is that there were fifty-five murders that happened here that were never solved. So maybe people killed somebody and they're worried—but the way to heal something is to discuss it openly, and make friends over it. If we hide it, we'll never heal from it."

I said I'd heard the suggestion, from one Indian on the crew, that the film might make for better communication between the reservation and Kadoka as well.

"Well . . . I had a meeting with the mayor there recently over the redneck attitudes, the discrimination—and it turned out he'd never been on the res in his life. They're afraid of us . . . I think in '76, some magazine did a survey said Pine Ridge was the tenth most dangerous place to live in the world, and I guess we've never lived that down. But I don't carry a gun, I don't feel unsafe here. Where I live in Manderson, it's a small community, we all know each other; we know who drinks, we accept that—and we help each other out."

The phone rang again. He got briefly embroiled in trying to hustle $129 for a bus ticket to get a kid back to his mother in New Mexico. Then another call came, someone needing buffalo meat for a funeral.

He joked at some point that they had a budget of $43,000,000, and if anything worked out right he'd be going round in a stretch limo. He talked on the phone in the lilting click of Lakota; then someone called from New York, wanting to know if he needed a permit to hike on the reservation. Alex told him, "No, you don't need any permission to come in here. But come now, it's pleasant in June—it'll get hotter than the dickens soon."

When the call was done, he said wistfully they should be charging for that kind of recreation. Especially since *Dances*, there being so much more interest—and now *Thunderheart* . . .

He said, "It's important that movie portray us how we are. On the East Coast even today, when they think of an Indian, they still think he's on horseback with feathers all over the place. But we're ordinary people. We wear clothes, we drive cars; we retain our religion, but we're just people. When we say we want to go back to the traditional ways, that's not feathers and tepees, it's *values*."

So I asked him if they could get the Black Hills back, as well as their values.

He said, "We'd like the whole 7,300,000 acres back, but we realize that's impossible. A lot of those people, ranchers, they've bought their land there—and we know they love that land the way we do. So first

what we want is the 1,200,000 acres of federal land back—and that'd get
our foot in the door. After that, it's a hundred-year goal to purchase the
land back, at its present value. Which isn't ambitious—it's actually very
lenient, given what was done to us. And we'd tell the miners and so on
that they had leases, and the leases were limited, so they'd know when
they'd have to stop. And sure, we've been offered new money to forget
it—$120,000,000—but how can we take that? We're not pimps, we can't
prostitute our mother.

"The Black Hills," he said, "are not for sale."

Well, I said, he must know there'd be a lot of white people who'd
dismiss this plan.

"I think," he said, "it'll be accepted in the end. See, never has one
positive thing been done to us in five hundred years—but that's going
to change. We're educated in the white man's way now, and we're going
to use that way to get back what's ours."

The phone rang again. He smiled and said, "It's the boss." He listened
for a while, then told her, "Okay. But I got a bloke from Great Britain
here just now. A bloody bloke."

I raised my eyebrows at the colloquialism.

He whispered aside from the phone to explain, "I always read 'Andy
Capp.'"

He had to go kill a cow for his dinner. One of the women in the office
said, "That's why he's got that knife." He was testing a short, sharp blade
across his thumb.

Another woman said with an ironic smile, "You know he's supposed
to eat the liver, if he's a true warrior?"

Alex White Plume laughed. He said, "I take one bite, then I give it
to the women."


"The Lakota people mastered the horse to survive; today we are
mastering the airwaves and riding them to a better future for all the
Lakota people."

So said the KILI-FM calendar on Jody Hummer's office wall. It was,
she said, the strongest community station she'd ever heard. Kili, said Jim
Garrett, means "way above"; the station with its mast sits high on
Porcupine Butte, "100,000 watts of Lakota power."

It plays an eclectic and fetching mix of country, rock, and traditional
Lakota music—the latter being haunting, rhythmic, wailing chants over
a background of soft, deep, pounding drums. It also plays a regular string
of community messages, in both English and Lakota: general material on

the dangers of alcohol, or the promotion of Lakota culture, along with specific announcements about forthcoming events, Desert Storm parades, a sobriety ride, or tomorrow's powwow by the college at Kyle.

The station was housed in a striking, single-story wooden building with a steep-angled roof jutting from the side of the butte. Under a blanket of grey rain out of lowering, blue-black skies, I drove there through Wounded Knee from Pine Ridge, and found Buzz Two Lance on solitary duty in a ramshackle little studio in the back. He wore glasses, with fine black hair grown long in a tail down his back; he was a round-faced, soft-spoken guy, running things on his own without fuss or fluster.

The station started in 1983, a direct outcome of events in the seventies. Buzz said, "Back then there was a lot of miscommunication, misinformation, a lot of distortion—you know how it comes about, from send to receive. What's said in the beginning isn't what's heard at the end, and that causes dissension."

And KILI was about setting that right.

He took a call, running a taped announcement about tomorrow's powwow at the college while he was busy; then a guy came in who'd be dancing there, so Buzz went to talk with him too.

I looked around. The studio was roughly lined with sound-proofing foam; tapes stood neatly stacked on freestanding shelves of bare wood knocked together along one wall. Buzz wandered back in and ran another tape, a lyrical poem about how once the young men had been "fronters," brave warriors always to the fore in every battle. But what was the battle with now, in which the Lakota nation needed brave fronters once again? It was against alcohol and drugs.

Buzz said, "One of the things the KILI board decided early on was to declare war on booze and drugs. It's been quite a struggle—but people are not afraid to say they're sober now, so we're getting back. I have a friend that was living here ten years ago, a white boy from Iowa; he came back two weeks ago, and he said he saw so much change. Because people want control of their lives now. So we're willing to accept that we have our ills, and to seek solutions: we won't just sit and bitch anymore.

"See, we grew up in this dependency culture, we got used to never having to lift a finger—and as long as we had to depend on them, they had us where they wanted us. But now, we know we have to make a choice, and we *can* make choices.

"Long time ago, the bureaucrats sat in Washington and said, We know what's good for them—but they never came and asked us. Now it's, Wait a minute, Washington—this is what *we* want. Because sure, we run powwows, we wear feathers, we dance. But we can run the rest of our show too."

And there was, I said, more attention from outside to their situation now . . .

He smiled, with a mild and knowing irritation. He said, "You know the last Wounded Knee ride? The anniversary ride, to put the spirits to rest? We had nine European TV crews here—Danish, Austrian, nine crews all talking to us. And there was just one, maybe two crews from this country.

"But they've got blinders on here. They're worried about Russia and China, they've got their hands in Africa and South America and Asia where they don't belong . . . It's like a guy lives over there, his fence is falling down, the grass is a yard high—and he's telling everyone else to fix *their* yards. Like human rights, they're always talking about that—but what about here? What about Pine Ridge? For that matter, what about the ghettoes in Chicago, places like that? Why don't we take care of our own, instead of meddling with everybody else?"

He said, "Take Desert Storm—where's the money to free anybody here?"

It was getting late. I left him sitting on his own up on the butte in the gathering night, playing his music and messages; I set off back for Rushville. On the way, I gave two kids a ride, Dale and Cathy White Face, teenagers; they were going to Wounded Knee, and I asked what they were up to.

Dale said, "We're going there because a friend died."

I said I was sorry, and asked what happened.

"Alcohol."

On the radio there was a tornado warning, for somebody, somewhere . . .

In Rushville that evening the Lazy River seemed thin, hollow, two-dimensional. For all its griefs and trials, the reservation was taking me over. I went to bed early. The TV in my room didn't work.

The Oglala Lakota College is a small cluster of buildings set in open hills just southwest of Kyle; the powwow there the next day was the 18th Annual Lakota College Graduation Wacipi & Dance Contest.

A hundred yards behind the college on a low flat-topped rise, the powwow ground was a circle of grass surrounded by four tiers of wooden benches. The seating was arranged in the shade of a rough arbor of pine branches, laid over big wooden beams; sets of benches were interspersed with plastic folding chairs set in rings around fat drums. You had to have at least six drummers per drum; drummers were being called over the sound system to register, as only the first ten to do so would have the good fortune of getting paid.

I arrived shortly after midday; the Grand Entry was scheduled for one. In a larger circle around the powwow ground, the reservation's battered pickups and vans were gathered in numbers already; four white tepees stood to one side, decorated with paintings of buffalo masks, shields, feathers, and the sun. Concession stands were getting busy; the Indian Taco Wagon had a sticker saying it took Visa and Mastercard.

The sky was a padded roof of bunched grey cloud; green hills rolled away on all sides to pine-dotted crests spattered with bare pale rock. In the middle distance a teenager appeared over a crest, bareback on a horse. All about, rattling kids scurried through the growing crowd in brilliant costumes of bright red and deep blue, turquoise and brown, rich orange, blazing yellow and glossy green. They wore dramatic feather headdresses, arching from the crown of their heads to the base of their backs; they tinkled with breastplates and anklets of ringing little gold and silver tin horns. Circles of drummers warmed up here and there, wailing and thrumming on the taut soft skin; soundchecks fizzed and crackled.

Flags blew hard on the hurrying wind—tribal flags and veterans' flags, the college flag and the state flag, the Stars and Stripes. The Gulf War flag was a yellow ribbon on a white background with red letters saying WELCOME HOME; the Vietnam flag was more somber, black, and said only FORGOTTEN WARRIORS.

"Testing, one two three four."

Inside the college Harold Salway, the tribal chairman, addressed the new graduates, stressing the hopes that went with them for the future of their people.

"All dancers, all dancers—let's start lining up for the Grand Entry."

And in they came, from both the Dakotas, from Oklahoma and Montana—led by Vietnam vets and Gulf War returnees bearing the colors—until the ring was filled with a whirling profusion of color, way over a hundred dancers in a foot-stomping, drum-thumping, spinning parade of feathers and plumes, tassles and beads, flashing mirrors and flowing furs, flapping bandanas and flailing fans, women and men, young and old, in shades and headbands, in furry boots and beaded moccasins, all bell-jangling with the rings and tubes of bright tin on their wrists and their calves, faces intent, faces smiling, faces *sober*. The chanting pulsed and surged over the sound system . . .

And you know what it was like?

It was like the Boise City rodeo, or the living historians with their battle at the Caney Mayfest.

It was more vivid, for sure, and more strange to white eyes—and it celebrated a culture whose central tenets are fundamentally opposed to the grab-it-and-grow-it ethos of the white tide, the dig-it-up-and-tear-it-down, the restless lust for progress . . . but still it was the same.

It was the same because they weren't charging money at the door. It was the same because they were doing it for themselves, to preserve and pass on a way of life to their children. It was the same because in a dry and windswept place barely fit for habitation, against the worst kinds of odds, these people had survived. They were proud and stubborn as hell, and—like Alex said of Manderson, like Mary Tiff and Moni Hourt said of the Plains all round—they looked out for each other.

So if only the white and the red could see each other, and look out for each other too, because you never know: The white man might learn something . . .

I had more people on Pine Ridge tell me things were getting better than anywhere else. Sure, you could say it couldn't get much worse—but the shrinking white towns are no model of social or economic health either, are they?

I tried the idea on Jim Garrett—that whatever the differences, there were essential characteristics the Indian and the white man shared on these plains and in these hills, in the heart of America.

He said, "You know what the common element is? It's the weather. The weather here makes you the toughest sons of bitches around, no matter what color you are."

Then he told me a story.

He said, "My grandma married a Frenchman named Fred Dupree. They ran cattle on an allotment up on Cheyenne River, and they had twelve kids, six boys—so the boys grew up cowboys. Anyhow, in 1896, the Lakota people were starving out, and someone went way into the Badlands on the western edge of North Dakota, and they spotted a small herd of buffalo in there. So they petitioned the agent to let them go hunt. But my grandparents sent some of the boys with them, with special instructions to rope some of the calves and bring them back alive. They brought back three heifers and a bull calf, and they raised them up till my grandparents died. So the executor of the estate sold them; there were thirty-five by then, and next to none left any place else. He sold the herd to Scotty Phillips over near Pierre, and by the time he died, there was two hundred and some. His boys sold them on to different places again, William Randolph Hearst got some, Custer State Park, the 101 Ranch in Oklahoma . . .”

So the buffalo I had walked among with Alan Shields in No Man’s Land might very likely have been descendants of the buffalo saved by Jim Garrett’s grandparents.

Jim said, “About the time they saved those four calves, that could very well have been it, the end—I’ve always been very proud of that. And a lot of guys get down on white guys, so I remind them of that. That it was one white guy, and one Indian woman, and they saved the buffalo.”

In the college hall applause rang out for the people graduating; outside, the sky cleared to shining blue. To the south, another horseman came in off the sweeping ridges, hooves kicking flares of dust. On the powwow ground, little girls took their turn dancing to the beating thud and the ululating chant; four judges stood intent among them with clipboards as they bobbed and whirled.

“Okay, let’s give these beautiful girls a round of applause here.”

Jim was with Jody Hummer, down from Kadoka recruiting extras; he introduced me to a kid named Joe Sierra, who’d done the first Big Foot ride with his mother five years back. In the cold, Jim said, they slept out on the ground, all circled round the fire, and everybody had a pile of wood. Each time the fire burnt down, somebody’d wake up and chuck their pile on. Joe Sierra, that year, had been nine . . .

And among Indians, it’s rude to point. They do it, said Jim, with a less intrusive facial gesture instead, a pushing-out pout of the lips, and a directed nod of the head.

As he told the story, other teenagers round Joe Sierra remembered, and smiled. Because Joe, when the ride was done, got interviewed on TV out of Rapid, and they asked why he’d done it. So he said he’d wanted to know how it felt for those people, way back; then he pushed out his lips, and tossed his head back ninety-five years through time.

“Right there on TV,” Jim laughed, “just like an Indian.”

He said during the ride, “We were looking for the trail at the top of Big Foot Pass in the Badlands wall, we couldn’t see it anywhere. So someone said the animals would help us—and sure enough, we must have spooked him, but a coyote came out, and he ran right down that trail. So then we could see it."

He sat contentedly at the *Thunderheart* recruitment desk in the warm and windy evening; it was six o'clock, there'd been dancing for five hours, and after dinner it'd go right on through the evening. So the music pounded on, the Indian Taco Wagon served its fine tacos—Best Concession Stand in the Heart of America—and the people came and went between powwow ground and college. Kids queued, some uncertain, some excited, to fill in the movie application forms.

"Oh man," said Jim, "this is tough duty . . . beats the hell out of Kadoka."

Then he grinned; he and Jody, he said, had a problem.

"We can't find enough mean-looking longhairs. It's ironic. Kadoka's scared—and here we are having trouble finding enough mean-looking guys."

I found Alex White Plume whittling on a stick with his cow-killing knife in the soft-drinks stall his wife was running. He said after the fifth ride, the centennial, when it had grown to three hundred riders, they'd asked the Great Spirit whether they should do it again.

And the answer was no. He said the spirits of Wounded Knee were laid to rest.

Looking out through the crowd under the arbor of pine at the dancers stamping and weaving, the drummers pounding and chanting, Alex said, "I tell you something. You're going to be lonesome when you leave this place."

And I thought, that'd be right.

Oglala Chairman Harold Salway was thirty-five, a handsome man in a black bomber jacket and smart creased trousers. He'd grown up on Bear Creek in the Black Eyes community; he was three-quarters Indian, one-eighth Irish, and one-eighth French. He'd been a policeman, then got on the executive board five years ago; he'd been chairman for a year.

The announcer told the crowd about Jody and Jim looking for extras; he said, "You know the first qualification is you got to have the nose. Like Kelvin here. You just got to have the nose."

Salway smiled. He said, "I'm not going. I want a main part."

I asked him how things went for the Lakota people.

He was wincing with pain, due in hospital in three days to have his gallstones out—but he submitted to my questions, rather like Mike Nuss did in the wreck of his house, with a careful good grace all the same.

On the reservation, he said, the pressures were still there, the forced policies, the forced laws; he said the agenda was still the same, though the methods were more sophisticated. And, he said, regardless of what measures the Indian might want to take, the secretary of the interior could always block them. "Five years I've been on the council now—and they prevent any real self-determination. Always."

So I asked what he thought the future held.

He said, "Right now I'm positive. I think there's an intellectual uprising taking place, a grassroots resurrection—and unification measures too, so we can have one voice to tackle the national issues."

So—the big question—could they get the Black Hills back?

Buzz Two Lance had said, "Yes. Maybe not in my lifetine, but I see a day coming . . . eventually, yes."

At the college a few minutes earlier a guy called Martin Red Bear had told me, "I'm hoping so. It's looking good. Not tomorrow, sure—but the tradition's going to win out in the end."

Now Harold Salway said, "We will get them back eventually. Because morally, spiritually, legally, they belong to us.

"But you take it issue by issue, detail by detail. See, there are a lot of ways to develop, and attain our goals—but the first is the empowerment of our people. Inherently, we have the power; it just has to be implemented, by using the laws of the government against them. And we're getting more trained, more experienced individuals who can do that now."

And they could preserve the environment against the rampage of corporate techno-progress too?

Salway said, "The pride in all the people who've been through all the wars—per capita, native Americans have served more than any other ethnic group, and I say that with pride—that same pride will prevent the desecration of the land. It's quiet, it's humble, it's respectful—but it's a pride that has all the courage necessary to protect and defend our heritage and our land."

The Lakota people were on the upswing.

"Yes. Since Wounded Knee in '73 there's a recognition of who we are. We're proud to be Indian, and to speak our language. In the early years, with the churches coming in, and the Depression, people even changed their names—they changed from good names like Looking Cloud to

Smith, say, just to get a job. My own name, it isn't Salway, it's Left Heron—and I promised my uncle I'd change it back . . ."

Why hadn't he?

"When I get out of politics. I don't want to defile it, it's a beautiful name—and politics has so much negative associated with it."

But from what he was saying, AIM had been a good thing.

"It's my viewpoint that it was—they helped bring the pride into being Indian again. And eight years ago, six years ago," he said, "no leader would have said that."

# 10.

# USA '91

*Gearing Up*

I couldn't face Rushville again; I went back to Kadoka instead, through Wambli and the Badlands and across the White River.

In the City Bar, one of the film crew was griping about the trials of life on location in Lagos. Terry Stout told him, "You know where *sympathy* comes in the dictionary? Between *shit* and *syphilis*."

It was Saturday night. I was on the pool table for hours, teamed up with a local woman—she had the skill, I had the luck—and we lost only twice. Sam Shepard, in straw hat and Wranglers, was on the other table; we arranged to talk over breakfast the next morning.

Shepard was still in the bar when I left, indistinguishable from the cowboys. Apted said he was talking about buying a place out there; after we talked the next day, he was going into the country to look at some quarter horses. Another of the crew, watching him among the locals on the night of the Fireman's Ball, wondered idly how the man did his work—did he go back to his trailer and write Pulitzer prize–winning plays in the small hours?

We had a late Sunday breakfast in the Best Western; the waitress brought sausage patties, hash browns, eggs over easy, mounds of toast and jelly. Feeling grimy, I drank gallons of coffee; I'd slept the night in the whale-truck by Jim Garrett's trailer. Shepard said he'd left the bar soon after I did; otherwise, he said, "It can get silly."

He was forty-eight, born in Fort Sheridan, Illinois; his father was in the air force, so he grew up in Texas, New Mexico, the Mojave Desert in California. He said, "I was here too, at Ellsworth by Rapid, when I was five or six. They got B-52s there, Stealth bombers . . ."

He shook his head. "Man, they're gearing up. It's really frightening

. . . I think the whole Gulf War was just to see how those weapons worked. I mean, you had the perfect enemy there. It was just, Let's tear their ass apart with every technological experiment we can, 'cause who'll give a shit? That was *destined* to happen—if not them, some other festering pocket over there. And Bush has just galvanized people with it; all this flag waving and parades, it's pathetic. But American people are so gullible in that way, it's very weird. I thought once there was some promise of America getting a conscience, but the Gulf War's obliterated that. Bush has set us back a hundred years."

I asked him what he thought about what was happening out here—about the way the heart of America here, where so much of the myth was born, was withering away now.

He said, "The strange thing about this country is that different territories have absolutely no understanding of each other. It's like different nations. There's no way a born-and-bred New Yorker's going to understand a Kansan, or vice versa. Or Arizona and Massachusetts, or Oregon and Alabama . . . but it started way back, with all the migrations. And a lot of information that comes out of this central part of America now, it's seen as somewhere almost exotic; a lot of people don't give a shit about what happens here. It's expendable country. As far as the coast cities are concerned, it can just bleed away in the dust. Yet as far as morality goes, or racial attitudes, it's more representative of the United States than any other place. This is where the original stock is—and this part of the country is more racist than the Deep South. At least the South has a tradition of managing it, whereas here it's still so blatant, so extreme. The fear here, the age-old fear of the primitive savage . . .

"Still, as a kid, this is the kind of country I grew up in—and I love it."

He said, "The overriding thing about this country is the sheer vastness of it. To look around 360 degrees, and see storms happening all around the horizon—it's like you're in the center of the planet. So it's very easy to see how the Indians related to it spiritually. You get out in the middle of the prairie and you hear a meadowlark singing, you listen—he's *saying something*. Or storms, or clouds changing . . . It's very easy to see how a race of people could live in a relationship with that, and coexist with it.

"So that's one of the great tragedies here, how that sense of being related to the environment has been demolished. That's the tragedy of the Indian—not just the demolition of the race, but the assault on the spirituality. But then, that's the great poverty of contemporary America as a whole—the sense of spirituality replaced just by hysterical preachers on TV. I mean, you go through the Badlands, that landscape, and all these interconnected tribes—then you see a sign for Flintstone National Park. Cartoons carved out of rock? You think, Fuck—*people died for this?*"

At least, I said, I'd come up against a sense of the positive on the reservation now, of forward movement . . .

He said, "That may be true for a certain faction. But for all these cultures in the United States, what they're up against is an overriding despair. And how you turn that around is no easy task. What do you say to them? Stop drinking yourself to death and do handicrafts? You're dealing with generations of despair. . . . Dennis Banks said an interesting thing about the alcoholism. He saw it almost as a kind of deliberate declaration, that they were not going to live in the white man's culture."

Or not going to live, period. . . .

Sam Shepard said, if I wanted to talk about similarities between the red and the white peoples of the Plains, "The alcoholism isn't only the Indians. It's through the whole white population, who also recognize the despair—that they're living under this incredible gun of the federal government. You go into some of these cowboy bars— they drink like there's no tomorrow. Not just to have a good time, but to *obliterate* . . ."

I asked him what he thought about *Thunderheart.*

He said, "It has a lot of potential. If nothing else, just simply to let people know what went down, and the conditions here. Because when that stuff hit the fan in the seventies, people, me inclusive, were ignorant of the severity of what happened here. By then, we were so used to little pockets of uprisings that we didn't realize the extremity of it, we didn't know just how many were killed. So if nothing else, it'll illuminate some of that. As an illustration of what happened, it's well intentioned."

Harold Salway had said he thought the film was a good thing. But he also said, "I worry it's been watered down, and they're not getting the whole message across. I told them, Tell it the way it is, tell it how it happened. I don't know if they will or not."

Jim Garrett had the same fear. "But," he shrugged, "that's Hollywood."

Shepard said, "As far as its internal morality goes, it's somewhat sentimental; it's weak in that regard. As far as the movie concerns the

Indian, it might lead us to believe everything's going to turn around—and that's a false hope. Indians getting power in their own hands? It's not happening. They're as much under the gun as they ever were.

"Because historically, what this government's always been terrified of is the internal threat. There's nobody going to sneak up on the beach or fly over either, we've got that all covered, the military machine's so strong there's really no outside threat. There's just the threat from inside—and it scares the shit out of them. So all these groups, the Panthers, AIM—anyone with inflammatory inclinations was squashed. I mean, *squashed.*

"And particularly the Indian thing, because there's this huge tract of land, Pine Ridge is huge—and for a militant group to get a foothold on that land, which is theoretically sovereign . . . well, the paranoia got totally out of hand. SWAT teams, helicopters; it was, Let's kill this thing before it ever gets on its feet. And now it's been destroyed, the possibilities of working *within* the so-called system . . . there are some, but it's under the thumb, always. Under the thumb of a government that really doesn't give a shit about them. Because when you get right down to it, they're not citizens—they're just a problem."

So they wouldn't get the Black Hills back.

"Well . . . when the real shit hits the fan, when there's a collapse—maybe certain things will be returned to their rightful owners then. In the long run, they probably will get them back; things'll come around. Because look at what's happening in Middle Europe, all these *collapses*—and it'll happen here. Hell, I think we're in a state of collapse *now.*"

In a field of dreams.

"The cosmetics, the media, the TV, all the voices convince people we're okay—but I think the collapse is taking place now, I think it's starting to unfold. Particularly when a so-called democracy is so absolutely dependent on the military to enforce its identity. It's like, Yup, we're democratic, we can *prove* it—with all this frightening machinery . . ."

Machinery that could either slow-cook us in the greenhouse, or flash-fry us on the tip of a missile—machinery that could, one way or the other, be the end the world.

Shepard said, "We were filming the other day, and I was waiting for the shot—so I was just pushing my feet round in the dirt, and I turned up a little bone. And one of the Indian guys said, Yeah, that's a dinosaur bone, you can tell by the crystallization of the marrow. And I thought, we're filming on something tens of millions of years old here . . . so, you know—how many worlds have ended already? How many more will?

"And when you look at the weather out here, the way the sky changes, the way the storms move in and out—it's impossible to believe something doesn't keep on persisting, in even the most incredible destruction. You look at the night sky here—it's absolutely religious, in the real sense, this land. Nature is filled with spirituality here, it hooks you into a sense of being part of this vastness, this huge, overwhelming *fact* of nature. We're not something apart from that."

So when it came to a case like the Black Hills, in the end, it was spiritual power versus military power. It was soul versus mere muscle and metal . . .

Shepard said, "I think those guys are right. The Black Hills will be returned."

### When the Fourth Wall Falls

Ed Starr had told me a creation story. But later, when we talked about the way we were messing with the earth, he told me a destruction story too, a Revelation at the other end of the Indian book. I'd asked him what he thought the future held . . .

He said, "There's a Lakota fable. Inyan and Maka, they were living in a tepee way out on the Plains—and in the distance they saw a big cloud coming. So they decided to build four walls around them to protect themselves. Then out of the cloud a herd of buffalo came, for days and days, coming and coming—and they broke down the first wall, and they broke down the second wall, and then the third. When they broke that, that was the time of the flood, Noah's time. And even at that time, the people still had choices.

"But now the buffalo are still coming, and the fourth wall, it's pretty well shattered. And this story was told, I don't know—in '48, '49? So we're pretty close, by now, to whatever's going to happen."

I asked what it would mean, when the fourth wall falls.

He said, "The end of the world, maybe . . . I try to make a choice to go back, to smoke the pipe, to learn how to go back to the Great Spirit. In the alcohol treatment too, we learn how to discipline ourselves. Because it's like getting prepared for . . . for whatever. The worst.

"The end time."

*Entropy*

Twelve hours into the bus ride back to New York, I was accosted by a crazy in the Burger King in the Greyhound terminal at St. Louis. He was, I think, named Don . . . well, we'll call him Don anyhow; he was one of life's Dons.

He was short, balding, splay-footed, whey-faced, a tad on the tubby side; he had tiny eyes, and tiny hands. He wore a faintly grubby Chicago White Sox T-shirt, a lightweight orange anorak, and trousers of an indeterminate grey-green. Vital items hung on bright coiled telephone wire from his belt loops—a miniature flashlight, a keyless plastic key-ring, a small, rolled-up woman's umbrella with a lilac floral design. He sat down opposite me, utility belt clacking.

He said, "You know what bothers me about America?"

It's six in the morning, you been on a bus all night, you got twenty-six more hours to go, you got to eat in a Burger King 'cause that's all there is, which is *definitely* the end of the world—and now you got to listen to Don, too? Tell me, you say, what bothers you about America . . .

"Pretty much most everything. You know what the federal government is?"

Uh-huh.

"You know what state government is? You know what county government is?"

Uh-huh.

"Well where you gonna go for justice when it's all corrupt?"

You sure as hell got me there, Don.

"I write to the United Nations a lot. I'm cosmopolitan. I got nine nations in me, I got Indian blood in me here. Where you from?"

I'm British.

"That could be Irish, Scottish, anything. Where you *from?*"

I'm from Wales.

"From Wales, huh? I'm from an institution, me. I had *many mothers* there. I've had five heart attacks in the last six years. Doctors bring 'em on with their medications."

He showed me scar-raddled calves. A nice sight, over your breakfast slop-in-a-bun.

He said, "You know what bothers me about America?"

And Don was okay; Don knew what was going down. He rummaged in a knapsack, and produced from its tattered contents—clothes, weath-

ered address books and leaflets, balls of string—a Casio personal orga-
nizer. Then he typed, in a brief fever of busy fingers, the answer to the
big question—an answer so secret, so important, so alarming that it
couldn't be uttered aloud.

"You know what bothers me about America?"

He shoved the little screen in my face. On it he'd written one word:
Entropy.

He said, "When you lose your energy, you don't get it back."

He said, "Greece. Rome. Portugal. Spain. France. Britain. Us."

Don knew what was going down.

He paddled away, clattering, into the weary throng of the poor, the
fat, the mad, the Mexican and the black on the concourse of the Greyhound terminal at St. Louis.

### Techno-progress

Five weeks after I gave Sharon away to Twitch, I walked from a long
and late breakfast with Sam Shepard on to the front lot of the Best
Western in Kadoka. The noon heat was blazing, glaring, the asphalt
toffee-soft under a remorseless, hammering blue sky. I find I've written
in my notebook at this point, "I've done it all here now."

But there was one thing more yet to do. . . . I headed west on I90. It
was eighty-seven miles to Ellsworth Air Force Base.

From a long way off before I got there, the Black Hills rose to line the
horizon. Under a weird barrage of creamy-grey, almost glimmering
raincloud, the hills *were* black, a crinkled wall, a striking silhouette. I
could see rain in columns gushing down, and through a turquoise gap
between the cloudbursts, thunderheads climbing far in the West. There
was a Severe Thunderstorm Watch for southwest South Dakota . . .

I pulled up at the gate, four miles north off the interstate; lightning
was popping over the hills, thunder rolling. In the security post, a
narrow box on the traffic island between the roads in and out, the phone
rang; it was a call from Pactola Reservoir on the other side of Rapid
saying they had hail an inch across over there. High above, a long thin
tongue of cloud came licking our way ahead of the storm. The military
police guy, a Hispanic kid from Texas, fretted over the chances of his
car getting pulped; the soldier with him, a blond lughead from Philadelphia, grumbled that South Dakota was a shitheap in every way.

I said I was writing a book; they called the duty public affairs officer, and he came over to help me gladly in any way that he could. . . . Even the death factory has a PR brigade, right?

It was Sunday; he'd been painting his house. He wore a beat-up pair of jeans, a paint-flecked grey T-shirt, and the inevitable baseball cap. He was Lieutenant Robert Carver, and he was twenty-six years old.

He said he'd give me a "windshield tour"—but a flash of lightning forked down then, and there was rain coming, so we went to talk first in Bandit Lanes, the base's bowling alley, until the weather was past.

Ellsworth was, said Carver, the largest operational base in Strategic Air Command. In its drab, functional, military way, it wasn't so much a base, in fact, as a small city with nukes and bombers in it: Rapid's ugly sister, with a population around 7,500.

The place was home to the 28th Bombardment Wing; they had B1 bombers, supersonic B-1B Lancers, EC-135 airborne command posts, KC-135 refueling tankers. Then, since August '89, there was the 99th Strategic Weapons Wing, the Strategic Air Command's training and tactics development unit. That unit had been, said Carver, "very important in the Gulf War. We sent five hundred over there, so we had an important role in that. Most of which I can't talk about . . . but B-52 crews train here. Some guys did as many as twenty-six missions. They did," he said brightly, "a good job."

Given that the top of the news just then was how many of Saddam's key facilities had survived intact, this seemed to be pushing it a bit. A good job? Pal, they *missed* . . .

And, of course, they missed Saddam too. America, peeved and bewildered, kept asking itself in the middle of its hysteric celebration how come the guy was still there. . . .

Meanwhile, as well as the bombers, Ellsworth was home to the 44th Strategic Missile Wing. They had, said Carver, 150 Minuteman 2 intercontinental ballistic missiles, spread out around 13,500 square miles of South Dakota.

Then he said, "We may not have them much longer. There's a proposal to phase them out in the force structure realignment."

That would, I said, clobber the local economy.

"It'll have some impact. But the drawdown plan's phased over three years—if it comes to pass at all." There had been, he said, one form or another of Minuteman there for twenty-seven years.

He said they'd try to make it as painless as possible—but it was, he admitted, "sensitive. The local rural power companies, for example, are concerned they'd be losing big customers, 150 silos, 15 launch control facilities—it's understandable.

Then there was everything that went to keeping the boys happy—the 812th Strategic Support Wing running the civil engineering, the recreational facilities, the security police, the street improvements; just now they'd been building a new commissary, a grocery store. And the bowling alley, the golf course—these things were, said Carver, "MWR: Morale, Wellness, Readiness."

They were, I imagine, jobs for South Dakota, too.

I asked him, coming from North Carolina, what it was like to be stationed out there, under the weather of the Plains.

Carver said, "It can change in a heartbeat. And the hail, that can tenderize your car some. But it could be worse—like Clark and Subic Bay, it'd be kind of tough to work with lava flowing over your desk.

"But the weather," he said, "has never interrupted our ability to do the mission."

And the mission was?

"To keep planes and missiles ready to go to war if necessary."

And wasn't it a bit odd, sitting bang in the heart of a target zone?

"It's something that takes a little getting used to. I'm also a missile launch officer," this amiable fellow now blithely informed me, "so I'm pretty close to it. And it's strange—but being ready means preventing war. You realize you're training hard to prevent it, 'cause the other guy knows you're ready."

I felt breathless. As Carver entered cheerfully into the twisted logic of deterrence, I tried to figure out what it meant, and how I felt, sitting drinking Coke and eating fries in a bowling alley with one of the guys who turns the key that ends the world . . .

He said, "I'm doing it so I never have to do it. It's a very strange paradox. But it's worked."

Nothing works for ever . . . and he would, I asked, turn the key?

"I would be the one who'd turn the key. Myself and my partner. And twenty-eight other guys. And women."

But what on earth could that be like?

"We turn them every day in training. Every day we go on the simulator, we turn the key. It's just an action. Just a turn of the wrist."

And the world ends. Just a turn of the wrist—and Robert Carver and his colleagues create ten thousand irradiated Auschwitzes . . . It was not,

I said, just a small matter of turning a key. It was not, by any stretch of the imagination, a simple action.

"Well, not to trivialize it . . . It's a very important action. But firing a gun at someone's a very important action too."

Hardly in the same league . . .

"There's two hundred of us on the base here. We don't talk about it much 'cause . . . well, it's our job. And not everybody gets to do it, you have to be qualified. You have to be an officer."

But did he not, I asked, think about the consequences of this turn of the wrist here?

"What are the consequences if we're not here to make sure it doesn't happen?"

But what if it does?

"I don't know. I guess the average person knows as much about it as I do."

He went to the pay phone now; I was making the guy nervous, he needed some authorization to carry on with this conversation. But it was Sunday, he couldn't raise anybody; so he took me over to his office to try again from there.

While he was on the phone I studied a video on the shelf by his desk: *Oliver North, Fight for Freedom*, copyright 1987 American Freedom Coalition. "See and understand what motivated this courageous man to strive for democracy in Nicaragua, and for truth in the chambers of the U.S. Congress . . . the story of a real-life American hero whose magnetism and patriotic conduct could change the course of history."

Carver got through to someone eventually, and got an okay to show me around. Outside, the weather had cleared.

"This isn't an official tour," he said, that small hint of anxiety still lurking, "I'd have to call D.C. for that."

We drove through a scatter of dull, yellow-green hangars. He pointed one out, "The largest freestanding cement structure in the world. In the free world, anyhow. It was originally designed to take three B-36s, and they're *big*."

Nearby was a Minuteman, "actual size."

It was like a woman on a cooking program, Here's one I made earlier . . . a white missile pointing motionless at the cloud-scudded sky.

We passed the new commissary: it was Wal-Mart–size, a food hangar. There was a water tower, and dreary offices and apartment blocks. LIVE BAND & COMEDIAN ONLY AT BURGER KING.

I went back to what he did for his living.

Carver stressed, with his cautious anxiety returning, "These are only opinions, these are *my* opinions—this isn't the Air Force view. I don't think I've given anything away ... but it's just a job that needs to be done, and I feel very strongly that it needs to be done. The mission is to keep our bombers and missiles ready in order to prevent a war."

And if war happens?

"We'll follow orders. We're trained to execute the mission, and if we're ordered to do so we'll do it."

Jesus. I was driving around the death factory with a zombie. Surely, I said, he had *feelings* . . .

"People have feelings, who doesn't? But the realization of the importance of the mission is the primary . . . what's the word? Thought. It's what drives the process."

But he knew what it would involve . . .

"We're not uninformed individuals. We keep track of what's going on in the world. I'd like to think we're fairly bright. You have to be an elite individual to become an officer in the U.S. military. In fact the U.S. military is one of the best educated forces in the world. You don't have stupid people in positions of authority."

So look, I say, you've got all these nukes here . . .

"I have to say this—officially the government can neither confirm nor deny the presence of nuclear weapons anywhere."

So what are you keeping in that silo with the metal tit on top there, Robert? Wheat?

He said on an official tour I'd have seen . . .

A guy in a white room full of computers turning a key?

"It's kind of an off-green room. Not lime green, not really grass green—it's kind of . . . it's a light pastel green. It's not ugly. I wouldn't paint my house that color, but it's not ugly. And there are red chairs. There's carpet, and nice fluorescent lighting, they have a nice bed module they're put in—and there's a small refrigerator, and a microwave, and a little TV, thirteen inches, color. So you can watch the ballgame. It's a good working environment."

God save us. You can toss a burger in the microwave, and watch Wrigley Field flare to fire and ash as you turn a key and the world ends.

And the fourth wall falls . . . I got in my truck and followed Robert Carver out of Ellsworth Air Force Base, past the B-52 and the two armed men at the gate—then I hurried the few miles south to rejoin I90 heading west.

In the next two weeks, I drove 4,367 miles.

*The Fourth of July*

On the Fourth of July, at the Colonial Inn in Dyersville, Iowa, I watched a discussion of the Black Hills issue on CNN. The introduction to the debate said, "Many see the dedication of Mount Rushmore (on its fiftieth anniversary) as rich with irony."

In 1975, the Supreme Court described the usurpation of the Black Hills as "the most rank and rife case of dishonorable dealing in our history." They awarded a settlement of one hundred twenty million dollars.

The Lakota people haven't taken the money. At the Oglala Lakota College on Pine Ridge, Martin Red Bear said, "Should we take the money? No. It'd be distributed, it'd vanish, it's just money—and the majority are against that. See, the Black Hills are sacred."

He said, "It's like if you was a Catholic, and someone took all your cathedrals."

On the Fourth of July, a Lakota leader called Mel Lone Hill was interviewed in the shadow of the Mount Rushmore carvings. Asked to reflect on the significance of the day for his people he said, "We don't have no independence. We're more a prisoner of the United States than independent. And I feel sad . . . As long as we don't have no Black Hills, we don't have no independence."

Debate was joined between the Republican Larry Pressler, a South Dakota senator, Ward Churchill of AIM from Boulder, Colorado, and a Cheyenne woman whose name I missed. They were asked, Should the Black Hills be returned?

The senator's opening shot was, "These lands should be open to *all* the American people."

The Cheyenne lady was emollient—"He is a good senator"—but the answer to the question (which he'd not answered) was, Yes, they should.

Churchill said the issue was not whether they should be, but whether they *would* be. "We've heard a lot of stuff from George Bush about liberating occupied lands. So if there's a *shred* of integrity, they'll get out of the occupied land here."

He also pointed out that besides the money being unacceptable in the first place, it was, compared to the billion or more's worth of gold and other minerals extracted from those hills, a pathetic sop anyhow.

Pressler got glib; that, he said, could go to the Court of Claims. Then he got slippery. Suggesting that "rank and file Indians" wanted the money, he blamed "militants, radicals"—without directly leveling those slogan words at Churchill—for stirring things up against the interests of their own people. It was a practiced evasion, ducking the question, lobbing out the groundless, discrediting smear instead.

The Cheyenne lady said, "It's not militants. It's Senator Inouye, it's Ben Night Horse Campbell [a Colorado congressman]—it's many reasonable people."

Short of a case here, Pressler retreated into sarcasm. He said, "Maybe we should all move back to Europe."

The moderator raised the dire economic condition of the Indian nations—and Pressler seized on that for a way out. He said that rather than agitating over land claims, people should focus on the real problems of poverty—which rather begs the question of whether they mightn't be less poor if they got the land back . . .

Pressler said the economic situation was, "very bad—and I've been one of those working hard . . . There's much more we need to do for our Indian people."

Quick as a whip Churchill shot back, "We are not *your* Indian people."

And what did it all mean, on America's birthday today?

Pressler said, "We're all Americans on the Fourth of July"—which, in the face of Don's entropy and Shepard's collapse, seems to me now a wholly meaningless statement.

The Cheyenne woman had the last word. She said, "We *are* a free people, and we're looking for justice. And there can be justice—and the republic will still stand."

I drove south through flag-dotted and partying little Iowa towns scattered in green oceans of corn. At Casey's General Store in the town of Wyoming, the counter girls were in a trembling chatter of excitement; there was a couple getting married today, so yesterday the best man had buzzed the town in an F-16.

"Happy Birthday America," said the radio. "And say thanks to those in uniform. They stood in front of the flag, instead of behind or beside it."

Rush Limbaugh, a crazed reactionary talk jockey who loves himself and thinks he's very funny, asked his adoring millions why he—a rich Republican—was working with the peons on the Fourth of July.

He was working, he said, because it was the ultimate act of patriotism—and because, "I *am* America."

Well, sometimes he is funny. Why had Bush started jogging again?

'Cause Sununu took the car.

Where did the debt-laden Donald Trump get the money for Marla's quarter-million engagement rock?

He put her breast implants up as collateral . . .

And sometimes he isn't funny at all. He mentioned the Indians who "think they *used* to own America! Ha ha ha!"

An Indian had got up after Bush at Mount Rushmore and said the thing should be torn down. Said Rush, "Isn't diversity a wonderful thing? What a great country. It'd never happen in Japan."

I crossed the Mississippi at Muscatine, and followed it south along the Illinois shore. Past Nauvoo the road ran close along the bank, and the river was huge, a flowing lake of a thing scattered with clogged green beds of reed and water lily. I crossed it again at Keokuk, and stopped at a gas station just over the line into Missouri. In the booze-packed store a thin old black guy croaked, "It's getting hotter'n a dog out there."

I headed south-southwest across Missouri; on County V past Hunnewell, the odometer told me I'd done six thousand miles. The backroads twisted through trees and golden grass; under the fierce blue sky I rode the bridges over the bright arms of Mark Twain Lake.

From the town of Mexico I took 54 through Jefferson City; a flock of balloons rose like glossy baubles in the raging sun. Like Mike from Miami, Oklahoma, I'd sure have liked a ride in one of them things.

But not that time . . .

The evening was coming down pink and orange as I came into the Ozarks. I zipped with eyes averted through Lakeview and Camdenton, a neon medley of full motels, fast food joints and fishbait stores—then, where 73 forked south off 54, I pulled up for gas.

The guy in the store was named Oral. He'd been to Egypt, and four days after he got there, Sadat was shot. He kept getting stopped at roadblocks, " 'Cause I had a beard." Then he went to China—and Tiananmen Square went down. He said, "Figure I'll stay home this year."

We shot the breeze over a cigarette under the last rose-vermilion of the sunset outside; there was a deafening roar of crickets in black banks of trees, and the pops and flashes of fireworks going up over Branch and Tunas and Macks Creek. Oral told me there were three motels in Buffalo, twenty-two miles south on 73. As I drove down there in the humid dark, the bugs were so thick the sound of them smashing and dying on the windshield was like heavy rain.

All three motels were full—but what Oral didn't know was there was
a fourth one, Jeno's—and Jeno's was empty. It was six battered wooden
cabins, tended with forlorn optimism by an ancient crone who began to
get fretful about my personal safety. I'd come 429 miles, and it was time
to Buy That Man a Miller—but, she said, I didn't want to go in those
bars. This was hill country here, those bars were *rough* . . . Besides, she
made out like the walk into town was an undertaking of Himalayan
proportions.

It took ten minutes, tops; I went in the Eastside Tavern on the central
square, and there were five guys there. They all had backaches and gut
gripes, and couldn't have beat up on me if they'd acted collectively.

And, hot from Mount Rushmore, George Bush had been to the parade
in Marshfield, a little town thirty miles to the south of here—but none
of these guys had been down there.

"Who wants to be in a crowd?"

For all George Bush had to do with these people, he might as well
have been the man in the moon.

The barmaid was from Louisiana—and these people here, she said,
were the most racist she'd ever met. With only one black family in the
town, she didn't understand it. . . .

And this whole patriotism thing, she said, wasn't shared by so many
Americans as the world might think. She said all this Gulf whoopee was
deeply resented, by veterans of Korea and Vietnam in particular. And
she said many, many felt worried about all the base closures now,
thousands and thousands would lose their jobs, *and there aren't other jobs.*

Sam Shepard: "A so-called democracy so absolutely dependent on the
military . . ."

On the TV there was another of those hype-the-Gulf army ads, with
rock video–style footage of the roaring choppers and speeding tanks in
the desert dunes; a throaty bass voice threateningly intoned, "Courage.
Competence. Commitment."

And they say the other guys went in for propaganda . . .

I went outside, and stopped to read the historical marker by the town
hall in the center of the square. Seems Dallas County in Missouri here
was "ceded" by the Osage in 1808, then settled in the 1830s and '40s
. . . A knot of drunken yahoos were firing rockets from a pickup across
the street. Seeing me reading the sign there, they started firing them
at me.

So here I was on this lavishly beautiful night, with the crickets still whirring thunderously in the trees, and the huge sky a brilliant bed of jangling diamonds cut through with shooting stars, hectic streaks of flaring sudden white . . . and I had rockets going off in the air and on the asphalt all about me.

Bangers banged and brakes squealed in the midnight dark; the yahoo kids hooted. I walked across the square and down the street back to Jeno's Motel, the sharp screams and cracks of the orange-sparking rockets following me, exploding against walls and windows and on the sidewalk, around my head and around my feet, to a scratched and sullen soundtrack of brain-dead whooping.

But there you go. When you're looking for the heart of America, you better be able not to flinch. . . .

Actually I was thinking, that's it. I'm out of here.

# 11.

# Survivors

There's a singer who, one gathers, is something of a rogue, who sits down one time with his good buddy to write the perfect country & western song. What, they ask themselves, are the essential ingredients of country?

Drink, prison, and Mom . . . so the opening line announces that he was drunk the day his mom got out of prison.

## Country Living

In Coffeyville I sat on a bridge over the Verdigris, the oily brown surge of the river shoving past between high banks of dirt and stone, the water strong and lazy under dense stands of bright trees. The woman I sat with began to tell me her story. . . .

Her father was a Pentecostalist. Her mother was a drunk who got married seven times, including twice to the same guy—who beat her, and "laid hands" on her daughters. I asked, did her mother always drink?

"Yeah. I remember watching cartoons when I was little and she'd just, *whup,* she'd whack me. And I'd say, I'm not doing anything. And she'd say, That's right. You're not doing a damn thing around here."

She was born to the first marriage; she had no idea how old she was when her parents divorced. "I don't know whether I can't remember, or I don't want to."

She stayed with her mother, who married the guy that beat her—so she went to the police about it. This was in Altus, Oklahoma; she'd have been twelve or thirteen. And the guy got out on fifty dollars' bail—so she jumped from an upstairs window, and cleared off before he got back. The guy reported her as a runaway; a policeman came to take her in.

She was downtown and she said, I'm right here, I'm not running any-where—so every time he got her in the car, she got right out again. A crowd gathered; he handcuffed her, but still she kept getting out. The policeman asked someone to help.

"This great big old fat guy came in the car and held me down, which made me mad, so I started kicking . . . and they set the bond at fifteen hundred dollars. Unbelievable. They shouldn't even have had me in there. And I don't know how much time passed, it was several days—but my mother came to pick me up and I said, No, I refused to go home. I didn't want to go back with her."

She was put in a halfway house—then sent to her father in Raymond-ville, Texas.

"I didn't even know he was coming till he got there. We sat and talked, and he knew that I smoked. He said, That's okay—we'll try and persuade you to quit. Then as soon as we were in the car and across the state line, he threw my cigarettes out the car. 'Cause they were religious . . .

"They decided I was demon-possessed. When they sang in church, they'd raise their hands in praise and I didn't want to do that, I didn't enjoy their church, and I'd just walk straight out. So they got me in a room, it was a totally empty room—except for one chair, like an old school chair with the wood seat, the wood back, sitting in the middle of the room with a silver pot and a roll of towels. 'Cause when the demon's cast out supposedly people spit and choke and stuff, I've seen people do it—and I suppose they expected me to do it too.

"So ten elders of the church and the preacher stood all around me and started yelling at me, not yelling at me for anything I did, but I guess yelling at the demon that was supposed to be in me. Just yelling. Not all the same thing at the same time—it was crazy. Madness. Satan leave her, demon be gone . . . crazy. And I got scared, with all those people, so I ran out. Which thoroughly convinced them that I definitely was possessed.

"That's when my stepmother cut off my hair with a butcher knife. She said it was my hair . . . See, her daughters had short frizzy hair, one of them wore braces, they were what we'd call nerds now. So she was jealous actually, is I believe why she did it. They were nobodies, and I was band queen, I got asked out . . . But she said God told her, God showed her it was my hair, it was the way I looked that caused my rebellion against God. I remember she had me by the throat on the floor telling me, You know what black trash is? Well, you're white trash.

"I tried to commit suicide then. I took pills and drank bleach. So they put me in a home in Corpus Christi. They packed a suitcase—not my clothes, I wasn't supposed to wear those kinds of clothes—and they put me in a home. It was twenty-four-hour religion. You had speakers in your room that piped in religion. You were required to memorize chapters at a time out of the Bible. Then if you ever broke the rules—got caught cussing, whatever—they'd hit you, and they'd always quote scripture at you first. 'Spare the rod, spoil the child,' or, 'Beat the child, he will not die'—I think it's found in Deuteronomy. We'd sit outside that room and count the blows, thirty on up. They hit you with a board. I was hit because I was writing a letter to my mother. I was supposed to receive and write no one but my dad and my grandparents. They hit me fifty-four times with a board."

Where?

"On the back of your legs, on your butt, wherever they could land it. I mean, you were jumping around there. Then after they hit me they put me in what they called lock-up—they handcuffed me to the pipes that come out from underneath the sink. For three days. You took a bath handcuffed to a pipe welded between the wall and the faucet, and they wouldn't give you a plug in case you tried to drown yourself, so you washed with one hand and the water running—and all the time scripture piping in . . ."

I asked if she knew why they'd done these things.

"I don't understand it. The older I get, the more confused I get. What were they thinking? When I was younger I tried to reason it out—maybe if I'd done this, maybe if I'd done that, maybe if I'd have raised my hands in church . . . maybe it was all my fault. But now I look at it and I just think, *What were they thinking?*"

She ended up in another home in Tecumseh, Oklahoma.

"It was totally opposite. At the first place you couldn't smoke, no tea, no coffee, no shorts—it was all dresses, they had to be at least three inches below the knee—and no makeup, no jewelry. But this other place, it was anything goes. The only thing you weren't allowed was razor blades and cameras. But we had our own pool, our own rec room, we had our own fast food restaurant, we had a roller rink, I was MVP on the basketball team . . ."

So it was good.

"Well, they weren't trying to push anything off on us. It wasn't bad—you just couldn't leave. There were only two things I hated. When you first got there they did a lice check, they put all this gunk in your hair . . . yeuucch.

"And the other thing was the queers, oh God. It scared me to death, I remember seeing it for the first time, and it about made me puke. I thought they'd beat the shit out of me if I didn't do it too. Every Friday you had to go from school and clean your room, and the housemother came to check there were no spots on the mirror, no dust in the drawers—and I passed inspection, so I went to watch TV. And I didn't know what they were doing, I was that stupid—but there was this white girl eating this black girl out on the floor in front of the TV. I'd never seen anything like it in my life.

"Anyhow, I got out because I graduated a year early. I graduated valedictorian in my class, Number 1 Grade Point Average—I won't tell you how many were in the graduating class . . . but that helped. And I had cousins in Oklahoma City, they'd started visiting, and they asked me to go live with them. Oh, I had fun then. I was seventeen, I guess, I modeled clothes, and I was an '89er Diamond Girl, a cheerleader—it was fun. We made appearances at boxing matches, at malls, in hospitals—it was *fun*.

"But I left 'cause my sister got pregnant, and the man left her, so it was me that took her home. To my mother . . . it was about the last place I wanted to go, but I did it for my sister. It's hard to believe, and I don't know why—I mean, if anybody would have been selfish and full of hate and full of ugliness, it would have been me. Really, it would have been me.

"But what I had, modeling, being a Diamond Girl—that didn't mean nothing compared to seeing my sister hurt, seeing her cry. And I didn't know what we'd find when we got home—I didn't know whether we'd find my mother at all.

"But that's when she married that asshole again. I'd gone to church camp, and I came back and there he was. And I wasn't going to live with him. Well, they wouldn't let me in anyhow—it wasn't him, it was my mother standing at the door telling me I couldn't go in—he wasn't big enough to do that himself. So the police came and I got my stuff, and I went to live with a girl I'd been at camp with. I went to Neosho, Missouri, and I stayed with that girl, and she took me to her church— and that's where I met my first husband at.

"He was the preacher's son; I married him in June 1980, I was twenty years old. We divorced eighteen months later . . . I'd just had my first child, a girl, and he comes in and says we have to talk. I say, okay. No, he says, we have to *talk* . . . and he's been cheating on me. Imagine—he was the song leader of the choir. So I left him and went back to that friend in Neosho just as soon as I'd filed for divorce.

"And we'd catch him watching us, me and the girl I lived with. I'd took my daughter with me—and he'd call every hour, him and his father both, offering thousands and thousands of dollars just to give my girl back and take off and never go back. We caught him one time with infrared binoculars behind somebody's car, watching us, watching to see if he could catch me in something to get me in court to get custody.

"I couldn't stand him bothering me all the time, so I left and went to Coffeyville. But I'd left some stuff in Neosho, so I went back to get it—and I called him to fix and meet, so he could see my daughter.

"When I hit the city limits there was a sheriff's car, and he pulled me over. He said, We got an anonymous tip-off you're carrying marijuana. Are you kidding? I never touch that stuff. But this cop goes in my dash and pulls out this Wal-Mart sack and he says, This is it. He didn't even *look* for it.

"But the girl I'd been living with, she'd filed for divorce too—and her husband smoked. So him and my husband, they'd set me up. And they took me and put me in a cell—and after all this bullshit he *still* didn't get my girl. 'Cause I called my girlfriend, and she collected her.

"Meantime in the cell was the biggest black woman I've ever seen in my life, she was in there for helping her boyfriend kill some guy—they chopped him up and put him in a trash can. You talk about scared, I was *scared* . . .

"Anyhow, they did an inventory of my purse and stuff, I was in there about two hours—and this guy comes to the door and he had a roach in his hand. He says, What is this? I say, What is *what*? He says, It's a roach. I say, You didn't find that in *my* purse. He says, You sit down and shut up . . . so I went to court. But there was no lipstick on the roach, no prints—and the judge said, Stop, this is a farce. So I picked up my daughter, and I went back to Coffeyville.

"Then I went back to him."

Why on earth . . .

" 'Cause it was the first time I'd ever been married, and 'cause of my daughter, and 'cause I wanted to make things work. But then after I'm back there a month, it turns out I'm three months pregnant—and that's not allowed, *no way*. He can have an affair, but me—that's adultery and grounds for divorce.

"So by the time we get to court I'm sticking out like this, pregnant—

and nobody goes with me, it's just me and some strange lawyer. But there's my husband with his dad the preacher, and everybody he could pull out of the woodwork. And that's where I come to find out, that sheriff that arrested me was one of his dad's good friends . . . I would swear on a stack of Bibles, he knew all along what was going on."

And the husband got custody. I asked how she'd felt . . .

"Oh God . . . I don't know. I sat in my car and cried. My husband came over and asked when they could take her, and I just screamed at the top of my voice so I wouldn't have to hear them."

She had the second child, a boy, and she brought him up; eight years later, at the beginning of 1990, she married again.

She found her second husband out in a lie two days after the wedding; he talked dream jobs that never materialized, took money from her purse, and from her son's pocket money too. When I met her, she'd left him.

Yet after all this story, after getting hit by the freight train over and over—she still had little religious messages framed on the wall in her kitchen. After what had been done to her in the name of God in Texas, and by a preacher's son in Missouri . . .

She said, "I still believe in God. Not in one denomination or another, but I still have faith. I still believe what the Bible says. And it's not all bad. I was near to marrying a guy from Michigan one time, I went up there, and the preacher was a Methodist, a very cool man, he rode a Harley. And he made us sit down with him for counseling. I didn't want to do any stuff like that, but he had to have four sessions with us talking before he'd marry us—and by the end of the second visit I could see I didn't want to marry that guy at all. So that preacher saved me from getting in it all again, least that time. It's not all bad."

Last thing I knew of this woman, she was going back to her second husband. Because, she said, you had to keep on trying to make things work.

You had to keep on trying, in that storm country there.


## What This Country's About

Moni Hourt said, "D'you know in this country women buried whole families and still started again? Cholera, diphtheria, whooping cough . . .

"I talked to a little old lady some years back, she was ninety years old, and she'd buried four children in three months. Four children aged from two months, to thirteen years. And she couldn't have any more. She never told me why, the older women don't tell you why—but she couldn't have any more.

"So she said she lay down on her last son's grave; she said she lay down there 'cause she wanted to die. There was nothing else, there was nothing else for her. She said she lay down all day, and the sun started going down, and she lay there and she kept thinking, it was time to die.

"But it wasn't. It wasn't time to die—it was time to milk the cows. So she got up that evening from the grave, and she walked down the hill, and she went home and milked the cows.

"During World War II, that lady wrote thousands of letters to the soldiers overseas—and over the years, many of them came to visit her here. That was her family then."

Moni Hourt said of those women: "They dug houses out of dirt banks, and they stomped the floor down, and they put down doilies, and they survived. And that's what this country's about."

## One Day at a Time

Larry Bettelyoun was thirty-four, and lived in Wambli; he'd got a job on *Thunderheart* as Michael Apted's driver. He wasn't a large man, but he was wiry, muscle-packed; he wore cowboy boots and jeans, a thick belt with a big buckle with his name on it, a red T-shirt and shades, and the long, glossy black hair of the Indian in a tail flowing way down his back. We talked in the sun outside the Kadoka auditorium.

He'd been sent to boarding school for five years till he was eleven. "People were still trying to erase the language then, so I'm real sad—I can't speak Lakota as good as I'd like. I can understand some, from my grandmother—I picked up some. And my mother's a full blood—but my Dad was a half breed, and he wouldn't let her teach us.

"So now I'm a Sun Dancer, and a lot of the people that dance with me, they speak Lakota. This summer I'm going to be tied to the tree for four days, and pierced—but sometimes I worry, how am I going to know when to do the push-ups, how am I going to know when to raise my arms to the sun? It's going to be hard for me, 'cause the sacred songs . . . It's going to be hard for me. But my wife speaks it, so she's helping me."

Of the Sun Dance he said, "You don't have no food or water for four days; just at dawn and sundown, you go in the steam lodge for half a dipper of water. And this is my fourth year, so I've accomplished my pledge—'cause four years ago my father was real sick, so I went to this medicine man to ask if I could learn the ways, to pray for the people that are sick, and the people that are on alcohol and drugs. That was the hardest thing I ever did, to accomplish the dance.

"After that, the hardest thing was the treatment center. I went this February to a forty-five-day program for Indians at Sergeant Bluff, Iowa, a real good program. I left a lot of things behind me there that I carried about for years. So I got no guilty conscience now, I feel clean. I was a closet drinker, I did it at home, or I went way off; I didn't want to wake up one day and find I'd killed someone, killed one of my friends. But I've been straight four months now.

"And this job really helps, this helps me stay straight. Also I been married thirteen years . . . I had three kids. But I had one daughter who died after twenty-three days, a crib death—I did a lot of my drinking over that. But when we went on the program, we really sat down, we had one-on-ones about it—so I left that there. It's over. Though it's kind of hard bringing it up . . ."

He paused; he was close to tears. He said he was sorry; he didn't talk about it a lot of times.

It wasn't what I'd expected our conversation to turn up. I said I was sorry too, and changed the subject.

I asked Larry Bettelyoun how he felt about *Thunderheart.*

He said it was going to be a great movie. "I read the script, I couldn't put it down. Reading it I could see myself, I could see those times—it's truthful. How can they call it fiction, when I lived that life?"

He said, "Our family—one of my brothers got shot in the back by one of my relatives, he was fifteen, sixteen; he didn't die, but it tore a real big hole above his tailbone. Then another time, my younger brother went with my elder sister and her husband to see a rodeo contractor that was using one of his bulls. And my little brother was sitting in the pickup, and this older guy came and tried to drag him from the truck with his friends; well, my brother was so scared, he got the rifle and shot him in the stomach. He died.

"But Bruce [Ellison] represented him, and we proved them wrong in court, our family cooperated; we proved we didn't look for no trouble, we was mellow. My brother still did about six months, it was real torment, they put him in the psycho ward—but he went along, and in the end they let him out. He proved he was okay, and honest. It went our way ... but I remember people used to come by our place in pickups, they used to shoot the place up after that."

It was Ellison who'd said I should talk to Larry. He said, "That guy's family used to lie on the floor with rifle rounds coming in."

Larry said, "My sister-in-law, sitting right there—one of my cousins hit her in the stomach, and killed her baby. So we went through a lot ... but I got seven sisters and four brothers, and we're real close. We stuck together. I'm just glad my kids don't have to go through it now."

So I asked how things were now.

He said, "The feuding's over, the killing's over, that's gone. The jobs are still needed—but there's a big effort right now. And there's a lot that are quitting drinking. There's still a lot that aren't ... but me, I'm working."

And he said, like Jacki Johns had in Minatare, he was taking one day at a time.

He said, "Some days you work real hard—but I go home, and I feel good about it. I've accomplished another day, and I'm still sober.

"See, when I was drinking, I'd blank out—but I always got home. I should have been dead, a lot of my friends are dead that way—but somehow I always got home. So God must have put me here for a reason.

"And now," he said, "this here is an opportunity. It's more money than I ever could make around South Dakota."

But his idea of what to do with it was different from the white man's. He said, "If you have a lot of money, cast it out—'cause it always comes back." He joked that his wife didn't trust him with his wallet—but, he said, "If you have it, give it."

He smiled, a diffident smile in the hot bright sun—the sun to which he'd raise his arms, pierced and tied to the tree, to pray for visions, and for the health of his people.

Larry Bettelyoun smiled, taking one day at a time.


## Don't Give Up

When the tornado hit Barneveld, Wisconsin, at one in the morning of June 8, 1984, among those who came to help in the aftermath were the Mennonites—some of them from as far off as South Dakota. One of them said in Barneveld, "If we had a day and didn't come, what kind of people would we be?"

When they were leaving and someone asked how they might repay them they said, "Help someone else."

Iowa had twenty-six tornadoes that day—then, in the evening, a storm crossed northeast toward Barneveld . . .

The tornado destroyed 90 percent of the town; aside from people's houses, twenty-nine of the town's thirty businesses were wiped out, all three churches, both schools, and the fire station.

"I was at the top of the stairs, looking at the landing half way down, where there was a little window; the lightning was flashing continuously so that there was a kind of blue glow. I couldn't go down because the stairway was swaying back and forth. There was a pressure, like a huge force pulling at you, just like it was going to pull you apart . . . There is fear, and then there is terror—and that was terror."

"I jumped up immediately and made a dash for the hallway that led to my daughters' room, and when I opened the door into that hallway, that side of the house had already blown away, and all I could see was a tree bending in the wind. I stood there and I screamed and I gasped and I prayed to God. There was nothing there. I was at the edge of nowhere . . ."

Nine people died—a farmer, a dairyman, the high school athletic director, a brother who was visiting his sister and the sister too, an ambulance attendant, his wife and their eight-year-old daughter, and a two-year-old boy.

"We had no clothes on, no shoes, and our feet got pretty well cut up because there was so much glass—we'd holler for help and nobody would answer . . . We didn't know if anybody was even alive anymore."

"We sat there in that rain, that cold rain. I felt around and found some insulation that had blown in from the walls—I said, 'Let's wrap up in this; it'll be better than sitting here in our underwear, even if it is a little itchy.' And that's what we did. We didn't know what to do, or what was going on."

"No words could describe the sick feeling I had in my stomach. I knew there must be death. How could there not be?"

The two-year-old that was killed died in his mother's arms; a piece of debris went through the back of his skull.

A year later, Barneveld had a service of memorial and renewal—and the father of that little boy was asked by a TV reporter, "Is there something the rest of the country could learn from what happened here?"

The man paused in the eye of the camera. Then he said, "Don't give up."

## *Hasta la Vista* Baby

On July 5 I left Jeno's in Buffalo some time before seven, and was into Harrison, Arkansas, for breakfast at nine.

Over the state line, 65 through the Ozarks was a feinting, weaving twister of a road, the surface a lousy mess of raddled potholes—and, what was worse, it was clogged with a holiday throng of campers and dawdlers. I got angry and bucked through them doing sixty to seventy, shunting and cursing and punching the radio, which did nothing but hiss and pray and tell me barbecue recipes. Then I found Booker T & the MG's as I pulled clear into Harrison. That and some heavy cholesterol cheered me up again.

But not for long. Farther south, deep in the dense green of the low mountains, a sign warned, CROOKED & STEEP NEXT 37 MILES. By Welsh standards it was a motorway, an interstate with a bend or two . . . but that's the thing with heartland Americans: Give them anything more demanding to drive on than an airport runway and, with the honorable exception of the drunken rednecks, they're immediately reduced to driving in a frozen state of twitching, rabbit-in-the-headlights panic. I mean, car culture? If they got out and walked, they'd get there quicker.

I weaved through Arkansas, snarling at the seed caps and blue hairs hunched anxiously over the steering wheels in front of me—then suddenly I realized: It was all a sinister plot.

There was a secret society, the '45ers, all driving round the country at a steady forty-five just to screw up the rest of us . . .

At last, I found some open road. I accelerated—but there was a battered old camper on the side of the road up ahead, with a worn sticker on the back announcing SNAPPER CAMPER—and he pulled out in front of me at the last possible moment. I jammed on the brakes—and he settled down to a steady forty-five.

First chance I could, I put my foot down to pass him. As the truck sailed alongside, I looked to my right at the Snapper Camper driver—and it was this leering, rotten-toothed psycho in a sawn-off denim jacket, his red-pocked face a scabrous stew of stubble, and in his grimy tattooed hand he had a shotgun pointed my way. The barrel spat fire; my right hand exploded in a sudden spray of blood and bone over the inside of the windshield . . .

Only kidding. I'm sure Arkansas is full of wonderful people—but I only spoke to five of them. I spoke to a bank teller, a waitress, two guys in gas stations, and a guy in a body shop when I took a wrong turn . . . so all I know about Arkansas is it's a forest three hundred miles long with some trailer homes in it.

Then I was in Texas headed west on I30—passing a sign for a town called Fate—and compared to the '45ers puttering about in Arkansas, Dallas in the rush hour was the Indy 500. Now *that* was driving—careening round the free-form multilane at seventy with one hand on the wheel, taking pictures of the skyline through the splattered bug-death on the windshield with the other, Simple Minds, ZZ Top, Jimi Hendrix, and Joe Walsh full blast all the while on the radio . . .

I drove 714 miles that day. If psychosis is your thing, it was fun. . . . I got to a friend's place in Austin around eleven, drank a six-pack, jabbered about America, and passed out.

America screws you up.

America's like that girl you had that thing with when you were twenty, that girl who drove you crazy . . .

Sometimes she says she loves you—other times she's out the door and gone for weeks, months, no word of explanation. She's far too self-willed—far too *free*—for you ever to have any more with or from her than just the moments you get—but those moments are so spiced, so charged that even when you know the parting's coming and it'll be bad and intense, still you can't help yourself wanting more, more . . .

So I bought a 1981 Ford F100 half-ton pickup truck, and I put 7,449 miles on the clock around the heart of America. I wore a baseball cap, I listened to country music, I guzzled gas and beer and fine fat breakfasts, I talked to cowboys and Indians, weathermen and oilmen, preachers and teachers, movie people and a missile man. And I came to the conclusion that, like that girl you had that thing with when you were younger, you can't say America's good or bad, or right or wrong.

You have to say instead that it's bigger than good or bad, bolder than right or wrong—that it's elemental and electric, spiritual and crazed—

and it's on its way out the door again even now, just when you thought you'd got a hold on it.

On its way out the door, spinning and screaming in the winds of history . . . What's that you say? You never had a thing with a girl like that?

Man—*you haven't lived.*

In Austin I went to see *Terminator 2.* It's the perfect American dream for the end of the millennium—a violent and indestructible robot with a heart of gold. Saddam never would have got away from *him,* George.

I drove back to Coffeyville. Somewhere in Oklahoma, Tom Petty sang that coming down was the hardest thing . . .

I sold the truck back to John Schmidt, then drank beer and tequila for forty-eight hours till it was coming out of my eyes. Twitch took me to the Horseshoe Lounge, where Jimmy L. Blankenship had met up three nights before with Shelli Smith, then gone on with her from there to the Touch Of Class. There, he got in a fight in the parking lot with Jeff Packard, and stabbed him to death.

Shelli Smith told Fritz Green for the *Journal,* "Everybody's a little confused."

In the Horseshoe now there was a catfight, women rolling and screaming, scratching and punching on the grubby floor.

A football player at the college put a gun in his mouth and blew his brain all over the wall. No one knew if he meant to do it, or if he was just fooling around and made a Big Mistake. Gretchen Pippenger took pictures. Not, she said, of the stuff on the wall . . .

Twitch gave me a red bendy plastic thing on a key ring with a Coffeyville logo on it. He said, "Glen Welden wanted you to have that," and grinned. "The key to the city."

The key on the ring was broken.

And Fritz gave me a pair of lucky dice. He said I had a porch I could sleep on in that town any time I liked.

The Jefferson Lines bus to Kansas City left at 5:50 in the evening from the Kwik-Stop Cafe on Elm; from there, it was Greyhound to New York.

The air was thick, hot and close. As I waited for the bus a mass of bulbous, blue-black cloud spread over the town from the southwest. Wind whipped litter round the empty parking lot as the light died, and the huge sky thickened to a marbled black.

There'd be heavy rain on the road that night, and lightning popping and flaring all the way to Kansas City.

The bus pulled out of Coffeyville, north on 169; the storm came in over the fields and pasture. In the murky light, as the heart of America fell behind me, I sat in the back and watched the weather, not wanting to leave.

*About the Type*

The text of this book was set in Janson, a typeface designed by Anton Janson, who was a punch cutter in seventeenth-century Germany. Janson is an excellent old-style book face with pleasing clarity and sharpness in its design.

| DATE | | | |
|---|---|---|---|
| | | | |
| | | | |
| | | | |
| | | | |
| | | | |
| | | | |
| | | | |
| | | | |
| | | | |
| | | | |
| | | | |
| | | | |